ROUTLEDGE LIBRARY EDITIONS: CHINESE LITERATURE AND ARTS

Volume 2

THE BOOK OF CHANGE

THE BOOK OF CHANGE

A New Translation of the Ancient Chinese I Ching (Yi King) with Detailed Instructions for its Practical Use in Divination

JOHN BLOFELD

LONDON AND NEW YORK

First published in 1965 by George Allen & Unwin Ltd
Second edition 1968

This edition first published in 2022
by Routledge
4 Park Square, Milton Park, Abingdon, Oxon OX14 4RN

and by Routledge
605 Third Avenue, New York, NY 10158

Routledge is an imprint of the Taylor & Francis Group, an informa business

© 1965, 1968 George Allen & Unwin Ltd

All rights reserved. No part of this book may be reprinted or reproduced or utilised in any form or by any electronic, mechanical, or other means, now known or hereafter invented, including photocopying and recording, or in any information storage or retrieval system, without permission in writing from the publishers.

Trademark notice: Product or corporate names may be trademarks or registered trademarks, and are used only for identification and explanation without intent to infringe.

British Library Cataloguing in Publication Data
A catalogue record for this book is available from the British Library

ISBN: 978-0-367-11183-0 (Set)
ISBN: 978-1-032-23151-8 (Volume 2) (hbk)
ISBN: 978-1-032-23161-7 (Volume 2) (pbk)
ISBN: 978-1-003-27600-5 (Volume 2) (ebk)

DOI: 10.4324/9781003276005

Publisher's Note
The publisher has gone to great lengths to ensure the quality of this reprint but points out that some imperfections in the original copies may be apparent.

Disclaimer
The publisher has made every effort to trace copyright holders and would welcome correspondence from those they have been unable to trace.

THE BOOK OF CHANGE

A NEW TRANSLATION OF THE ANCIENT CHINESE
I CHING (YI KING)
WITH DETAILED INSTRUCTION FOR ITS PRACTICAL
USE IN DIVINATION

BY

JOHN BLOFELD

London
GEORGE ALLEN & UNWIN LTD
RUSKIN HOUSE MUSEUM STREET

FIRST PUBLISHED IN 1965
SECOND EDITION 1968
SECOND IMPRESSION 1970

This book is copyright under the Berne Convention. All rights reserved. Apart from any fair dealing for the purpose of private study, research, criticism or review, as permitted under the Copyright Act, 1956, no part of this publication may be reproduced, stored in a retrieval system, or transmitted, in any form or by any means, electronic, electrical, chemical, mechanical, optical, photocopying, recording or otherwise, without the prior permission of the copyright owner. Enquiries should be addressed to the Publishers.

© *George Allen & Unwin Ltd, 1965, 1968*

ISBN 0 04 181001 5

DEDICATION

For Chin and Smoe with warm affection

PRINTED IN GREAT BRITAIN
by Photolithography
UNWIN BROTHERS LIMITED
WOKING AND LONDON

CONTENTS

	page
FOREWORD TO THE BOOK OF CHANGE (I CHING)	5
TRANSLATOR'S FOREWORD	10
INTRODUCTION	13

PART ONE: EXPLANATORY CHAPTERS — 21

1. An Approach to the Book of Change — 23
2. The Background of the Book of Change — 38
3. The Symbolical Basis of the Book of Change — 48
4. The Method of Divination — 59
5. A Guide to Interpretation — 72
6. A Summary of Instructions — 79

PART TWO: THE BOOK OF CHANGE

(Text and Commentaries) — 83

1. Hexagrams 1 to 30 — 85
2. Hexagrams 31 to 64 — 148
3. Postscript — 212

APPENDIX: TABLES AND DIAGRAMS FOR ASSISTING INTERPRETATION — 213

1. The Trigrams with their Principal Attributes — 216
2. Fu Hsi's Arrangement of the Trigrams — 217
3. Fu Hsi's Circular Arrangement of the Trigrams — 217
4. King Wên's Arrangement of the Trigrams in Family Relationships — 217
5. King Wên's Circular Arrangement of the Trigrams — 218
6. The Trigrams in the Arrangement Used in Charms for Warding Off Evil — 218
7. Parallel Diagrams Indicating the Interaction of Yin and Yang — 219
8. The Hexagrams in the Sequence in which they Occur in the Book of Change — 220

THE BOOK OF CHANGE

9. The Hexagrams Arranged According to the Base Structure — 221
10. Fu Hsi's Diagram of the Derivation of the Sixty-Four Hexagrams — 223
11. The Hexagrams Arranged According to the Number of Yang Lines in Each — 224
12. The Seasonal Correspondences — 225
13. Table of Ruling Lines — 226
14. Table of Approximate English Phonetic Equivalents of the Names of the Trigrams — 226

FOREWORD

to the *Book of Change (I Ching)*

By Lama Anagarika Govinda

Among the great books of the world the *I Ching* occupies a unique position. Not only is it among the oldest books that ever were written, but besides this it represents a conception of the world that differs widely from all other systems of thought found in the East or anywhere else in the early records of humanity, without contradicting them. The reason is that the *I Ching* is not based on a religious doctrine, a divine revelation or on tribal law and folklore, but on the observation of nature and human life, the interaction of universal laws and individual behaviour, of free will and destiny.

Instead of emphasizing the eternal, the unchanging, the immutable, as the highest aim and ideal of man, or by personifying it in the concept of a divine and eternal being, in contrast to an ephemeral and more or less unreal world of doubtful value, the *I Ching* is the only book of ancient wisdom that makes CHANGE itself the centre of observation and recognizes TIME as an essential factor in the structure of the world and in the development of the individual. Time here is not merely conceived as a negative or destructive agent, to be feared and denied, but as the very essence of life and therefore not opposed to the eternal, but rather that by which the eternal is being revealed.

The originators of the *I Ching* (which is not the work of a single author, but the accumulated wisdom of many generations, successfully applied and proved workable for a span of not less than 3000 years) accepted change as the natural order of things, the true nature of life. And they realized that it is not merely a principle of transiency and instability and a cause of suffering and unhappiness—as it appears to those who desperately cling to the idea that only the changeless is eternal and worth striving for—but that change itself gives meaning to life and contains an element of stability, an inherent law or eternal principle, which people tried to find outside the world in a realm of transcendental reality.

Thus they realized that change is not arbitrary or accidental and they discovered the laws of transformation, according to which each thing or state of existence can only change into something already inherent in its own nature (and not into something altogether different), and the equally important laws of periodicity, according to which change follows a cyclic movement (like the heavenly bodies, the seasons, the hours of the day), representing the eternal in time, converting time quasi into a higher space-dimension, in which things or events exist simultaneously, though imperceptible to the senses. They are in a state of potentiality, as the invisible germs of future events and phenomena that have not yet stepped into actual reality.

Therefore the *I Ching* maintains that those who know the "germs" and the laws of transformation are the masters of their destiny.— But how is one to know the germs which are hidden to the senses and inaccessible to the intellect, as they are still in a state of unformed potentiality?—Here a faculty of the human mind comes into play, which modern man has neglected or almost forgotten: the mysterious forces of our depth-consciousness, our intuition, which the ancients evoked through trance-like states or in meditation, religious rituals and divine oracles, in which the individual consciousness was extinguished in favour of a greater, more universal consciousness.

In all these states of mind thoughts and sense-impressions are excluded, the depth-consciousness is freed from ephemeral desires and purposes and from the distractions of the peripheral or surface-consciousness, which generally is occupied with the limited concerns of our daily life; and thus we become aware of the germs that determine our future and are revealed in symbols, in archetypes of profound significance. These symbols may vary according to the racial, linguistic, cultural and historical background of the individual, unless they belong to those universal archetypes which are valid for all human beings, irrespective of race, culture and social conditions. The evaluation of these symbols, therefore, depends on a thorough knowledge of the meaning of symbols and a discrimination concerning their origin and applicability. In ancient times this evaluation was the function of priests and seers, and if nowadays we wish to avail ourselves of the knowledge laid down by them in books like the *I Ching*, we have first to study carefully the symbolic language employed by them and try to translate it into the psychological language of our time, a language as much conditioned by the religious tradition in which we grew up, as by the historical background of our respective civilization.

Though the *I Ching* grew out of the practice of ancient oracles, there is a second, equally important, aspect of it, which in the course of millenniums transformed the oracle-book into a philosophy of life, namely, the formulation and definition of the laws of transformation.

FOREWORD

While the ritual action and the resulting answer of the oracle so to say pinpoint a certain situation by making conscious what was hidden in our subconscious mind, the knowledge of the laws of transformation makes it possible for us to foresee the probable course of future events, according to the direction we choose to take from the starting-point of the present situation. In this way the law itself, instead of becoming a cause of our enslavement, becomes an instrument of free will.

Thus the *I Ching* combines intuition and experience with a logical method of applying both to a given situation, which allows us to exert our reason (as a safeguard against a merely emotional approach or 'wishful thinking') and gives us the freedom as well as the responsibility of a final decision. It is this that raises the *I Ching* to the level of a spiritual science and a philosophy of life and distinguishes it from a mere system of soothsaying or fortune-telling, in which man is deprived of his free will and conceived as a play-ball of fate, going to a predetermined future, upon which he can have no influence.

While soothsaying for this reason is without moral value, the *I Ching* uses divination not for determining the future, but for raising the already present hidden tendencies of the human mind into the light of conscious awareness, in order to give the individual a glimpse of the various possibilities before him and a chance to choose the best course of action, according to circumstances. In this way the individual, instead of disregarding or opposing the acting forces and realities around and within himself, co-operates with them and makes them his partners in the creation of his future. A sailor cannot control the wind or the current of the water, but he is able to utilize their forces by skilfully co-operating with them.

How we can co-operate with the forces of destiny or the realities of our present situation, is shown in the *I Ching*, in which the laws of transformation have been defined by a method which is as ingenious as it is simple, by using only a plain and a broken line to indicate the polarity of all phenomena of life, and six positional values to show their relativity in the sequence of time and their relationship in space.

Just as the invention of the decimal system with its positional values and the introduction of the concept 'zero', was one of the most important steps in the development of mathematics, leading to the discovery of new spiritual dimensions, so the hexagrams of the *Book of Change* created a system of symbols, capable of expressing a vast variety of combinations and permutations, indicating their inherent movements or transformations, which practically cover all situations in human life. The advantage of these symbols is that—like those of mathematics—they are independant of language and therefore universally valid. They form the stable framework or skeleton around which the living flesh of organic thought and creative vision have been growing, and in this process a symbolism of verbal concepts and similies and pictorial (visible) forms originated according to the cultural genius and the environmental conditions (landscape, flora and fauna, climate and seasons) of the Chinese people. As this symbolism is enshrined in the Chinese language and in the ideograms of the Chinese script, only a thorough knowledge of both can guarantee the correct interpretation of its intricate relationships and their deep meaning.

Nobody could be more qualified in this respect than the author of this new translation, who speaks and writes Chinese with a fluency rarely attained by Westerners, and who has the added advantage of being thoroughly acquainted with Chinese life and culture on all levels, as his autobiographical book *The Wheel of Life* (Rider, 1959) and his charming description of pre-communist Peking under the title *City of Lingering Splendour* (Hutchinson, 1961) amply demonstrate. These books are the fruit of twenty years of life and work in China. As a translator of classical texts of Chinese Ch'an literature he has made a name for himself by the translation of the sayings of one of the most famous Masters of Meditation: *The Zen Teachings of Huang Po* (Rider, 1958).

Due to his deep involvement in the spiritual life of China he was able to recognize the importance of finding the right approach for those who want to consult the *I Ching*, whether for purposes of divination or for general advice in important situations of life (and only such situations justify the use of this book). In regard to this I may quote the author's own words from a letter dealing with his *I Ching* translation: 'I have very strongly stressed the religious ritual way of approach to divination and interpretation and shown that the whole process is in some important respects equivalent to a form of yogic meditation. It is just because the *I Ching* (in Richard Wilhelm's translation) is rather widely used in the West on a level not much higher than that accorded to any cheap fortune-telling book that I felt the urge to prepare a new version so worded that those who use it will have no faith in the responses *unless they do approach both enquiry and interpretation in a truly religious manner*.'

FOREWORD

It is, [therefore], with the greatest confidence that I recommend to all lovers of Chinese wisdom this new translation of one of the most profound books ever written in the remote past of this ancient civilization.

TRANSLATOR'S FOREWORD

Can any reasonable man suppose this universe to be mere chaos? The correspondences between the behaviour of all things great and small—from the celestial bodies rolling in space to the minute constituent parts of atoms—seem rather to point to a universal pattern of movement, governed by an Immutable Law of Change. Indeed, there is much reason to assume this Law to be eternal, to suppose that universes may take form and dissolve, aeon upon aeon, without deflecting its action any more than the birth and death of mayflies.

From this it is clear that, could we but analyse the pattern of changes governed by this Law and could we but relate our affairs to the right point in the everlasting process of ebb and flow, increase and decrease, rising and falling, we should be able to determine the best action to be taken in each case. Then, by peacefully according with the necessity to advance, remain stationary awhile or retreat, by cheerfully accepting the promise of gain and loss when each is due, we could come close to being masters of our lives!

This is precisely what the ancient Chinese Book of Change purports to teach us how to do. Its authors believed that they had succeeded in analysing Change itself into sixty-four constituent processes, each subdivided into six stages and all interacting upon one another. They invented a method for relating individual affairs to the stages and processes most closely affecting them, thus fashioning a key whereby future generations could unlock the secrets of the future and determine the surest way to live in harmony with the circumstances prevailing. For more than two thousand years, those who have learnt to use it have testified to the marvellous results obtained. That key is now in your hands—use it well and you will not be disappointed.

JOHN BLOFELD
Sala Santitham
Autumn 1963
Bangkok

INTRODUCTION

Since soon after noble Anthony allowed himself to be seduced by the languorous joys of Egypt's court, we barbarians from countries even closer to the Western Ocean's rim have nourished our children on stories about the fabulous treasures of the East. But all too often we have been thinking of such attractions as subtle perfumes, brocaded satins, carven jade, fragile porcelain, damascened swords or gorgeously set jewels. Doubtless a few of our ancestors sought in the East for treasures of the spirit or the mind, but it was not until the middle of this century that many of us began to thirst for spiritual refreshment from sources remoter than the Sea of Galilee. The groups of English-speaking people who actually practise teachings brought from India and the Further East are a new phenomenon and they are still few and small compared with the throngs of Asians teeming westwards to discover the secrets used in subduing nature's external forces. Driven by urgent necessity to seek remedies for disease, illiteracy, poverty and cruel want, many Asians have abandoned their traditional struggle to subdue the forces within man's own mind so as to concentrate on subjugating the external forces threatening their children with avoidable suffering. This is most understandable, but yet a cause of sadness to one who knows the value of what they have given up. On the other hand, it is heartening to observe a growing trickle of our own people hastening East in search of those who can still teach them how to conquer what lies within themselves. Meanwhile, perhaps partly induced by their search, less vital Asian influences are now percolating to many corners of the world; they are affecting architecture, interior decoration, landscape gardening, the fashioning and painting of porcelain and, above all, the art of cooking.

Some of those whose interest in Asia is stimulated by these influences must sooner or later long to discover what really lies behind, say, the ability to create an extraordinarily moving arrangement of rocks and moss or to give life and movement to forms delineated with a few sparse brush strokes executed in plain black ink. As recent publishers' catalogues will show, many of our contemporaries have gone deeper than those eighteenth-century dabblers who were content to augment their knowledge of exotic bric-à-brac with the merest sprinkling of Chinese philosophy. Amidst a welter of charlatanism in literature and life, something is taking root in the west of that spiritual activity which expresses itself in such varied (and to us exotic) forms as Zen and other kinds of Buddhist mind control, Hindu yoga, Tibetan tantra and Sufi mysticism. At least some students of these spiritual and mental disciplines have come to care less for conquering the world about them than for seeking within the silence of their own hearts the very meaning of life.

Though organized religion may be declining in many of the traditionally Christian countries, one of the great questions propounded by Jesus Christ continues to haunt us: 'What is a man profited if he shall gain the whole world and lose his own soul?' A sinister echo of this poignant question now posing itself with growing insistence is: 'What shall it profit a people to plumb the profoundest secrets of the material universe if such knowledge leads to the expunction of life from the surface of the earth?' Besides, even were this threat removed, our preoccupation with such activities as spanning rivers and increasing the yield of crops would still leave us helpless in the face of our worst sufferings, for these prey less upon the flesh than upon the feelings and the mind; indeed, people wealthy enough to escape most physical discomforts seem peculiarly liable to mental and emotional afflictions. Suppose there were full attainment of the chief goal at which so many nations now aim, namely the complete satisfaction of every citizen's material needs, the resulting triumph might well fall short of expectations. Of course the fight against disease, hunger, poverty and illiteracy must go on, especially in the many countries where these are still life and death issues, but why should we not aim at simultaneous conquest of the without and the within?

There are already numerous English translations of Eastern works whose authors devoted most of their lives to self-conquest and self-understanding; for books such as these, the *Book of Change* (*I Ching*, pronounced YEE JING) is not a substitute, since it has a specialized function; but its worth is incalculable in that, besides being permeated with the highest spiritual values, it enables any reasonably unselfish person who is capable of fulfilling a few simple conditions both to foresee and to CONTROL the course of future events! By rightly interpreting and strictly following the *I Ching*'s interpretation of universal laws, we can make ourselves as farsighted as the lesser Gods! Though, because of its peculiar nature and immense antiquity, it may not be felt to make good connected reading; it can be used to explain the present and predict the future with almost terrifying precision! For those who wish to live in harmonious accord with nature's decrees but who naturally find them too inscrutable to be gathered from direct observation and experience, its guidance is unexcelled.

In China, as in Japan, Korea and Vietnam which have a predominantly Chinese-style civilization, the *Book of Change* has been in constant use from remote antiquity until the present. Confucius himself set such store by it that the leather thongs binding the tablets on which his copy was inscribed were three times worn out! Once he exclaimed that, had he fifty years to spare, he would devote all of them to studying the *Book of Change*! In Japan, right up to the time of the Meiji Reformation less than a century ago, even military tactics were strictly based upon a pattern inspired by this extraordinary book. The *Encyclopædia Britannica* mentions this in the slightly contemptuous manner quite commonly adopted by Western savants faced by something beyond their comprehension, but then adds that the Samurai (to whom the whole passage refers) formed one of the best fighting forces the world has ever known! Many Japanese believe that the naval victories they won in the earlier part of the Pacific War owed much to the fact that books of strategy based upon the Book of Change were required reading for the higher ranks of Japanese officers. As one of my Japanese friends wryly remarked: 'If the people at the very top had not been too "modern" to consult the *Book of Change*, all those tremendous victories would not have been thrown away.'

It is doubtful if anyone in Mao Tsê-tung's China is encouraged to read the *I Ching*, unless as part of a course in ancient literature—yet I should be only mildly surprised to learn that the strategy of his generals owes something to its inspiration. Certainly the movements of the Chinese army along the Indian frontier in 1962–63 possessed characteristics reminiscent of the lessons traditionally drawn from the *Book of Change* by strategists. In Japanese universities, it retains something of its traditional place; indeed, among the populations of the Far Eastern countries at almost every level, its exponents and admirers are innumerable. For example, only two or three days before this was written, Mr Charles Luk, the famous Ch'an (Zen) scholar of Hongkong, sent me a newspaper cutting describing how a child who had wandered from home on a mountainous island near Hongkong had been discovered a few days later 'thanks to the inspired action of the parents in consulting the *I Ching*'.

My aim in making a new translation of this work is to produce a version in the simplest possible language containing clear instructions for its use in divination, so that any English-speaking person who approaches it sincerely and intelligently can use it as an infallible means of choosing good and avoiding evil. I must make it clear that it is not one of those ordinary fortune-telling books which forecast future events and leave us to sit back passively awaiting them; indeed, its authors did not regard the details of the future as unalterable, but as liable to follow general trends and tendencies. Instead of rigid prophecies, it makes suggestions, based on an analysis of the interplay of universal forces, not about what WILL happen but what SHOULD be done to accord with or to avoid a given happening. It makes us the architects of our own future, while helping us to avoid or minimize disasters and to derive some benefit from every possible situation. It is a book for those who prize virtue and harmony above profit. It will not, for example, help us to get rich or to injure our enemies (unless they happen to be working against the public good), but it will help us to make the best of our lives and to live in harmony with prevailing circumstances, whatever they may be.

Professor Richard Wilhelm's translation of the same work, together with an admirable foreword by the great C. G. Jung, has long been available in both German and English. My version neither competes with nor duplicates his; it is intended to serve a somewhat different purpose. Apart from being shorter and simpler, it differs from his in several other ways. For one, my explanatory chapters deal with but one of the several aspects of the Chinese original and are thus rather modest in their scope. Whereas Wilhelm's version is to some extent a textbook suggesting how the words of the text were derived from the symbolic diagrams to which they refer, my version is almost wholly concentrated on the aspect of divination—not because it is the most important, but because the deeper aspects of the *I Ching* are so profound that even were I qualified to deal with them, a thousand or two thousand pages would be needed to do them justice. That is why Chinese scholars have fought shy of stepping where Wilhelm dared to tread. Some Chinese literati with whom I discussed the matter were at first shocked by or contemptuous of my audacity in declaring that I intended to bring out a SIMPLE version of the *I Ching*. 'Simple!' one of them exclaimed, 'Then why not aim at making big money by bringing out a simple version of the teachings of Einstein?' However, they were mollified when I added that I would deal only with the divination aspects in my notes and explanatory chapters; and, later, one of them even undertook to correct the mistakes in my translation. I do agree with them in feeling that Wilhelm should either have said

INTRODUCTION

very much more about certain aspects of the book or else left them alone. What we have now is sufficient to excite our curiosity but not to allay it.

Another difference between the two versions is that my translation usually makes some kind of sense, whereas many passages in Wilhelm's make none. (Some examples chosen at random are: 'Someone does indeed increase him; ten pairs of tortoises cannot oppose it.' 'The inferior man molts in the face.' ' "Laughing words—ha ha!" Afterward one has a rule.' 'The underbrush is of such abundance that the small stars can be seen at noon.' 'He dissolves his blood. Thus he keeps at a distance from injury.' 'Release yourself from your big toe.' 'The way of wood creates success.') These mysterious passages may be the result partly of a desire to be wholly faithful to the original text and partly of failure to understand it. Curiously, my avoidance of entirely meaningless phrases is not altogether an advantage. Apart from the fact that those extraordinary passages of Wilhelm's I have quoted may be regarded by some people as rather appropriate to a book of auguries and thoroughly in line with the mysterious utterances of sibyls in other parts of the world, there is the more important matter of the terseness of the Chinese original. Its exceedingly terse style in many places justifies a number of widely varying translations; nor is it unlikely that in some passages several simultaneous meanings were deliberately implied. Moreover, the Chinese text includes hardly any pronouns at all, so that my arbitrary inclusion of them for the sake of reasonably good English puts a quite artificial limitation on the meaning. My readers, in using this book for divination, should always bear in mind that, for example, 'For ten years he performs no useful function' can equally mean 'For ten years, she (I, you, we, they) perform (performed, will perform) no useful function' and quite possibly 'For ten years, I (you, he, etc.) could not (cannot, will not be able to) be usefully employed (or usefully find employment for myself, himself, etc.).' Usually, the context of a sentence in an ordinary Chinese book makes it quite clear as to what pronouns and tenses are intended; but, in the case of the *I Ching*, there are many isolated phrases with no context to help us. Quite arbitrarily, I have often used 'he' in what I have called the Text and 'we' in the Commentary attached to it; the idea being that the Text tells us, so to speak, a little story with a symbolical meaning and that the Commentary relates this story to our own circumstances. I think most people familiar with the Chinese original will regard this strategy as justified by the intention of the authors. Another pitfall is the vagueness of certain individual words—such as 'evil', which might be 'evil men' or 'evil doing', etc.

While on the subject of Wilhelm's version, I must record my debt to him. Though I have hardly ever followed his translation except in places where it was obviously the best possible way of rendering the Chinese, I am indebted to him for quite a lot of my vocabulary, especially for the names of many of the hexagrams and even for those most useful words 'trigram' and 'hexagram' to distinguish KUA composed of three or six lines.

Throughout the translation, everything placed in brackets has been added by myself—either for explanatory purposes or because I feel that the words are implied in the Chinese version. However, in some cases where the Chinese text implies additional words positively demanded by the sense or by English grammar and style, I have avoided using brackets. I have also bracketed explanatory remarks about the structure of the hexagrams. Thus 'The fifth line is central (to the upper trigram)' contains an explanation which the Chinese reader would find unnecessary, not so an English reader unfamiliar with this work.

I cannot always guarantee the accuracy of my translation. Judging from several Chinese versions of the *Book of Change* in my possession, even expert Chinese commentators have widely varying and even contradictory explanations of the more difficult passages. The most I can do is to assure the reader that my renderings of even the abstrusest passages are reasonable attempts and that any Chinese experts who disagree might be hard put to it to prove me definitely wrong. Moreover, the translations of the Text and Commentary connected with each hexagram and with each individual line were all sent to Hongkong to be vetted by a Chinese friend well-versed in the *I Ching*, Mr K. S. Fung, whose English is excellent. Such is Mr Fung's great respect for the *I Ching* that he was not content to trust even his own understanding of it, though based on many years of study; so, in turn, he passed my translation to Professor Chan Charm Chuen, Mr Ngan Shiu Tung and Mr Wong Shing Tsang.[1] Needless to say, they found a number of faults in my original draft; but, as I have now incorporated their corrections, it is to be hoped that few, if any, very serious errors remain. However, English being far less terse and ambiguous than Chinese, I may have failed sometimes to give the WHOLE sense of the original; i.e. my version conveys the truth, but perhaps not the whole

---

[1] These gentlemen are not responsible for my explanatory notes, which they have so far not seen.

truth. Whatever I know of the Chinese language has come to me from living very long in China and very close to Chinese people. This has in many ways been good for me and for my knowledge of the language; but the style of the *I Ching* is so archaic that I cannot help regretting my lack of scientific training under a highly distinguished sinologue of the calibre of Arthur Waley. Such a training would have been most valuable in enabling me to be sure of allotting to each character what was probably its contemporary meaning at the time when the *I Ching* was written. If my rendering does contain some errors that bring smiles to the lips of the sinologues, I hope they will be smiles of compassion.

JOHN BLOFELD
Sala Santitham
Bangkok

Rainy Season, 1963

PART ONE
EXPLANATORY CHAPTERS

CHAPTER I

AN APPROACH TO THE BOOK OF CHANGE

It was not until fairly recently that Asian scholars began to interest themselves widely in the material sciences which—for better and for worse—have done so much to transform human life, especially in the West. Formerly, Asia's thinkers were chiefly occupied with the search for life's meaning (or, at any rate, man's true goal) and for ways of utilizing that vital knowledge for self-cultivation and self-conquest. One of the most valuable, though far from the most coherent, of the aids to understanding life's rhythmic processes, with a view to bringing man back into harmony with them is the Chinese *Book of Change*. As to its date of origin and authorship—questions to which more importance is attached in the West than in Asia—opinions vary. Confucius, who lived some two thousand five hundred years ago, regarded it even then as an ancient work and it is safe to assume that some parts of it are at the very least three thousand years old. Indeed, it must be one of the very oldest extant books in the world. The authorship of the basic Text is attributed to King Wên (1150 BC) and his son Duke Chou and that of the Commentary which now forms an integral part of the whole to Confucius and his disciples. There is no conclusive proof either for or against these claims; all that can be said is that the book is certainly of very great antiquity and that recent scholarship indicates that the Chinese have been right about such things rather more often than was formerly supposed. In any case, the matter seems to me of scarcely more than academic interest; what does interest me enormously is that the *Book of Change*, when properly put to the test, responds in such a way as to remove all doubts about its value as a book of divination.

My calling it the *Book of Change*, instead of using the more usual plural form, the *Book of Changes*, is something of an innovation. The Chinese language, of course, is free from the complication of number, gender and so on, so both translations are valid. My choice of the singular form arises from my conviction that the Chinese authors selected the title to reflect their concept of Change as the one unchanging aspect of the universe normally perceptible to human beings. In this universal context, individual changes are relatively unimportant; it is the process of change itself which needs to be emphasized.

Whether we use the *I Ching* for divination or to study the principles involved in it, if we allow ourselves to be governed by its teaching, we shall thereby enrich the content of our lives, free ourselves from anxiety, become harmless or even intelligently helpful to others and pleasant companions to ourselves. It is a source of inner harmony and of communion with those great forces whose interplay creates all visible and invisible worlds except for their own Parent, the T'ai Chi or Absolute Itself. It sets for us a marvellous ideal, that of the Chüntzû or Superior Man—one who is perfectly self-controlled and self-sufficient, wholly free from self-seeking and able to stand firmly and serenely among forces which toss lesser men to and fro like shuttlecocks, despite their tears and screams. Cheerfully impervious to loss or gain, he acts vigorously when action is needed and willingly performs the much harder task of refraining from action when things are better left alone. Able to reconcile whatever can be reconciled, he knows how to stand aside rather than waste his effort on the impossible. Well disposed to enjoy the pleasures of eating, drinking, sleeping, travelling and so forth, he is capable of meeting stress, pain, disability, bereavement, illness and death without repining. In him, compassion and patient acceptance are united. Fools will take him for a bigger fool than themselves: wise men will know him for an incomparable sage. (Incidentally, students of Zen who know what to look for in an accomplished teacher will recognize the Chüntzû at the moment of meeting him. Of course, everybody can recognize one if he knows how to look.)

For well over two thousand years, the *Book of Change*, presumably more or less in its present form, has been used for divination and, in an earlier and briefer form, since considerably earlier than that. It is this seemingly occult aspect of the book, so easily taken for granted by the Chinese, which is likely to call forth disbelief and even scorn from Westerners who have never put it honestly to the test. I have no means of convincing sceptics unless by asking them to test its powers in all sincerity, which their very disbelief will make virtually impossible for them. Correct interpretation of the oracles requires a particular state of mind—here again, students of Zen possess a special advantage—in which respect based on belief is a vital factor. My own experience is that the oracles, properly sought and properly interpreted, are unfailingly correct; so that, if the injunctions implied by them are followed strictly, everything will come to pass exactly as foreseen.

The world-famous psychologist, C. G. Jung, whose illuminating preface to the English edition of Wilhelm's version is a joy to read, courageously dared the scorn of his fellow scientists by publicly asserting his belief in the *I Ching*'s predictions. He even went so far as to attempt to show why they are correct. His argument, as far as I can understand it, is that whatever happens at a given moment is bound up with the entire universal situation then prevailing; hence, even if the (to my mind) rather inadequate method of coin-tossing is used for consultations, there need be no doubt about the result; for the way the coins fall will be governed by that prevailing situation. In this connection, he also employs the phrase 'exploring the unconscious', apparently suggesting that the function of the *I Ching* is to draw from the unconscious to the surface of our minds whatever is necessary for a correct understanding of the problem posed and its solution. I must confess that, much as I admire C. G. Jung, I cannot accept this explanation—perhaps because I do not really understand it. What seems to me a flaw in the argument about coin-tossing is that, while it is true that everything occurring at a given moment is closely interrelated with the prevailing universal situation, the *I Ching* gives equally apposite answers to all questions, regardless of the time of asking them. Thus, if I ask how Nigeria will fare in the years 1970–80, a correct prediction cannot be much affected, if at all, by my asking the question at ten a.m. on December 24, 1963, or at seven p.m. on January 17, 1964. If Professor Jung were still alive, he would probably be able to satisfy me on this point; as it is, we shall never know. Anyway, what is particularly striking is that a great man who set much store by scientific method frankly testified to his conviction of the book's divinatory powers. His scientist's integrity was revealed by his willingness to jeopardize his reputation among his fellow scientists rather than suppress what seemed to him to be the facts.

Like Jung, I have been struck by the extraordinary sensation aroused by my consultations of the book, the feeling that my question has been dealt with EXACTLY AS BY A LIVING BEING in full possession of even the unspoken facts involved in both the question and its answer. At first, this sensation comes near to being terrifying and, even now, I find myself inclined to handle and transport the book rather as if it had feelings capable of being outraged by disrespectful treatment!

As to how the book succeeds in giving answers which produce this uncanny effect, I do not know. A number of explanations may all be near the mark, as with the opinions of several witnesses who have observed the same traffic accident from different places in the street. If you say that the oracle owes its effectiveness to the subconscious of the one who asks the questions, or to the unconscious (which is probably universal and therefore common to all men), or to the One Mind (in the Zen sense), or to God or a God or the Gods, or to the philosopher's Absolute, I shall be inclined to agree with every one of these suggestions, for I believe that most of all of these terms are imperfect descriptions of a single unknown and unknowable but omnipotent reality. Rather than attempt an explanation of my own, I bear in mind two sayings—Laotzû's 'He who knows does not speak; he who speaks does not know' and the old English adage 'The proof of the pudding is in the eating'. In other words, I am entirely satisfied with the results produced by the *I Ching*, but do not presume to explain the lofty process by which they are achieved.

I had spent many years in China and had acquired some knowledge of the Buddhist classics as well as a much slighter knowledge of Taoist works before I began to feel much interest in the *I Ching*. No doubt one of the reasons for this delay was that the Chinese text is so difficult as to be largely incomprehensible to anyone who has not made it the object of special study. What first caught my attention was the discovery that so many Chinese scholars, despite intellectual backgrounds so varied that they stretched almost all the way from Laotzû and Confucius to Karl Marx, spoke of the *I Ching* with respect and let it be seen that they would have much to say about it if they believed me really interested. In the end I bought copies of the Chinese text and of the English version of Wilhelm's translation. The first I soon put on one side as beyond my powers of understanding and the second, for some reason or other, I put away in a cupboard with other books without reading much of it. Then came the Communist revolution and my departure from China, perhaps for ever. By a curious chance, the Wilhelm version found its way into the trunk containing the relatively small number of books I decided to carry away with me. It was not until I had been in Siam for something like ten years that a chance remark made me study the book with some care and try my hand at using it for divination. The very first time I did this, I was overawed to a degree that amounted to fright, so strong was the impression of having received an answer to my question from a living, breathing person. I have scarcely ever used it since without recovering something

AN APPROACH TO THE BOOK OF CHANGE

of that awe, though it soon came to be characterized by a pleasurable excitement rather than by fear. Of course I do not mean to assert that the white pages covered with black printer's ink do in fact house a lively spiritual being. I have dwelt at some length on the astonishing effect they produce chiefly as a means of emphasizing how extraordinarily accurate and, so to speak, personal, are its answers in most cases. Yet, if I were asked to assert that the printed pages do not form the dwelling of a spiritual being or at least bring us into contact with one by some mysterious process, I think I should be about as hesitant as I am to assert the contrary.

To clarify this a little, I propose to offer three examples of the *I Ching*'s answers to enquiries. The first is an example of a question properly put and accurately answered, while the other two demonstrate the book's disconcerting but humorous means of rejecting questions that are improper in themselves or put to it in improper circumstances.

My interest in the *I Ching* was fully awakened towards the end of 1962 at about the time when hostilities between India and mainland China commenced in the Tibetan border region. Before long, the newspapers in Bangkok (where I live) were prophesying that the Chinese armies would continue their rapid advance, swoop down onto the plains of India and perhaps occupy some major cities there before India's friends could come to her defence. The contrary view was never expressed in the newspapers that came to my notice. As I had been very happy both in China and India and felt a keen affection for both peoples, I was deeply disturbed; finally, in a spirit of sincere enquiry, I consulted the *Book of Change*. The answer was so contrary to other people's predictions that I decided to write it down word for word. I do not have the record by me now; but, as far as I remember, my interpretation, which was closely based upon the actual wording of the book, ran something like this, though it was considerably longer and more detailed. An army in the hills (the Chinese) was looking down upon the marshy plain below (India). If its leaders were wise, they would halt their attack at the very moment when everything was going well for them, refrain from advancing further and perhaps withdraw in some places. A week or two later, this is precisely what happened. Moreover, the *I Ching* had given reasons for this advice, namely that the lines of communication were already too long for safety; that the opponent (India) was likely to receive powerful support from its friends; that the moral value of calling a halt before any necessity for it became generally apparent would be greater in the long run than fresh military gains; and several other reasons which I cannot now recall. I remember that every one of them was later adduced in newspaper articles to explain the unexpected behaviour of the Chinese and I vividly recall the astonishment of my friends when I showed them what I had written down in advance of the newspapers. It could of course be claimed that a good deal of the accuracy of my answer was due to my particular interpretation of the actual words below the two hexagrams and the two moving lines involved; but, as I had not at all expected the Chinese to call a halt or reasoned out the possible reasons for their doing so, it is hard to see how I could have made myself the dupe of autosuggestion.

The following is a reconstruction from memory of the way in which I obtained these results. The response consisted of Hexagram 48 plus moving lines in the first and second places of that hexagram plus Hexagram 63 (which results when those lines 'move' and thus become their own opposites).

Hexagram 48 signifies a well. My knowledge of the Indo-Tibetan borderlands, where the mighty Himalayas slope sharply down to the dead flat plain of north India, led me promptly to equate India with the well and to think of the Chinese as looking down into it from above. Of the two component trigrams, one has 'bland' or 'mild' among its meanings, while the other means 'water'. Taking water, the contents of the well, to be the people of India, I found it easy to think of bland or mild as representing their declared policy of non-violence and neutrality. Thus, the significance of these two trigrams convinced me that I had been right to suppose that the well represented India (or the whole of that country except for the Himalayan border region). The Text attached to that hexagram contained three ideas which seemed to me appropriate to the situation. That the well suffers no increase or decrease suggested that India would lose no territory lying south of the mountainous frontier region; the rope's being too short suggested that the Chinese could not safely extend their lines of communication further than they had already done; otherwise, their 'pitcher' would be broken, i.e. they would suffer a serious reverse or defeat.

Next, I examined the texts and commentaries attached to the two moving lines (lines 1 and 2) of that hexagram. The commentary on the first of them suggested that a further Chinese advance would not succeed and that the time had come for a wise commander to 'give up', i.e. to halt and perhaps to withdraw somewhat. The commentary on the second moving line suggested that, in addition to the tactical

AN APPROACH TO THE BOOK OF CHANGE

reason for halting already given, there was also a strategic or political reason, namely China's inability to win a favourable response from other countries, hostile, friendly or neutral as the case might be.

The main Text and Commentary of Hexagram 63 reinforced the conclusions I had reached. 'Success in small matters' suggested that the Chinese would not forfeit their local gains in the Himalayan region. The reward promised for persistence in a *righteous* course appeared enigmatic, until I remembered that the Chinese had never accorded recognition to the McMahon Line; thus they could argue (and certainly believed) that they had a legal claim to certain border areas, to which past Chinese governments had also laid claim; whereas there could be no shadow of legality to back up an advance into the Indian plains (i.e. down into the well). The last sentence of the main Commentary attached to this hexagram states: 'It is clear that good fortune will accompany the start; but, ultimately, affairs will be halted amidst disorder because the way peters out.' The last four words of this passage are often taken to mean: 'thenceforth, heaven's blessing is (or will be) withdrawn.' In other words, for the Chinese to advance into the plains with no moral claim whatsoever to support them would be to court disaster. Thus, in a nutshell, the whole response conveyed to me the idea that the Chinese would gain local successes, but that there were tactical, strategic and moral reasons for supposing that no further advance could be made with impunity.

My second example concerns a time just a few days after this prediction had been fulfilled. Flushed with this and some other successes, I soon put a question that was suggested by an incident described in C. G. Jung's preface to Wilhelm's version. I asked the *I Ching* whether I could now consider myself as a qualified interpreter of its oracles and freely make use of its power to influence the lives of those of my friends who had faith in it. In other words, the question resulted from an impure motive—self-esteem! The answer was as salutary as it was deflating. In effect I was informed that one who sought to interpret the *Book of Change* for people who would rely upon his reading of the answers must possess a considerable number of intellectual and moral virtues, several of which were named directly or by implication. The really shattering sentence came at the end. According to my interpretation the *Book of Change* added: 'Do you really suppose that you have these qualities in any marked degree?' My cheeks could not have been redder if I had been unexpectedly reproved by a living person whose high opinion I particularly desired.

The only other time I have so far made this sort of blunder was during a dinner party at my house. One of the guests persuaded me to demonstrate the powers of the *I Ching* for a French lady. I should of course have refused. In the first place, no serious Chinese admirer of the book would dream of testing its powers for the sake of an experiment any more than you or I would deliberately test in public the knowledge of a professor staying under our roof to discover whether he really knows his subject or is a charlatan. Then again, though none of us was drunk, we had all had quite a lot to drink and were incapable of the proper degree of seriousness and composure of mind upon which successful interpretation of the oracles depends. As I had no real desire to convince the French lady either of the *I Ching's* powers or my own, my agreeing to carry out the test was frivolous and for this I was well punished. With the air of an adult basically unfond of children who politely consents to take part in a children's game, Mademoiselle consented to ask me to foretell the events of the coming year as they affected her. For a reason I did not understand until later, the answer, on account of numerous moving lines and some unexpected delays, took so long to come out that everybody in the room had come to share her boredom by the time I was ready to read out my interpretation. From politeness conversation had almost ceased and for almost an hour my friends sat gazing at the uninspiring sight of myself busy with pen and paper. Somehow I was so busy dealing with each small segment of the answer that it was not until I came to read it out that I really took in its meaning as a whole. My scribbled drafting and re-drafting had covered several sheets of paper and, as I found it hard to decipher such hasty writing, the process of reading the answer in itself took quite a long time. Sentence after sentence, I stumbled through it and, when at last I reached the end, I found that all I had written added up to no more than this:

'If you wish to be virtuous, behave virtuously in word and deed. If you want to enjoy yourself, do whatever you enjoy doing. If you want to travel, travel. If you prefer to stay at home, stay at home'—and so on!

All my efforts and all the boredom my friends had endured were rewarded with nothing better than a series of dismal platitudes! For weeks afterwards I could not meet Mademoiselle without blushing at the recollection.

This moral tale should be taken to heart by those who hope to get interesting and valuable results from consulting the *Book of Change*.

AN APPROACH TO THE BOOK OF CHANGE

It is a book which must on no account be treated lightly. As a Chinese friend of mine wrote recently:

'The responses to be won from the *Book of Change* are sometimes of such tremendous import that they may save us from a lifetime of folly, or even from premature death. It must be treated with the deference due to its immense antiquity and to the wealth of wisdom it contains. No living man can be worthy of equal deference, for it is no less than a divine mirror which reflects the processes of vast and never-ending cosmic change, those endless chains of actions and interaction which assemble and divide the myriad objects proceeding from and flowing into T'ai Chi—the still reality underlying the worlds of form, desire and formlessness. It has the omniscience of a Buddha. It speaks to the transient world as though from the Womb of Change itself—Change, the one constant factor amidst all the countless permutations and transformations of mental and material objects which, when the eye of wisdom is closed, appear to us as meaningless flux. That their infinite number can be mirrored in so small a compass is because they all proceed according to adamantine laws and all are facets of that spotless purity and stillness which some men call T'ai Chi or the Tao and others the Bhūtatathatā, the Womb of the Tathāgatas (Buddhas), the Source of All.' (Extract from a Chinese newspaper article.)

More or less to repeat what has just been said, but in slightly different terms, everything observable by the senses is subject to change and therefore in motion, for the Unchanging which Christians call the Godhead or God is imperceptible, unless to those experiencing the state variously called Unity with the Godhead, Supreme Enlightenment, Absorption in the Tao. It is the function of the *Book of Change* so to interpret the various interlocking cycles of change that the progress of individual transformations can be deduced from them and the enquirer thereby receive a firm support which will help him to avoid being swept through the vortex like a leaf carried by angry waters. Though we cannot, by holding up our hand and using Words of Power, bid the winds and waves to cease, we can learn to navigate the treacherous currents by conducting ourselves in harmony with the prevailing processes of transformation; thus we can safely weather successive storms in this life and in all lives to come until that probably remote time when, having penetrated to the very heart of change, we enter the immutable, undifferentiated stillness which is at once the womb and the crown of being.

An attitude of reverence—though indispensable—is not the sole condition for correct interpretation of the *Book of Change*. Not the least of the various obstacles is the exceedingly archaic mode of expression which adds to the difficulty of understanding what must have seemed strange even to readers contemporary with the book's authors; for, as with oracles the world over, the meaning is so esoteric as to baffle the mind until intuition, careful thought or some unforeseen experience provide a sudden illumination. Probably the authors were sometimes deliberately obscure, for it has always been usual for Eastern sages to cloak their teaching in terms which hinder its misuse or profanation by non-initiates. However, the main reason for the difficulty we have in interpreting the *I Ching* is that Confucius and his disciples, not to speak of King Wên and his contemporaries, are separated from us by such a vast period of time. Thus, even for the Chinese, the language requires prolonged special study; as for us, the strangeness is greatly enhanced by the disparity between our two cultures—the one based largely on those intuitive thought-processes which stem from a consciousness turned inward, the other deriving from an outward-turning of the mind in accordance with the principles of Greek logic and the empirical sciences. How should authors separated from us by such great distances in time and space not seem obscure? In my translation, I have sought to minimize the difficulty, but I have not dared go too far for fear of being unfaithful to the original or distorting the true meaning by clumsy and incomplete interpretations. Moreover, I have accounted only generally for the way in which the Chinese authors derived each sentence from the construction of the lines and hexagrams forming the pre-textual symbology, for the scope of that subject is too great and my knowledge of it far from adequate.

Those readers who positively like their oracles to be couched in terms so obscure as to be inscrutable will prefer Wilhelm's version to mine, as parts of it are obscure enough to satisfy the most ardent devotees of mystery. A certain loss of picturesqueness is the price I have had to pay for making my rendering as easily intelligible as the Chinese text allows.

Another serious difficulty is that of relating the answer given to the question asked. For this, use of the intuitive faculty is essential, but intuition is the very faculty which among Western people is generally the least developed. Consequently, any previous training the reader

AN APPROACH TO THE BOOK OF CHANGE

may have had in Zen or analogous systems of supra-intellectual development will be most helpful. In most cases, some weeks or months of practice will be necessary for acquiring reasonable proficiency. Without that practice, though our interpretations may often be correct, the danger of misunderstanding will make it inadvisable to base weighty decisions upon the predictions obtained. On the other hand, proficiency can be acquired by anyone able to achieve such stern impartiality as to preclude any modification of the real meaning by wishful thinking. If at first some of the *I Ching*'s predictions seem to be faulty, they should be noted down together with the questions asked and the numbers of the moving lines and hexagrams composing the answers; later, it will be seen that the faults lay not with the predictions but with the interpreter's lack of skill. A really skilled interpreter who consults the *Book of Change* correctly will find that the answers given are NEVER WRONG! C. G. Jung quotes the example of Confucius who, in all the years he leant upon its advice, did find the *I Ching* 'wrong' just once. What really happened was that it advised him to modify a certain heaviness of character of which he himself was not sufficiently aware.

It may be thought that, as the *Book of Change* contains only sixty-four hexagrams, the number of possible responses must be very limited; actually the total number runs into many thousands. As will be seen, the first hexagram elicited by manipulation of the divining sticks usually contains one or more moving lines, each of which adds to or modifies the basic meaning of that hexagram and, by merging with its own opposite, contributes towards the formation of a second hexagram which has also to be taken into account. Even so, a book is of course a static object; once printed, the words are fixed in their places and the total vocabulary limited accordingly. Thus if someone were to ask the *I Ching* whether to send his son to Oxford or to Harvard, it could not plainly answer 'Oxford', since that word is for obvious reasons not to be found in its text. Provided the question were backed by weighty reasons and serious intent, a correct answer would undoubtedly be given; but its wording might overtax the skill of most interpreters; so it would be wise to rephrase the question and thus reduce the hazard of misunderstanding. For example, two separate questions could be put, one relating to each university.

Other questions liable to produce cloudy answers are those in which the time period is left too vague. The *I Ching* generally foretells events without clearly specifying just when they will occur, so it is advisable

c

to phrase the question accordingly. We may ask what will happen to such and such a project or person within three months or three years or whatever period of time seems apposite. A highly skilled interpreter might scorn to use this simple method. Not long ago, a Chinese friend who had recently joined the Ministry of Foreign Affairs at Taipei asked me to enquire when he would obtain his first posting abroad. The first answering hexagram implied that the oblation had been made but not the sacrifice and the second spoke of crossing the great river. Presently, my friend took the *I Ching* from my hands and, within a minute or two, pronounced himself satisfied with the answer, though I was still puzzled by its apparent vagueness. He explained the matter as follows.

'Most officials in our Ministry look forward to being posted abroad, so, for fairness sake, such posting largely depends on length of service, though this is by no means a hard and fast rule. That an oblation has been made but not the sacrifice means that I entered upon my public duties only a little while ago and that I have not yet performed enough service to amount to a sacrifice for the public good. Just as, in ancient times, the worth of each sacrifice of oxen and so on was precisely fixed, so is it now a different kind of sacrifice. In other words, I may hope for no special favours in the form of an unusually early posting abroad. Crossing the great river can certainly be taken to mean crossing the sea, for times have changed since the territory south of the Yangtse was the furthest anyone thought of travelling. Besides, as you see, the Chinese editor notes that some of the words in the text imply that the prediction will be fulfilled as soon as possible. Taking the two together, it is obvious that I shall not be sent abroad before I qualify by length of service, but also that I shall not be kept waiting (as so many of us are) beyond that time.'

This anecdote illustrates one vital aspect of the *I Ching*'s philosophy, namely that performance of duty to the state or to the people is commensurate with performing sacred duties to the Lord of Heaven. The connection between my friend's entering the government service and making a preliminary oblation before the commencement of the sacrifice is a very precise one. The answer he received contains several nuances that a Western interpreter might overlook, which suggests that the *I Ching* may not function quite as well in Western as in Chinese hands. This may indeed be so AT FIRST, but long practice in

AN APPROACH TO THE BOOK OF CHANGE 35

divination and careful study of the text will gradually acquaint us with the underlying meanings of its symbolism. Moreover, since intuition plays a greater part than intellect in interpreting the responses, even the most obscure answers will cause no great difficulty to one skilled in exercising this power.

The *Book of Change* is more concerned with ways of attaining inner satisfaction and harmony with our surroundings than with helping us along the road to material success, especially if that success is likely to cause difficulties to others or adversely affect our character or peace of mind. Questions as to how to live in harmony with conditions over which we can exercise only limited control will bring forth more helpful guidance than questions aimed at discovering means of gaining materially. This does not mean that ALL questions concerning commerce and financial matters should be avoided, for obviously these may profoundly affect our true welfare and that of our dependants; but betting, gambling on the stock exchange and all means of self-enrichment involving no service to others are too foreign to the spirit of the *I Ching* to form suitable subjects for our questions. Reputable Chinese scholars very rarely consent to put enquiries of this kind, but the ordinary street-corner fortune-tellers seldom share their scruples, for their main concern is to set their fee. However, as they often put their questions mechanically and without bothering to attain the necessary receptivity of mind, the replies they give their clients are seldom of much value, unless through coincidence or the exercise of cunning. I suppose that all of us are human enough to be tempted to put questions in which a lofty moral ingredient is not conspicuous; it is really very hard to know where to draw the line—strict rules cannot be laid down. All the same, it is well to bear in mind that the most helpful answers are received by those who set some limit to the degree of selfishness their questions involve. Most Chinese experts are agreed that every misuse of the book for selfish or frivolous ends is likely to decrease, perhaps permanently, the enquirer's quality of 'LING', that is to say his ability to obtain and interpret responses so accurate and to the point as to suggest almost supernatural powers.

Readers steeped in Zen or in the teachings of Taoism may wince at this heavily moralistic approach and I am inclined to agree with them that so much sermonizing (exceedingly foreign to my habit) demands either an apology or an explanation. No doubt my attitude has been conditioned by the strong doses of Confucianism that anyone who works for months upon this book must inevitably absorb—for, after all, the Confucian Commentaries form approximately half of the whole book in its present form—but at least two other factors have played their part in dictating this approach to a book dealing with powers transcending mere morality. The first is that, in order to make my translation useful to as many people as possible, I am obliged to emphasize the important connection between the motives behind our questions and the value of the *I Ching*'s answers. Though we dismiss what might be called the superstitious belief that the *Book of Change* 'is not inclined to' give answers to improperly put or unsuitable questions, the fact remains that even the pre-Confucian passages are written from a lofty moral standpoint; they seldom tell us that this or that is sure to happen, but rather that the Superior Man (i.e. the well-nigh perfect man) will be well advised to do this or to refrain from doing that. The second factor is my conviction that the supra-moral view of Zen and of Taoism has to be understood in its proper context and that this point is all too often overlooked by Western would-be adepts. Though both these schools of mind training teach that all mutually opposed pairs of concepts, including virtue and vice, good and evil and so on, are illusory distinctions which effectively veil the face of reality, this high teaching was never intended to absolve us from all scruples and restraint or to allow us antinomian license to follow the flame of our desires wherever it may dart; for it is assumed that the serious adept (to whom alone such teachings can apply) has reached a stage at which he is incapable of desiring to deceive, hurt, unbalance or otherwise harm himself or others. Of my many Asian teachers—Zen (Ch'an) Masters, Tantric Lamas and Taoist recluses—not one failed to preach something very close to conventional morality to those of their pupils (including myself) who had not yet advanced beyond the need for restraint by rule.

There are, however, two distinctions between conventional morality as understood in the West and the morality common to the *I Ching*, to Taoism and to Zen. One concerns the nature of evil and the other has to do with the function of sex. Whereas the usual Christian view seems to be that certain thoughts, words and deeds are in themselves evil, Buddhists, Taoists and, I think, the authors of the *I Ching* hold that they are less the fruit of evil than of ignorance, in the sense that a man endowed with great insight is not tempted into harming others or himself. Most Eastern sages commend a happy acceptance of life as it is and prophesy nothing but sorrow and frustration for those whose cupidity leads them to swim against the current of circumstance or to

AN APPROACH TO THE BOOK OF CHANGE

attempt interference with the working of universal laws in order to gain peculiar benefits for themselves.

As to sexual behaviour, there are not a few Christian teachers who so closely identify extramarital sexual intercourse with the utmost sinfulness as to make it seem comparatively more evil than many other courses of conduct which a native of the Far East would be much more likely to condemn. To the latter, extramarital sexual relations are culpable only if they cause suffering either to one of the persons concerned or to others; chastity becomes a moral duty only when a man undertakes to devote his entire energies to achieving the supreme goal—Enlightenment, Absorption in the Tao or whatever he may have learnt to call it. On the other hand, cupidity and interference with the peace and happiness of others are both regarded as incompatible with even the most elementary forms of spiritual progress.

The purpose of this digression is to throw some light upon what the Chinese would or would not regard as obstacles to achieving a state of mind suitable for consulting the *I Ching*. Generally speaking, the ability to attain a thoroughly receptive and so to speak 'void' state of mind just prior to and during consultations is nurtured by a way of life in which deliberate deceit or other harm to living beings is unthinkable —a way of life in which self and selfishness undergo the same sort of diminution as a slowly deflating balloon.

CHAPTER 2

THE BACKGROUND OF THE BOOK OF CHANGE

The *I Ching*, though it deals with vast cosmic forces and though its pronouncements have a universal validity, is essentially Chinese in flavour. In China, a clearcut distinction used seldom to be made between separate duties to the family, to the state and to the Gods—all of them being considered as overlapping parts of a single whole. Similarly, few Chinese make much distinction between one religion and another. We are apt to speak of a Chinese acquaintance as being a Confucian and/or Taoist and/or Buddhist; whereas he, if for once he ponders the matter deeply, may smilingly confess that he is all of those and something more as well: for there are whole segments of the traditional Chinese religion which fit into none of those categories; they have most curiously existed for several thousand years without even acquiring a name! When an elderly or middle-aged Chinese refers to his Chiao (religion)—which, by the way, is remarkably seldom—he is generally speaking of a highly individual compound of Confucian, Taoist and Buddhist ingredients (and others even more ancient but nameless) which happens to suit himself. The *Book of Change* reflects this typically Chinese attitude towards religion, cosmology and metaphysics if only because much of it took final shape before distinctions between one religion and another had arisen. Buddhism is absent from its pages, for the Indian religion did not reach China until long after the *I Ching* took final form. Even the possibility of their being Buddhist interpolations is slight although some passages are interpreted in later commentaries in a manner not untinged by Buddhist thought. In spite of this, students of Zen Buddhism will find in the *Book of Change* much with which they are familiar, partly because those who have stood face to face with Reality are bound to describe what pertains to it in rather similar terms.

The actual Text of the *I Ching* (attributed to King Wên and Duke Chou) surely dates from a period long antecedent to the emergence of Taoism and Confucianism as separate entities. Whereas the Commentaries are decidedly Confucian, the Text contains the seeds or prototypes of both religions and in any case, the two are not contradictory,

BACKGROUND OF THE BOOK OF CHANGE

though (perhaps unfortunately) a difference in emphasis has caused them to diverge along the separate paths of public duty and inner fulfilment. Just as many of the basic concepts of Christianity and Islam have a common origin in those of the Jewish Scriptures which came to form the Old Testament, so are the fundamental principles of Taoism and Confucianism found intertwined in the ancient *Book of Change*.

I have neither wisdom nor space enough to offer a learned disquisition on each of these venerable Chinese religions, but something must be said about the concepts common to both for the sake of those approaching the *I Ching* without any knowledge at all of classical Chinese thought. I must begin shamefacedly by putting out of mind two disconcerting sayings attributed to the founder of Taoism: 'He who speaks (of the Tao) does not know (it) and he who knows (it) does not speak (of it)'; 'The Tao (Way) which can be expressed in words is not the real Tao'! With what little confidence these sayings allow me, I shall now attempt to set forth my understanding of the matter.

There is T'ai Chi—the Universal Principle, the Ultimate Cause, the Absolute, the Eternal, the Never-Changing, the Ever-Changing, the One, the All. Nothing lies outside it; there is nothing which does not contain all of it. All things come from it; nothing comes from it. All things return to it; nothing goes into or returns to it. It IS all things; it is no thing. Thus, T'ai Chi (or thus my audacity in presuming to define it).

T'ai Chi's most easily observable function is I (pronounced YEE) —Change. At the normally perceptible level of existence, there is nothing which remains without movement, without change. Every single thing is either coming into existence, developing, decaying or going out of existence. (Simultaneously, but from another viewpoint neither superior nor inferior to the first, nothing moves, nothing changes, nothing comes into existence, develops, decays or goes out of existence; but, with divination, we are concerned with what appears to us in daily life, namely the former level.) Change, which is never-ending, proceeds according to certain universal and observable rules. In relying upon the *I Ching* to reveal the future, we are not dealing with magic but calculating the general trend of events and seeking the best way to accord with that trend by relating whatever matter we have in mind to the predictable cycle (or cycles) of events to which it belongs.

I (Change) is brought about by the interaction of T'ai Chi's complementary aspects, the Yang Principle and the Yin—Yang, Heaven, active, positive, male, firm, strong, light, etc.; Yin, earth, passive, negative, female, yielding, weak, dark, etc. Their interblending in varying proportions accounts for the differences between all substances and all objects in the universe. Flimsy analogies between ancient philosophies and modern scientific thought are seldom profitable, but in this case the temptation is too strong to resist. The old theory that there are ninety odd irreducible elements which in compounded form give rise to all substances and objects has, as we all know, given way to the knowledge that all things can be reduced to atoms and that their individual qualities are due to variations in the proportion of protons to electrons in the composition of these atoms. How far this bears analogy with the Yin and Yang concept, I am too ignorant of modern science to say; superficially there is a striking similarity. Both schools of thought agree that all substances are basically one substance (if substance it can be called) and that the differences between them are wholly due to varying combinations of what in each case may be loosely called its positive and negative aspects.

In the *Book of Change*, which doubtless follows a system of thought that was old when the book came to be written, the process of change is visualized as stretching from One to infinity by a path which, for convenience sake, is held to comprise Two (the Yin and the Yang), Eight (symbolized by the trigrams), Sixteen (symbolized by certain of the hexagrams), Thirty-Two (symbolized by those and sixteen other hexagrams) and Sixty-Four (symbolized by all the hexagrams). In other words, each stage along the path consists of a doubling of the previous figure. That no stages are usually included between sixty-four and infinity doubtless results from an arbitrary decision not to make things too complicated for ordinary human understanding. (Even with this arbitrary limit on the number of symbols, the *I Ching* can provide four thousand and ninety-six possible answers to our questions, which is surely sufficient for most purposes.)

Parallel with T'ai Chi at what might be called the centre of things were T'ai Chi not infinite and therefore centreless, there is Tao—the Way. In many passages it appears more or less synonymous with its august parent; but, as its literal meaning suggests, the choice of this term places emphasis upon the functional as opposed to the static aspect of the Absolute, for where there is a Way there is likely to be movement along it. Though the two are not to be regarded as separate, except for the sake of convenience, the word Tao has many other

BACKGROUND OF THE BOOK OF CHANGE 41

meanings which, closely connected as they are, cannot be thought of as identical with T'ai Chi. To Taoists, the Tao is very often the Way that each individual has to follow if he wishes to accord with the great cosmic principles that govern life instead of putting up a futile resistance to them at the cost of needless pain, stress and frustration. Or the term may be used in the sense of 'the right Way for a given individual' or the 'only possible Way for him'; in which case it would not be improper to speak of the Tao of a fish or of a soldier, meaning respectively living and dying in the manner of fishes and living in a manner which now and then involves the duty of hacking enemies to pieces. On the face of it, the inclusion of the soldier's Way would seem to involve a contradiction; for hacking men to pieces, even when regarded as a duty, may not be universally held to accord with the concept of Tao in its loftiest sense, but I doubt if many Chinese would accept that there is a contradiction. With their traditional contempt for soldiers, they would surely agree that a man does wrong to become a soldier; but very likely they would add that, having become one, he must behave as a soldier and, if so required, hack men to pieces. By so doing he follows his soldier's Tao, which is the Universal Tao viewed from between the hedges bordering his line of march. (Japanese Bushido made much of this sort of argument.) Another commonly met connotation of Tao is the Way viewed as a safe path through life from which carelessness may cause us to slip and to which it may be difficult to return. Confucian writers frequently use the term Tao in any or all of the above so to speak 'Taoist' senses, but to these they add one of their own—the Path of Virtue viewed as a way of public duty rather than of inner fulfilment. The *I Ching*, being pre-Taoist and pre-Confucian uses Tao without making any clear distinction of meanings beyond what is provided by the context.

Closely associated with the loftiest connotation of Tao is the concept of Tê (or Teh) which, in its primary sense, is the functioning or power of the Tao within the mind of an individual. (Here again, there is some overlapping, for Tao itself can also be used with just that meaning.) If I empty my mind of its likes and dislikes together with all the other rubbish accumulated during a lifetime of folly, I may expect to be guided by the functioning of the universal Tao in me, that is to say by my personal Tê. From this concept is derived another of Tê's meanings—virtue, both in its moral sense and in the sense of a specific power as when we speak of a man or a plant as possessing the virtue of healing. It might reasonably be held that Laotzû uses Tê to denote the functioning of the supreme Tao in an individual, whereas Confucius employs it in the sense of moral virtue acquired by education, practice and perseverance, but I wonder if either of those sages would have acknowledged this distinction? In our attempts to understand them, we have unfortunately to rely upon commentaries written by men born in later periods when there were many distinct schools of religion and philosophy—at least in books and for purposes of discussion, though I strongly suspect that in their personal lives the Chinese have always indulged in the genial custom of combining any number of conflicting beliefs, however seemingly outrageous the resulting paradoxes. I am inclined to render Tê as 'virtue'; readers who use this book for divination will do well to remember that, besides its acquired moral sense, the basic meaning of 'virtue' is very close to that of 'power'. My effort to translate this sacred book may be regarded as a virtue in the moral sense, whereas the strong green tea which enables me to go on working long after midnight has virtue in the sense of a specific power. The latter meaning is best exemplified by the Biblical story which tells us that, when a woman touched the hem of His garment, Christ felt the virtue go out of Him.

A word of very great importance in the *I Ching* is Chih—the will. It may denote Heaven's will or the Ruler's will or the will of the Superior Man and thus, by implication, our will, since we are expected to take the Superior Man for our model. In practice, all these meanings of Chih are interrelated, for the wise man, whether prince or commoner, aims at such true conformity with the cosmic processes that there can be no conflict between Heaven's will and his own (or, ideally speaking, OUR own). I have been careful to use 'will' and not 'desire' to translate it, even at the cost of rather stilted English for the *Book of Change* pays us the compliment of supposing a lack of identity between our will (lofty and austere) and our desires (which, since we are human, must quite often be ignoble).

As to the Chüntzû or Superior Man, he is one who, desiring to live in harmony with the laws of Heaven and earth, seeks out the company of holy sages and eschews that of unworthy men—whose faults, however, he treats with lenience. Aiming at supreme wisdom and the highest virtue, he continually examines and corrects his own failings. He is generous, modest and reluctant to interfere with others, though his duties of state now and then bring him into conflict with rebellious evil-doers. His involvement in statecraft may seem to modern eyes very much as it did to the founders of Taoism, that is to say inconsistent with his desire to be a sage; but to Confucius and, apparently, to the authors of the *Book of Change*, a Superior Man's failure to put his wisdom at the disposal of a worthy prince would be unthinkable. We feel a greater sympathy for Confucius when we recall that, monarchist of monarchists though he was, he nevertheless taught that if a ruler behaves too badly Heaven thereupon withdraws its mandate, after which he is no longer a divine ruler but a mere robber whom any man may attack and even slay without deserving censure. To my mind, what distinguishes a Superior Man more than any other ornament of character is that he is one who knows WHEN NOT TO ACT. This outstanding virtue, which students of Zen will be quick to commend, requires a much greater degree of wisdom and self-control than the ability to act rightly when the need arises.

I am now going to venture an observation which some of my Chinese teachers and friends may find both shocking and ignorant. It is that, in my opinion, Confucius quite possibly did not fully understand the *I Ching*! Considering that the present version owes about half of its bulk to him or his close disciples and that he has long been accepted as a sage of almost godlike degree, the expression of such a doubt amounts to blasphemy. All the same, I see Confucius as a man standing somewhere between two very different types of people— those who, in these days, would be Zen adepts or Taoist, Sufi or Christian mystics, men for whom virtue is less a matter of accepting salutary rules of conduct than of perfect conformance with the dictates of an in-dwelling 'entity' higher-than-self; and, on the other hand, people rather like most present-day Christians, Communists and other upholders of Authority who take the strictly moralist view that certain things are obviously good and others clearly evil, from which it follows that, instead of presuming to allow our inner promptings to guide us, we should stick closely to a set of rules set forth by God or by men wiser than ourselves, without paying too much regard to the demands of a given set of circumstances. If I am right in so placing Confucius—I base my judgement on what I have read of Confucian works—it may be that the Commentary on the Text is not deep enough to do justice to the Text itself. In that case, the word Tê should almost invariably be understood to have a profounder meaning than moral virtue; and the Superior Man—the model all of us are called upon to imitate— should be admired not so much for stern morality and a profound sense of public duty as for what may now be called Zen-like accord with the inner promptings that arise when passions are banished and thought is stilled. I am far from suggesting that the Confucian Commentary be ignored in our interpretation of the *I Ching*'s answers; the most I would say is that it may be wiser to give a little more weight to the Text than to the Commentary.

We must be on our guard against regarding the Text as containing separate Taoist and Confucian strands. It was surely composed by men with a genuine insight into the workings of cosmic laws who had come very close to beholding the face of Ultimate Reality. It is a pity that the archaic language employed makes it difficult for us to distinguish whether certain phrases are arbitrarily chosen metaphors or terms most carefully selected to point at spiritual truths too deep for clear exposition. Some of the seeming metaphors are so bizarre as to suggest one of those secret languages to which only initiates have the key. (This is especially so with hexagrams 41 and 54, but it is more apparent in the original Chinese than in my rendering which tends to be somewhat of a paraphrase where a literal translation would make no sense at all.)

C. G. Jung rightly stresses in his preface to Wilhelm's version that the Chinese have traditionally been inclined not to think in terms of strictly causal relationships. If the laws of cause and effect really govern everything to the extent now generally assumed, then there is little room for employing the faculty of intuition; divining the future becomes a matter of observing the past and taking for granted that, given similar causes, similar results will ensue. In practice, however, this method is almost valueless for dealing with human beings, for the activities of mind resist all attempts to confine them in a causal straight-jacket. The traditional Chinese view is that each event is part of a concurrent situation in which the lines dividing one object from another are less real than they seem—though not necessarily unreal. Being practical people, they can hardly doubt that each of the 'myriad objects' does have its own real identity and they would not be surprised to learn that, when Dr Johnson kicked the table to refute Bishop Berkeley's idealism, he hurt his foot! On the other hand, they are disposed to think that the real individual identity of each of the 'myriad objects' does not preclude them from being one with another when viewed in another and no less acceptable way. Thus the cycles of progression and retrogression which succeed or run parallel to one another are not regarded merely as the totality of an infinite number of separate but interlocking causal chains, but also as a unified process in which the separateness of the component objects and events is real in one sense but unreal in another. Man may think he is planning his own life (which

BACKGROUND OF THE BOOK OF CHANGE   45

to some extent a few extraordinarily gifted people actually succeed in doing), but in reality he is being swept along by great winds and currents of circumstances beyond his control. When he peacefully accepts life as it is and allows these currents to carry him with them or even joins his small store of strength to theirs, he enjoys serenity and his schemes are apt to prosper. When he forces himself to swim against them, he suffers stress, frustration, anxiety, failure, disappointment and his plans inevitably go awry. It is not by chance that one of the most frequently encountered words in the *I Ching* is Shun—peaceful or glad acceptance of what has been, what is and what will be.

Taoism, perpetuating ways of thought and action that antecede Laotzû, its founder (500 B C approx.), teaches us to live close to nature, to observe natural processes and to model our activities upon them. The virtues of water are especially extolled. Water does not attack impregnable obstacles, but peacefully finds its way around them. Rivers, though they seek the lowest level and the easiest course, do not fail to reach the sea. The art of life requires knowledge not only of when and how to act but also of when not to act; wise action confines itself to dealing with whatever positively insists on being dealt with; were it to go further than that, it might stir up the need for more action and lead to involvement in things better left alone. If all the world were Taoist, sleeping dogs could sleep long. A wise cook neither wastes his energy nor blunts his chopper cutting through bone; he directs the chopper at the narrow spaces between the joints. A tree does not plan how to get water and when to drink it; it drinks what comes. Tigers do not kill for the pleasure of killing or because they glory in their strength; they kill when hungry. Wise men respond to needs when they arise, but carefully refrain from doing whatever would add to them. There seems no reason to doubt that Confucius accepted much of this doctrine, just as the Buddha accepted many Hindu tenets current in his day and as Jesus Christ accepted a large part of the Jewish religion. What principally distinguishes Confucius from Laotzû is that, whereas the latter emphasized self-cultivation coupled with withdrawal from worldly affairs, he himself regarded self-cultivation as a means of fitting a man to play his part in the widening circles of family, state and, ultimately, 'all beneath Heaven'—the whole known world.

The *I Ching* has much to say about wise government administration and the conduct of military affairs, for its authors viewed life as a whole, recognizing that there are certain ways of action which conform with the cosmic processes and others which do not, whether at the cosmic, national, family or individual level. In undertaking divination by means of the *I Ching*, it is useful to remember that, when a question unconnected with administration receives a response that looks like a lesson in statemanship, all the enquirer has to do is to transfer the principle involved to another sphere. Thus, to take just one example, in the case of an undergraduate or junior member of the teaching staff at a university, the 'ruler' may be taken to imply the Master of the College or the Head of the Faculty concerned; the 'minister' becomes the Dean or some similar personage, and the 'kingdom' becomes the class, college or university according to the sense of the question. No rule can be laid down, but the enquirer should have no difficulty in seeing how to transpose the universal principle involved to the sphere affected by his question.

Military action in the *I Ching* usually takes the form of chastising rebels—a matter concerning which many religious leaders prefer to remain silent, though they are seldom slow to wield sword or rod in practice. The chastisement of rebels will seem less out of keeping with the lofty and humane tone of the rest of the book when it is remembered that a perfect state is presupposed, one in which ruler and ruled are united in their desire to bring about the good of all; hence the 'rebels' are not just persons inimical to a certain ruler or opposed to a particular system of government, but people deludedly trying to sail their craft against the current of circumstance and to destroy the universal harmony, thus endangering themselves and countless others. Moreover, the various references to statesmanship and the art of war reflect the conditions obtaining in the many separate states which, in ancient times, paid only nominal service to the Emperor of China. Learned people, even literate people, were proportionately very rare. Each scholar felt that the best way he had of contributing to the public good was to obtain employment with a prince sufficiently well-intentioned to allow him to guide the administration of the state so as to promote conditions of peace, happiness and plenty. Most books written during that period were primarily intended as guides to ruling princes and their scholarly advisors. As printing was still unknown, each copy had to be handwritten and books could never be plentiful, so those written for administrators were felt to be of the greatest value. The *I Ching,* though it also had much wider purposes, was no exception. On the other hand, the Chinese conception of life as a single whole made it quite natural for individuals to apply the principles of books dealing with statecraft to their own private activities. Confucius, in teaching that the welfare of the state depends upon the right conduct of the families composing it and thus upon the self-rectification of each family member, was not mouthing a platitude but stressing the fundamental unity of the whole and its parts—a tenet common to most or all of the ancient Chinese systems of philosophy.

In these days of increasingly specialized education, new divisions and distinctions are for ever being created and it is only in the teachings of the very greatest scientific leaders of our age that we can now and then glimpse the fundamental unity which lesser men are busily hiding from our sight. The London Buddhist Society's slogan 'All life is one' reminds us of a voice crying in the wilderness. How many people, happening upon this slogan for the first time, pause to consider all its implications? That there are some is probable, for people are gradually becoming frustrated by the needless complexity of modern life and by the unsatisfactory state of modern education with its emphasis on isolated segments of existence, on learning much of something and very little of anything else. People already troubled by these things will not find the *I Ching* too strange and will be quick to benefit from its teaching. Those at the opposite extreme will be likely to condemn it as incomprehensible gibberish and to wonder why some of us, despite our having enjoyed 'all the benefits of a sound modern education', should bestow attention on the incoherent teaching of so-called sages belonging to a primitive feudal society which has long since passed away. Happy for them if their bewilderment is fruitful in leading them to reconsider their judgement and to begin doubting the wisdom of their own way of life!

CHAPTER 3

THE SYMBOLICAL BASIS OF THE BOOK OF CHANGE

The relationship between the sixty-four hexagrams and the appended Texts is a complicated subject to which justice can hardly be done in a few pages. King Wên and Duke Chou formulated a very precise method to determine the phrasing of their Texts from the mutual relationships of the lines composing each hexagram, but I must confine myself to describing only a few of the considerations governing their choice of words. In general it can be said that the hexagrams arranged in their proper order symbolize the entire sequence of changes through which everything in the universe, at all levels from the microcosmic to the macrocosmic, passes in continuous cycles. It is by relating our affairs to parts of this sequence that we are able to forecast with great accuracy how far they will prosper or decline and, in some cases, find means of affecting the issue to our advantage. The value of the forecasts, assuming that our interpretations of the responses are correct, will depend on how far we are willing (and temperamentally able) to proceed smoothly in the direction indicated, i.e. to accord gracefully with inevitable changes whether they portend increase or decrease. By struggling in the opposite direction to that indicated, though we may win some temporary successes, we rupture the harmony subsisting between us and the cosmic forces; such conduct must ultimately bring us no less frustration than would fall to the lot of an insect trying to move an elephant out of the way. We can no more permanently oppose the forces controlling life than we can choose not to be born or not to die; yet we can, in relatively small matters, *temporarily* hasten or retard some of their immediate effects—perhaps with enough success as to seem, now and then, to belie the forecasts in the *Book of Change*. Such a possibility seldom arises, for the book rarely declares that this or that will surely happen; rather, it points out that, circumstances being what they are, we shall be well advised to act in a particular manner. At times it shows us how to surmount difficulties lying ahead; at others, it warns us that those difficulties are insurmountable and that we shall do well to halt or retreat. The decision is left to us; after we have made it, events pass altogether beyond our control.

SYMBOLICAL BASIS OF THE BOOK OF CHANGE

The Lines

The sixty-four hexagrams upon which the forecasts are based are each composed of two trigrams making a total of six lines. Each line is either broken and therefore yielding or unbroken and therefore firm. The broken ones are generally called Yin lines; the unbroken are referred to as Yang lines. The former symbolize the qualities of the Yin principle —earthly, passive, negative, female, dark and so forth; the latter symbolize the opposite qualities—heavenly, active, positive, male, light, etc. Neither is in itself better or worse than the other, for the two principles have an equal part to play in the totality of existence. Under certain circumstances, they become moving lines, that is to say lines moving in the direction of their own opposites, with which they finally merge. A moving Yin line is expressed by ——×—— and a moving Yang line by ——○——. The hexagrams are first treated as being composed of stationary lines only. When some of the lines move and merge with their opposites, a new hexagram is formed.

The Trigrams

There are eight trigrams, this being the maximum number which can be formed with only two kinds of line. According to tradition, they were discovered by the Emperor Fu Hsi (2852–2738 BC), the first recorded ruler in Chinese history, who is now generally regarded as a legendary figure. It is said that he first saw them upon the shell of a tortoise. Whether or not there is actual or symbolical truth in this story, the trigrams are certainly immensely old, far older than the venerable *Book of Change* itself. Primarily they represent certain aspects of nature, both active and passive, such as thunder, wind, mountain, lake and so on. They are also identified with the elements, the seasons, the hours and many other things. Ch'ien (☰), which contains three firm lines, stands for the Yang principle and all its qualities; hence is supremely active. K'un (☷), composed of three yielding lines, stands for the Yin principle and all its qualities, including passive acceptance. Together, they represent the whole universe (literally heaven and earth) in its basic Yin-Yang form, which stands at only one remove from the perfect unity of T'ai Chi (the Absolute).

50   THE BOOK OF CHANGE

In another sense, they are regarded as the joint creators and hence the 'father and mother' of the phenomenal universe; the other six trigrams being their three 'sons' and three 'daughters'. (Details of this 'family', will be found in the appendix.) Each hexagram contains two of them; they stand in varying degrees of accord or discord with each other and thus form the basic determinants of that hexagram's precise significance. If they are in close accord, the hexagram will symbolize something pleasant, harmonious, fortunate, etc.; if there is discord between them, the hexagram will stand for something unpleasant, inharmonious, unlucky and so forth. A relationship somewhere between these two extremes will endow a hexagram with a significance neither wholly desirable nor altogether undesirable. Four of the hexagrams are held to be of outstanding importance; namely Hexagram (1), Ch'ien, Heaven, etc., which is composed of two Ch'ien trigrams and therefore of six firm lines; Hexagram (2), K'un, earth, etc., which is composed of two K'un trigrams and therefore of six yielding lines; Hexagram (11), T'ai, Peace, composed of a K'un trigram above a Ch'ien trigram and therefore of three consecutive yielding lines above three consecutive firm lines; and Hexagram (12), P'i, Stagnation, in which the positions of this pair of trigrams are reversed. The reason for their special importance is that the first, being purely Yang, is entirely positive, creative; the second, being purely Yin, represents the acme of passive acceptance; the third and fourth are composed of equal proportions of Yang and Yin, not intermixed but adjacent to each other. Naturally T'ai, which has the firmest possible base to support its three yielding lines has a very favourable meaning; whereas P'i, with three firm (hence strong and heavy) lines weighing down upon three yielding (and therefore weak and fragile) lines, is most unfavourable. The examples furnished by these last two clearly indicate one of the methods used in interpreting the hexagrams. Their symbolical forms are:

Ch'ien (2)	K'un (2)	T'ai (11)	P'i (12)

The Nuclear Trigram:

As we have seen, the hexagrams viewed in the simplest way are each composed of two trigrams, one above the other; of these, the lower

SYMBOLICAL BASIS OF THE BOOK OF CHANGE 51

is held to be the first and the upper subsequent to it, for trigrams and hexagrams are always read from the bottom upwards. Besides these component trigrams, each hexagram also contains two interlocking nuclear trigrams, the first composed of lines 2, 3 and 4; the second, of lines 3, 4 and 5. Thus, to take a hexagram at random, ☰̳ has ─── and ─ ─ for its component trigrams and ─── and ─ ─ for its nuclear trigrams. In certain cases, such as the hexagram ☰̳, one of the component and one of the nuclear trigrams are the same; in rare cases, both pairs or even all four trigrams may be the same. In determining the Texts of the hexagrams, the authors took both pairs of trigrams into account. If, for example, we find some word in a Text with a connotation suggesting 'beauty' and notice that neither of the component trigrams is Li (beauty, flame), we shall probably see that Li is one of the nuclear trigrams—but not necessarily so, as there are many other considerations governing the wording of each Text.

The Family Relationship

The trigrams, according to one arrangement already touched upon, comprise a family—father, mother, eldest, middle and youngest son and eldest, middle and youngest daughter. The family relationship between two trigrams within the same hexagram has an important bearing on its meaning. Thus, a textual passage about two women under one roof is derived from the juxtaposition of two of the daughter-trigrams. It forms a particularly clear example of the relationship between a hexagram and the appended Text.

The Sequence of Hexagrams

The traditional order in which the hexagrams are arranged is by no means arbitrary. Among other things, it calls attention to the vital part played by reaction in the system of cosmic changes; for it often happens that a particular hexagram is IN SOME SENSE the opposite of the preceeding one—though seldom in an absolute sense. For example, the hexagrams symbolizing Peace and Stagnation are not precisely opposites, but the one is desirable while the other is to be deplored. Their juxtaposition reinforces a lesson of history that prolonged periods of peace often give rise to stagnation. At best, during times untroubled by threat of war, our ingenuity is rather grudgingly employed in bettering man's condition; when war breaks out, purse strings are loosened and scientific and social changes proceed by leaps and bounds, so it may be fairly said that the speed of progress is closely proportionate to the degree of danger. We may derive some comfort from contemplating the relative positions of those two hexagrams, as the placing of Stagnation directly after Peace suggests that their relationship has for ever been a natural condition, from which it follows that we need not blame ourselves too severely for such a sad state of affairs. If, in dealing with any hexagram, we glance at those immediately before and after it, we shall be able to evaluate the total situation more effectively.

The Suitability of the Component Lines

Taking these various factors into consideration, we shall recognize that a yielding or a firm line, or two or three of one kind coming together, or a particular combination of both, may serve to indicate whether a situation is favourable or unfavourable. The Confucian commentaries on the lines often allude to the suitability or unsuitability of a certain line to the place it occupies. In my own notes, I have not added much explanation for fear of wearying the reader with technicalities; but, with practice, he will begin to distinguish for himself why a certain type of line is said to be specially suited or unsuited to its place in a hexagram. Thus, Hexagram (28) has this form

When it is viewed vertically, the yielding line at the bottom is found to be in a hopeless position, for it has to support with its inadequate strength the weight of four firm (and therefore heavy) lines coming immediately above it. When the whole is viewed horizontally, both the yielding lines cause misgivings, for the general effect is that of a heavy beam so weak at both ends as to be unable to support its own weight, let alone whatever structure depends upon it. In general and provided that other considerations do not materially alter the situation, a yielding line over a firm line is well placed, as it is easy for the heavy to support the light; the reverse situation is sometimes unsatisfactory. In every hexagram, lines 2 and 5 have a special importance as they are each central to one of the component trigrams, of which the three component lines, reading upwards, stand for Earth, Man and Heaven respectively. The fact that the central line of each trigram refers specifically to man may be one of the main reasons why lines 2 and 5 are so often singled out for special comment regarding the suitability or otherwise of their position. Omens in the Texts covering the whole range between supreme good fortune and calamity are derived principally from a consideration of the suitability or otherwise of the lines concerned.

The Interrelationship of the Lines

Each hexagram has one or more 'ruling lines', one of which generally, but not always, occupies the fifth place.[1] Moreover its remaining lines are very often held to stand in mutual relationships resembling those between a ruler, his chief minister, and his various officials and followers. Very often lines 1 and 6 are of the least importance, as they are held to lie beyond the confines of the main situation. Line 6 sometimes represents a sage no longer engaged in worldly activities. Lines 2 and 4 may symbolize women and/or sons, but at other times they symbolize subordinate officials. This type of relationship has as much bearing on the Text appended to a hexagram as the 'family' relationship subsisting between the two component or nuclear trigrams.

The Sequence of the Lines and Component Trigrams

The transformation symbolized by a hexagram, whether it is a complete change or just a segment of some wider change, is held to begin

[1] See Appendix 13 for a table of the ruling lines.

at the bottom line and proceed upwards. Hence, the lower lines and trigrams are held to symbolize the earlier stages of the whole process involved.

The Movement of the Lines

The following chapter, where it deals with the use of the divining sticks, discloses the circumstances under which a hitherto static line becomes a moving line. Moving lines are of special importance for at least two reasons: (1) their transformation into their own opposites brings to the fore a second hexagram of which the Text and Commentary modify those appended to the first; (2) in contradictory situations, the import of an individual moving line takes precedence over whatever is forecast by the hexagram as a whole. It may happen that, whereas the hexagram indicates that present conditions are thoroughly unfavourable to our plans and that our best course is to refrain from further action or even to retreat from a position already gained, the moving line may assure us of entire success if on the contrary we prosecute our plans vigorously. If so, we must disregard the previous injunction. In actual fact, no genuine contradiction is involved; for, whereas conditions may be generally unfavourable to the type of project we have in mind, particular circumstances (symbolized by the moving line) may make it desirable or even essential for us to go forward without delay—though, of course, the warning conveyed by the hexagram as a whole will tend to make us proceed with more than usual caution.

The Wording of the Texts

We have seen that the Texts appended to the hexagrams and to the individual lines are ascribed to King Wên and his son, Duke Chou, respectively. Whether or not they were the real authors is not of much importance. The system followed in abstracting the Texts from the symbols is discoverable, although complicated by a large number of considerations. In classical Chinese, articles, prepositions, conjunctions and those adverbs whose function is chiefly syntactical are few. Hence almost every word of the *I Ching*—nouns, adjectives, verbs and descriptive adverbs for the most part—is full of meaning and can be traced directly to the formation of the hexagrams. Moreover, lack of clear delineation between the different parts of speech makes it possible for

SYMBOLICAL BASIS OF THE BOOK OF CHANGE 55

the same word to do duty in different places for various parts of speech and facilitates the writing of passages possessing several equally valid meanings. Of even greater importance is the fact that the Chinese characters, having originally been for the most part pictorial, for ever retain something of this pictorial quality and thereby allow a decidedly complicated set of events to be set down with telegraphic brevity. So it is easy to understand why very few syntactical words had to be inserted between the operative words of the Text, each of which was derived directly from the arrangement of the lines and trigrams. It will be noticed that most hexagrams, though limited to six lines only, are followed by Texts containing many more than six words; it is clear that each line, in accordance with its place in the general arrangement, was made to yield several words, i.e. several meanings. In a sense it would be true to say that the hexagrams were treated as a very brief code from which messages differing in length and detail were deduced by following certain uniform rules. (The aptness of this analogy is demonstrated by the fact that some Western scholars used to suppose the *I Ching* to be a mere code book.)

People or things possessed of creative power—heaven, sun, ruler, etc.—are of course suggested by firm lines, while yielding lines commonly denote such qualities as passivity and acceptance. Which of many possible alternatives was chosen in each case depended upon a full assesssment of all the ruling factors. The Superior Man, for example, is not always derived from a Yang line, which is what we might expect; he may be deduced from a Yin line, provided it is in a position to 'assist' one or more Yang lines.

While, in general, there is no question of the Yang lines being superior to the Yin lines, yet where the latter denote persons of mean attainments or something else derogatory, as happens quite often, there does seem to be a strong suggestion of their inferiority; but it will be found that Yang lines can also stand for undesirable persons or qualities if they are unsuitably situated in a hexagram. In reality, the question of the superiority of either sort of line to the other does not arise, for the Yin and Yang principles are EQUALLY vital to all possible situations. Creativity or activity and malleability are both essential. That Yin lines very often have desirable connotations will be seen from the fact that most words meaning willing accord, glad acceptance, gentleness, gracefulness and so on are derived from them. Then there are concepts such as responsiveness and favourable correspondence which are derived from appropriate combinations of both sorts of line—Yin and Yang lines in mutually helpful positions. Similarly, concepts of discord, doubt, lack of confidence, unfaithfulness, etc., are often derived from unsuitable combinations of both sorts of line.

In the Texts appended to several hexagrams, it is said that the timely application of those hexagrams is of peculiar importance. Such statements, viewed only from the viewpoint of divination and bereft of their religious philosophical and cosmological implications, emphasize the fact that the success to be won from following the advice of the oracle will greatly depend upon correct timing. There are certain times when increase or decrease, going forward or halting, filling or emptying is either inevitable or much to be desired. Obviously, it is of great value to us to know in advance which of these alternatives to follow.

The inherent quality symbolized by each hexagram is called its 'virtue'. Whether it is likely to strike us as a desirable or undesirable quality will depend upon whether the arrangement of the hexagram's component lines indicates a situation suitable to the carrying out of what we have in mind. In truth, no hexagram denotes an undesirable quality, since all components of the cosmic process are indispensable; were some omnipotent being to suspend a single one of them, the result would be chaos. Filling without emptying, creation without destruction would lead to such an accumulation of beings and objects that life would become impossible.

A preface to one Chinese edition of the *I Ching* declares that the Text of each hexagram, besides elucidating its meaning, is confined to four factors—its virtue, form, substance and transformation. We have seen that its 'virtue' means its quality—creative, receptive, active, quiescent and so on. Its 'form' means its composition in terms of its component and nuclear trigrams; its 'substance' connotes the arrangement of the six component lines and its 'transformation' refers to 'the coming and going of the firm and yielding lines'. As to 'coming and going', the explanation given is that they refer to that which comes from outside and that which goes from inside—coming implies that something is about to happen; going that something is about to be dispersed.

The *I Ching*'s terminology suggests that, even in ancient times, Chinese religious belief was characterized by acceptance of a number of apparently incompatible objects—just as it is today. T'ai Chi, the Absolute, is not mentioned in the Texts because in its undifferentiated form it is never present to man's observation during his ordinary states of consciousness; it is only to be inferred from the interaction of Yin

SYMBOLICAL BASIS OF THE BOOK OF CHANGE

and Yang, which is going on continuously both within man himself and in the external world about him. Nevertheless, the whole tenor of the book's philosophy postulates an impersonal Absolute functioning through cosmic processes over which no deity or deities have control. This state of affairs is, nevertheless, not incompatible with the existence of the Gods; for the peoples of Eastern Asia do not conceive of Them as immortal Beings standing outside the cosmic process and independent of the universal laws; rather They are thought to be Beings Who, although endowed with superhuman longevity, special powers and somewhat etherial bodies, are neither creators, nor omnipotent, nor immortal. Like us, They have Their limitations—They are born and, after a very long time, They die; meanwhile They are subject to the same universal laws as other creatures, infringement of which brings pain, frustration and disgrace. What may seem strange is the *I Ching*'s mention of a Supreme or Heavenly Ruler, He to Whom the seasonal sacrifices were performed, usually by the feudal princes. Not very much is said about Him, but early Chinese literature makes it clear that, though not the Creator of the Universe, He has great power over the well-being of men, Gods and demons. Exactly how this Supreme Deity can be reconciled with the impersonal T'ai Chi is not made clear. It would be easy to draw a parallel with Brahminism which recognizes in Brahma both a Supreme Deity and an impersonal Absolute, but I do not know of any ancient Chinese books that provide grounds for this comparison. What seems more likely is that the T'ai Chi and the Supreme Ruler exist side by side because the Chinese, with their characteristic lack of interest in metaphysical matters, willingly accepted both the abstract cosmology of the sages and a more popular type of religion without finding them mutually contradictory or, rather, without bothering about the contradiction. It seems always to have been Chinese policy to treat supernatural beings with grave respect while having as little to do with them as possible. Another acceptable explanation with many analogies from elsewhere in the world is that the scholars of ancient China, finding it difficult to convey abstract principles to uneducated or poorly educated men, saw no objection to personifying the Absolute as a means of inculcating discipline, reverence and fear of evil-doing at the popular level.

Two phrases which frequently occur in the *Book of Change* are 'regret vanishes' and 'no error'. As to the first, when difficulty or danger threaten, we often feel remorse for our past actions, recognizing that, had we behaved otherwise, the unpleasant situation would not have arisen. Regret is thus added to our other sufferings. If, however, it is obvious that we are in no way responsible for the trouble threatening us, then we are spared regret. As this knowledge is often a source of courage and determination, the *I Ching* is careful to distinguish between troubles brought down by ourselves and those for which we are blameless. The phrase 'no error' is very similar; it means that we are not to blame, however troublesome the situation may become; it also seems to presage no added advantage or disadvantage to ourselves from continuing in our present course of action. On the other hand, such words as 'error', 'regret', 'serious trouble' and 'calamity' all indicate, with varying degrees of emphasis, that our present or proposed course of action must be changed.

Another phrase with which we meet again and again is 'righteous persistence' or 'persistence in a righteous course' which, in Chinese, consists of a single monosyllable—'chên'. Generally the implication is that determination to persist with our plans, regardless of setbacks, difficulties and obstacles of all sorts, will ensure success, *provided that our course is morally justified*. Had I rendered it by a single word such as 'persistence', 'perseverance' (Wilhelm's choice) or 'determination', I should have done violence to its real meaning. Mere perseverance regardless of the moral worth of our actions would never have commended itself to the authors of the *Book of Change*, who cared nothing for success as such, but delighted in the attainment of self-mastery and whatever tended to the public good.

It will be seen that the *Book of Change* has more to say about Hexagram (1) and (2) than about any of the others. This is partly because extra commentaries are included of which only the sections dealing with these two hexagrams survive; either the remaining sections were lost or else they were never written. Another reason for this fuller treatment is that the Creative (1) and the Receptive (2), being respectively composed wholly of Yang lines and wholly of Yin lines, are the prototypes from which all the Yang and the Yin principles in their abstract purity—unsullied Heaven and spotless Earth, sheer creativity and perfect receptiveness; whereas the other hexagrams symbolize situations derived from their interaction and stand in the same relationship to them as children to their father and mother.

CHAPTER 4

THE METHOD OF DIVINATION

All the instructions contained in this chapter are taken from Chinese editions of the *Book of Change*. They are given in full, because I have not presumed to make an arbitary omission of those perhaps not suited to Western taste. How strictly the enquirer follows them must depend upon his own judgement. If he declares that the *I Ching*, like any other book, consists of so much paper and printer's ink, bound between two covers, nobody can dispute these facts. If he goes so far as to use it for sitting on or to support his feet, obviously it will not suffer and feel outraged as would a human professor similarly mistreated. But a man who delights in what is seemly will scarcely do these things, even though, if he finds ritual distasteful, he may hesitate to burn incense and prostrate himself to the earth before undertaking an enquiry. In the East, however, ceremonials which missionaries contemptuously call 'idol worship' are acceptable to intelligent men, not because of the pleasing effect they may be presumed to have upon the object of 'worship', but because they are held to have a benign effect upon the mind of the performer. A striking example of this difference of viewpoint is afforded by the rites of Tantric Buddhism which many Western scholars deplore on account of their allegedly mechanical nature. Though it cannot be denied that a few mechanical practices have crept into that form of Buddhism—the turning of prayer-mills by water power is an instance—the truth is that all the important Tantric rites, with their material symbols, mantras and mental images, owe their undoubted efficacy to the mental forces which they at once symbolize and set in motion. This point is worth remembering when we come to consider how far we should follow the traditional Chinese ritual when consulting the *Book of Change*. If we prefer to dispense with parts of it, perhaps no loss will result, but to follow the instructions literally may be wiser than to err by curtailing them too much. It is understandable that some of these rites would make us feel bashful if we were called upon to perform them in front of an audience likely to scoff; but this situation need not arise as there is a much more important reason which favours consultation of the *Book of Change* in near solitude. Unless we have had long experience, the presence of many other people is unlikely to be conducive to our achieving that state of mental receptivity without which our interpretation of the oracle may be so faulty as to produce dangerously misleading results!

Care of the Book and of the Divining Sticks.

The *Book of Change,* when not in use, should be kept, wrapped in clean silk or cloth, at an elevation not lower than the shoulders of a man standing erect. When about to make use of it, the enquirer, after washing his hands, unwraps it and spreads out the wrapper like a tablecloth between the book and the surface upon which it is to rest. (The belief that a sacred object, when placed in contact with a ritually impure surface, loses something of its virtue is by no means confined to the Chinese.)

Ideally, the fifty divining sticks should be yarrow stalks between one and two feet long, but thin wooden rods shaped like knitting needles but unpointed make a good substitute. They should be stored in a lidded receptacle which is never used for other purposes. It may be simple or elaborate; its substance is of little importance, but it should be clean and pleasing to the eye.

Framing the Enquiry

If the enquirer is to put a question on his own behalf, he will naturally decide its wording before he begins the opening ceremony. If he has undertaken to divine something for another person, the two of them should frame the question together, for its form is of great consequence. Above all, the either/or type of question should be avoided. Some suitable question-patterns are as follows:

Is it advisable, under such and such circumstances, to go forward with such and such a project?

If this or that is done, what will be the result?

What is likely to happen to this or that project, person, organization, country, etc., during such and such a time (month, year or period of years)?

What is hindering the progress of this or that project?

How is so and so to be accomplished?

THE METHOD OF DIVINATION

The answers seldom indicate exactly how much time must elapse before some action or event becomes due; if necessary, the enquiry should be framed along the lines of the third of the above examples so as to set some limit to the time involved. Information about a specific hour or day is rarely received because, although in general the cosmic processes follow immutable laws, the details are variable and the outcome of an affair may be advanced or delayed or even somewhat altered by circumstances, including deliberate action by ourselves or others. The authors of the *Book of Change* did not regard the future as unalterable; they thought in terms of mighty sequences of change following a regular course with predictable results, like the process of the four seasons, or like a river, now gushing through a narrow gorge, now fighting its way through rocky shallows, now running smoothly and slowly—its water destined, sooner or later, to reach the sea. They were not fatalists teaching that man has no control over his own destiny; a man who swims with the current can, within reason, choose his course; and, even should he attempt to swim against the current and amidst treacherous whirlpools, his destruction can be advanced or delayed within certain limits by his own action.

Enquiries apparently needing a response limited to a single word or sentence sometimes receive unexpectedly detailed answers, for the *I Ching* is generous with its advice and there may be circumstances affecting the outcome of our plans of which we have hitherto been unaware. Moreover, there are relatively few vital questions which can be answered with a plain yea or nay. Usually it is better not to ignore any part of the reply received. Passages which at first seem irrelevant may have deep significance.

Commencing the Enquiry

In China, those in authority used to face South when granting audience. Accordingly the *Book of Change* should be placed ready for use on a table facing south and in the centre of the room. Just in front (i.e. a little to the south) of the book, on the same or a lower table, there should be an incense burner (or a small pot tightly packed with ash to hold the butt of an incense stick) and the receptacle containing the divining sticks. The enquirer stands with his face to the table and thus faces north. He first performs three full kowtows (prostrations to the ground) and then, from a kneeling position, inserts a stick of lighted incense into the burner. Next, he draws forth the fifty divining sticks and, holding them horizontally in the right hand, passes them three times through the incense smoke by rotating them clockwise. Meanwhile, he orally or mentally recites his previously prepared question with such perfect concentration that his mind is void of all else. If further kneeling incommodes him or hinders his concentration, he may then seat himself at the table until the closing of the enquiry.

The Manipulation of the Divining Sticks

The object, of course, is to obtain the *I Ching*'s response; this is sometimes confined to the Text and Commentary appended to a single hexagram; more often, it involves a hexagram with one or more moving lines, in which case several Texts and Commentaries must be studied: (*a*) those appended to the answering hexagram; (*b*) those appended to each of the moving lines; (*c*) those appended to the hexagram formed by changing the moving lines of the original hexagram from Yin to Yang or Yang to Yin lines as the case may be. Once the system of employing the divining sticks is mastered, it will be found much less difficult than it looks at first sight. With practice, their manipulation will become so nearly automatic as not to interfere much with our state of mental receptivity.

As soon as the fifty sticks have been passed through the incense smoke, one of them is immediately returned to the receptacle and plays no further part until it is time to repeat the rite in connection with another enquiry. Thus, though there must be exactly fifty sticks for ritual purposes, only forty-nine are used for discovering the responses to enquiries. Their number should be carefully checked each time, as one more or one less than the right number would upset the calculation and produce irrelevant replies. For what follows, an experienced enquirer will need only the divining sticks and his own two hands. Those less experienced will find it helpful to have in addition two trays (each about the size of a dinner plate). I shall refer to them as A and B.

The forty-nine sticks are bunched together on A. The enquirer, with his mind still concentrated upon the question or else in a state as near to void as possible, stretches out his right hand and swiftly divides them into two heaps lying one to either side of the tray.

Taking one stick from the right pile, he places it between the last two fingers of his left hand. Next, he diminishes the left pile by pushing away four sticks at a time until only one, two, three or four are left.

THE METHOD OF DIVINATION

This remainder, he places between the next two fingers of his left hand. Thereafter, he subtracts sticks from the right pile, four by four, until only one, two, three or four remain. (Sometimes, this third step is omitted as, once the system is well understood, the remainder from the right pile can be calculated from the size of the remainder from the left pile.) He now has in his left hand a total of either five or nine sticks, i.e. 1+1+3, or 1+2+2, or 1+3+1, or 1+4+4. These five or nine sticks he lays in a heap on tray B.

The same process is repeated with the remaining sticks on tray A, which are bunched together again with the right hand and then divided as before. This time, the total will be either four or eight sticks, i.e. 1+1+2, or 1+2+1, or 1+3+4, or 1+4+3. These four or eight sticks he places on tray B, but keeps them a little apart from the sticks already there.

Again the process is repeated with the sticks that remain on tray A. This time, the result will also be four or eight, compounded in the same way as for the second part of the process.

As a result of these three countings, tray B will now contain one of the following combinations (5 or 9)+(4 or 8)+(4 or 8). These three figures will indicate whether the bottom line of the answering hexagram is a Yang line or a Yin line, i.e firm (unbroken) or yielding (broken). They will also indicate whether it is a moving line or not. The following table shows: (*a*) all the possible combinations of numbers obtainable from manipulating the divining sticks in the way just described; (*b*) the type of line indicated by each of those combinations; (*c*) the names and descriptions of the various types of line; (*d*) the ritual number given to each. The Texts appended in the *Book of Change* to the individual lines of each hexagram always begin with the words: 'a six for such and such a place' or 'a nine for such and such a place'; because these lines only concern us when they are MOVING LINES and six and nine are the ritual numbers which indicate their movement. As there are four kinds of line, there are four corresponding *ritual numbers* to which, for the sake of clarity, I have prefixed the letters RN.

When the bottom line of a hexagram has been established in this way, the forty-nine sticks are again bunched together on tray A and the same process with its three phases is repeated in order to establish the second line from the bottom of the hexagram. This is done again and again until all six lines have been established. Altogether, there are six dividing and counting processes each consisting of three stages.

THE BOOK OF CHANGE

Divining Table

(a)	(b)	(c)	(d)
5+4+4	——C——	an Old Yang line (i.e. moving)	RN9
9+8+8	——×——	an Old Yin line (i.e. moving)	RN6
5+8+8 ⎫ 9+8+4 ⎬ 9+4+8 ⎭	——————	a Young Yang line (i.e. static)	RN7
5+4+8 ⎫ 5+8+4 ⎬ 9+4+4 ⎭	—— ——	a Young Yin line (i.e. static)	RN8

Example

We will suppose that the following answer is received:

5+4+8	—— ——
9+4+4	—— ——
5+8+8	——————
9+8+8	——×——
9+4+8	——————
5+4+4	——C——

First we study the main Text and Commentary appended to this hexagram.

Next we study those appended to its first and third lines because in this instance they are both moving lines.

Finally we study the main Text and Commentary (but not those appended to the individual lines) of the hexagram which results when the moving line or lines (in this case one and three) of the initial hexagram have 'moved' and thus been transformed into their own opposites, namely the hexagram

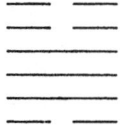

If one or both the moving lines of the initial hexagram appear to contradict something in the main Text, they must be given precedence over it, as this would imply that the fundamental situation is modified by exceptional circumstances which, nevertheless, form part of it. If no contradiction is involved, the meaning of the initial hexagram must be combined with whatever special meaning is indicated by the moving line or lines. On the other hand, if, on account of the movement of one or more lines, we receive two hexagrams in response to our enquiry,

THE METHOD OF DIVINATION 65

there can be no question of contradiction—however contradictory the two hexagrams may seem—for they refer to the earlier and later stages of the same event or sequence of events. Between them, they may indicate that our affairs will go well (or badly) at first, but that later a reversal will occur.

These seemingly complicated matters will at first interfere with the enquirer's mental concentration and his ability to understand the answer intuitively rather than analytically, but practice will reduce this obstacle.

If there are no moving lines, then the main Text and Commentary attached to the first (and only) answering hexagram contain the whole response to our enquiry. However many moving lines there may be, the response never exceeds two hexagrams.

Table of Numbers

Upper Trigram → Lower Trigram ↓	1 Ch'ien	4 Chên	6 K'an	7 Kên	8 K'un	5 Sun	3 Li	2 Tui
1 Ch'ien	1	34	5	26	11	9	14	43
4 Chên	25	51	3	27	24	42	21	17
6 K'an	6	40	29	4	7	59	64	47
7 Kên	33	62	39	52	15	53	56	31
8 K'un	12	16	8	23	2	20	35	45
5 Sun	44	32	48	18	46	57	50	28
3 Li	13	55	63	22	36	37	30	49
2 Tui	10	54	60	41	19	61	38	58

E

When one or two hexagrams have been received in answer to an enquiry, their numbers can be discovered from the table and the relevant Text and Commentary looked up without difficulty. As a hexagram is always read from the bottom up, the bottom line and the second and third lines from the bottom form the lower trigram; the remaining three form the upper trigram.

Divination by Means of Coins

Even in China, there are people who find divination with the yarrow stalks or divining sticks is too slow and cumbersome, so they resort to the use of six coins. However, these are mostly professional fortune-tellers, more interested in their fee than in the accuracy of the *I Ching*'s responses. Personally, I am not greatly in favour of this simpler method, although it saves time. Since we should consult the *I Ching* only on serious matters, it is well to set about it in a spirit of seriousness and to be prepared to spend an hour or so on each consultation, just as when we consult a lawyer or psychiatrist. Then again, the coin tossing method is so brief that it is easy to get in the habit of doing it perfunctorily without achieving the proper state of mind—thus defeating our own object. Finally, if the sticks are manipulated carefully according to the rules, it is not possible to make a mistake in using them; whereas any small accident, such as a slight unevenness of the surface on which it falls may affect the result of the toss. However, for those who prefer the coin tossing method, the following table indicates what lines to assign to the results obtained. Three coins of equal size are used. Strictly speaking, they should be a particular kind of ancient Chinese coin (with a square hole in the centre) which is inscribed on one side only. As these are now hard to find, we may have to use ordinary coins; but, as modern coins are inscribed on both sides, we have first to determine which side corresponds to the inscribed side of the ancient coins. My own view is that, since the main function of coin inscriptions is to reveal their value, that side which indicates the value should be regarded as the inscribed side. The three coins are placed together in the hands loosely cupped, shaken awhile and then allowed to fall simultaneously. The result of the first throw will reveal the bottom line of the answering hexagram; the second throw, the next line from the bottom, and so on. In this table, IN stands for what we have decided to call the inscribed side and BL for the theoretically blank side.

THE METHOD OF DIVINATION

Coin Table

BL+BL+BL	———O———	an Old Yang line (i.e. moving)	RN9
IN+IN+IN	———×———	an Old Yin line (i.e. moving)	RN6
BL+BL+IN	———————	a Young Yang line (i.e. static)	RN7
IN+IN+BL	——— ———	a Young Yin line (i.e. static)	RN8

Interpreting the Response

Whether divining sticks or coins are used to establish the answering hexagram(s), the only real difficulty comes later when we seek to interpret the response in the light of the question asked and of all the circumstances surrounding it. Success depends to a considerable extent on our experience, but the prime necessity is to allow intuition to play a larger part than analytical reasoning. Whereas most of the other stages can be perfected with long practice, this one demands both practice and a certain talent. However, the more mechanical aspect of interpretation must first be mastered. One brief method for accomplishing that much is to open the *Book of Change* at random from time to time, pretend that the hexagram appearing on the open page has been received in answer to a properly made enquiry and then study the Text and Commentary in the light of that pretended enquiry, without as yet making any attempt to employ intuition. When reasonable proficiency at this level has been achieved, the next step is to ask real questions by means of the divining sticks or coins and allow increasing scope to intuition in interpreting the answers.

There will be some people who, sooner or later, will long to try their hand at making interpretations directly from the formation of the hexagrams, i.e. without the assistance of the appended Texts and Commentaries. To reach such a high stage of proficiency would require many years of practice and a version of the *I Ching* with such full notes on the significance of the line arrangements as to require a thousand pages or more! A careful study of my own and Wilhelm's versions would be far from adequate preparation—though, of course, there is nothing to prevent anyone from 'playing at' this sort of interpretation just for the fun of it and it is possible that an unusually gifted person might have some success; this is one of the reasons why I have given a number of tables and diagrams in the appendix.

An especially important point to bear in mind while studying the general principles of interpretation is that the structure of the hexagram is based upon the assumption that intimate relationships exist between all things in the universe from solar systems lying beyond our ken to objects so small that even the microscope has not discovered all of them; that the same fundamental laws govern worlds, nations, groups of entities, single entities and microscopic parts of entities. Indeed, it is now generally known that close similarities are to be found in the behaviour of worlds rolling in space and of atoms revolving in a tiny piece of matter. It follows that, if the subject-matter of a response to one of our enquiries seems to have little bearing on it, all we have to do is to transpose this response into 'another key'. Thus, for example, military terms such as advance and retreat can be used in connection with almost all activities without undergoing much change in meaning and mention of the ancient Chinese sacrifices to the Supreme Ruler of Heaven can be taken to indicate sacrifices of a different kind. References to the chastisement of rebels can be understood to mean that firm (but always just) means are required for dealing with people whose self-interest puts them in opposition to the general good within the framework of our specific enquiry. Here, however, we are on dangerous ground, for it may be that we ourselves are more guilty than our opponents of pursuing our self-interest beyond the bounds of good behaviour; in which case we can hardly apply the notion of 'chastising rebels' to our efforts to subvert their plans. It is vital to remember that the *Book of Change* is so worded as to preclude its use for obtaining advice or assistance in carrying out nefarious undertakings. All its responses take for granted that we are prompted by reasonably virtuous motives; but, unfortunately, we human beings are so constituted as to be easily deceived by the whitewashing propensities of our own consciences; without frequent self-examination, it is not easy to be sure how far the alleged purity of our motives will stand the full light of day. Were we to rely upon the *Book of Change* to advise us how to attain a thoroughly improper goal, its response would lead us away from rather than towards that goal and we might end up by joining the ranks of those who regard such divination as 'meaningless superstition'!

The reader who, undeterred by these difficulties, has made up his mind to allow the *Book of Change* to play a part in determining his future courses of action is like a man about to undertake a voyage in strange waters. He may expect to find himself in places hitherto unknown to him, without having anything in the way of charts or compass beyond the inadequate notes and introductory chapters accompanying this translation. Some of the oracles will be so cryptic as to tax his powers of understanding; others, seemingly plain, may

THE METHOD OF DIVINATION

have deeper meanings which he must try his best to penetrate; and always the need for intuition will be paramount. Attempts to plumb the wisdom of the Far East through the logical processes which seem to many Westerners the only possible approach to knowledge are sure to be wide of the mark. The enquirer's mind should be so nearly void of everything but his question that even the desire for an answer must occupy his attention as little as possible. His mind comes to resemble a limitless ocean with no coastline or islands visible and with but one tiny craft—the question—floating unpropelled upon its surface. If this state can be preserved during the slight distraction caused by the process of manipulating the divining sticks and carried over to the interpretation of the answer, he need have no fear of receiving wrong or inapposite advice. The best course for him to take will reveal itself in such a way as to leave no room for doubt. For beginners, especially, it is well to allow the work of interpretation to be preceded by silent meditation in which the mind gradually subsides into stillness and intuition takes up the functions which intellect has, for the time being, discarded; otherwise, the intellect's monkey-like leaping will twist the meaning of the response in the direction most desired by the enquirer and substitute wishful thinking for truth. Silence. Emptiness. Receptivity. Absence of longing for what will come. Willing acceptance of that which comes. These are the ideal conditions for interpretation.

Closing the Enquiry

The instructions found in most Chinese versions of the *Book of Change* include the following ceremony. When a response has been obtained and its interpretation in relation to the question carefully noted down, if there are no more enquiries to follow, another stick of incense is lighted and the enquirer 'takes his leave of the book' with a threefold prostration (kowtow). Thereafter, the divining sticks are returned to their receptacle, the *Book of Change* is rewrapped in its coverlet and both are returned to their usual place.

A Final Consideration

Some Western scholars are inclined to scoff at the concept of placing reliance on intuition and to suggest that it is the ignorant and untrained man's substitute for learning and knowledge. Owing to the inroads made by modern education upon the ancient cultures of the countries of the East, man's natural power of intuition is being increasingly neglected even in that part of the world where it was once considered of paramount importance; so that, with most individuals, East or West, this power is steadily declining towards atrophy. That intuition is a power no less natural to human beings than sight or hearing is clear from that fact that, in those communities where it is still prized, it is either possessed or attainable by almost everybody. In Tibet, some of its manifestations such as telepathy are so widespread as to cause astonishment to newcomers from other parts of the world. In China and Japan, among Zen Buddhists and certain others who have not been beguiled into turning their backs on their own past, there are daily instances of intuition's efficacy. Indeed, most people of the Far East, where the process of atrophy has not been going on very long, show some indications of retaining at least vestiges of this power. Western residents in Far Eastern countries are continually astonished by the accuracy with which the local people gauge their true feelings towards them however much those feelings are outwardly dissembled. It is scarcely possible for a Westerner to make himself liked by a Chinese or Japanese, however well he acts the part of friend, unless his affection is real.

Intuition is no more a supernatural gift than the powers of walking, running and jumping; but, like them, its full development requires regular exercise. Whatever is coarsening to mind or body affects it for the worse; or, rather, since a distinction between mind and body is not acceptable to thinkers in that part of the world, it may be better to say 'whatever is coarsening' and leave it at that. A number of factors are responsible for coarsening the human entity, of which gluttony and other physical excesses are by no means the worst. Malice, envy, continual dishonesty, and—above all—physical and mental cruelty have an especially dire effect on the power of intuitive perception. The harm suffered by the victim of cruelty is scarcely more (and sometimes much less than) the harm inflicted upon the doer; ultimately, he becomes so coarsened and weighed down that his more delicate faculties wither away. Other unwholesome qualities produce the same sort of result, each in its own degree.

Were intuition to be left out of account in our dealings with the *Book of Change*, the responses would still, in most cases, make good sense; but only their external meaning would be apparent; whereas those who have acquired a really high order of intuitive perception will sometimes discover level upon level of meaning and benefit accordingly.

People in whom this power seems to be weak or virtually non-existent can cultivate it by taking two courses simultaneously. The effects of atrophy can be counteracted by limiting our self-indulgence and any of our propensities which are obviously harmful to ourselves and others if, in addition, we daily perform one of those mental exercises at the supra-intellectual level which, for want of a better English word, are generally labelled 'meditation' by Zen adepts and others who value them. If these exercises are continued over months and years, it may be possible to develop such keenness of intuition that we can foresee the future course of our affairs so clearly as to make further recourse to the *Book of Change* unnecessary!

CHAPTER 5

A GUIDE TO INTERPRETATION

There are two insuperable obstacles to providing a reliable guide to interpreting the *I Ching*'s responses.

The first is that so much depends on the various circumstances leading to the enquiry and upon numerous related facts, some of which may already be present in the enquirer's mind, while others are not recognized as having any connection until either the response itself or subsequent events demonstrate their importance. An elementary example is provided by the fifth line of Hexagram 3, Chun, Difficulty. If that happens to be a moving line, the response will include the words: 'Fertility cannot easily be brought about', which will obviously have different meanings for, say, somebody longing to bear a son or daughter, a man considering whether to buy a certain piece of land, a teacher hoping to enlighten a backward child, an administrator about to take charge of a new territory, a person expecting to benefit from a particular friendship or a business man mulling over a new policy. There may be other cases on which the words seem to have no bearing at all, as with the enquiry: 'Is it advisable for me to break my flight across India in the hope of receiving permission to visit the Dalai Lama?' In this case, the words (taken out of context) seem either to be irrelevant or else, perhaps, to mean that it would not be fruitful to attempt it. But supposing the enquirer's original plan was to fly straight across India on his way further east, hoping to persuade the Cambodian authorities to adopt his pet community development scheme; then the oracle might be taken to imply: 'You will have great difficulty in bringing your scheme to fruition', from which might follow the implication that a delay of two or three days in order to visit the Dalai Lama would scarcely affect the issue. However, that same moving line goes on to say: 'Persistence in small things will bring good fortune; in greater matters it will bring disaster.' Any previous doubt as to whether the oracle referred to the difficulty of getting permission to see the Dalai Lama or to the improbability of the enquirer's being able to put over his development scheme successfully can almost certainly be resolved in the light of those additional words, for he must know which of these two matters is of relatively slight importance to him.

A GUIDE TO INTERPRETATION

The second obstacle is that the *Book of Change* can seldom be accurately interpreted in accordance with a particular situation unless the faculty of intuition is allowed to play a decisive role. Naturally, it is impossible to portray the part of intuition when we are dealing with hypothetical cases.

Nevertheless, those unskilled in interpretation may gain some advantage from the following examples of how to interpret responses at their face value, that is without allowing either for a detailed knowledge of the background of the enquiries or for the role played by intuition. But, first, at the risk of repetition, I wish to warn the enquirer against mistaking his desires or expectations for intuition. It is true enough that what is discovered by intuition does quite often coincide with what people consciously hope or expect, but there is a very great danger of their allowing themselves to imagine this coincidence where it does not in fact exist. True intuition occurs only when the mind has been temporarily withdrawn from all conceptual and intellectual processes by means of Zen-like concentration, during which time our consciousness is cleansed of hopes, fears, expectations and so forth.

Case 1

Let us suppose that an enquirer is debating whether to leave his present employment in order to take up a post abroad which, though it would increase his income and improve his prospects, might cause him regret for other reasons. (For the sake of simplicity, these reasons will not be specified in our example; but, were the enquiry a real one, they would occupy an important place among the many factors bearing upon the right interpretation of the oracle received.) In response to his simple query, 'Shall I accept the post which has been offered me in Tokyo?', he receives Hexagram 3, Chun, Difficulty, together with a moving line for the fourth place and, as a consequence of the latter, a second hexagram, namely Hexagram 17, Sui, Following or According With (for this is what Chun becomes when the fourth line 'moves' and thus changes from a yielding to a firm line).

The Text of the former hexagram presages difficulty followed by the utmost success and promises reward for (morally correct) determination; but it also advises against seeking a new goal or setting out for a new destination and advocates consolidating the present position. The Commentary on the Text, as usual, reinforces the teaching of the Text itself and adds a warning about the difficulties which are liable to attend the growth of something new. Similarly, the Symbol indicates difficulty and suggests that this is a time for setting our present circumstances in good order (for, when the *I Ching* states that the Superior Man does so and so, this should be taken to mean: 'If you value wisdom and virtue, you will do so and so'). The moving (fourth) line recommends hesitation now as a means of ensuring prosperity in the future; while the commentary on that line, with seeming contrariness, urges the pursuit of what is desired by the enquirer. The Text of the second hexagram (H.17) also promises success and advises determination; it adds a firm assurance that we shall not be involved in error. The Commentary on the Text makes specific reference to the two component trigrams by speaking of movement and joy conjoined and ends with a firm indication that, in all matters, it is essential to attend to the timeliness of our actions, thus according with one of nature's fundamental principles. The symbolism suggests that it would not be timely to take action now.

The interpretation of these apparently conflicting points in the light of the specific enquiry requires some skill. Several passages, if taken by themselves, seem to imply that, despite some initial difficulties, it would be well worth while for the enquirer to accept the post in Tokyo in a spirit of determination to succeed; but other passages seem to advise against a journey at this time, while advocating consolidation of the present position and emphasizing that a move just now would be most untimely. My own interpretation (leaving out of account background details, the character and attainments of the man involved, and the part normally played by intuition) would run something like this:

The Text of Hexagram 3, taken by itself, indicates that he should not accept a post abroad at this time, since this would involve a journey and a new goal in life, but that he should rather seek to consolidate his position in the organization where he now works. The Commentary on the Text suggests that this opinion should perhaps be modified somewhat because of the emphasis it places on the success attending the birth of something new, once the initial difficulties have been overcome; but the symbolism reminds us that there are matters to be set in order before any novel action is undertaken. The moving line both counsels hesitation and urges the pursuit of what is desired. The Text of the second hexagram (H.17) confirms part of what we have already learnt from the Text of Hexagram 3; but, whereas the former advises against a journey, the latter's reference to the conjoining of movement and joy makes it appear that a journey is rather to be desired than otherwise; however, the stress placed upon the need for timeliness forbids impetuosity, all the more so as what is said about the symbolism clearly indicates that this is not the right time to make a major move. From all this, I conclude that the enquirer should not be in a hurry to accept the Tokyo appointment, but that he should keep it (or the possibility of obtaining some similar post) in mind and be firmly determined to seize a chance of bettering his prospects by going abroad when it becomes more certain that the right moment has arrived.

Case 2

Someone has received information that there is reason to suspect dangerous disloyalty on the part of a subordinate in the branch of administration which he heads. Yet, on the strength of the latter's past good record, he is reluctant to accept the fairly convincing but not altogether conclusive evidence of misbehaviour. Accordingly, he enquires of the *Book of Change*: 'Shall I dismiss, or at least transfer, this man, since there is reason to suppose that his activities are endangering the interests of the administration?' For answer, he receives: Hexagram 5, Hsü, Calculated Inaction, as well as two moving lines, the fourth and the fifth, and (consequently) Hexagram 14, Ta Yü, Great Possessions (or the Great Possessor). From these, the following main points emerge. The Text of the former hexagram (H.5) indicates three things—the advantage of refraining from immediate action, the wisdom of being firmly determined and the auspiciousness of making a journey at this time. The Commentary on the Text underlines the importance of remaining inactive but determined; it adds that considerable clarity of mind is required if danger is to be avoided. What is said about the symbolism reiterates the importance of not acting hastily. Line four suggests that, even if violence were to erupt, we should still be well advised to sit back and let things take their course. Line five recommends thorough relaxation accompanied by firm determination to act rightly at the proper time. The Text of the latter hexagram (H.14) promises success to those who are already wealthy and powerful. The Commentary on the Text echoes what was said earlier about the need for firmness and strength. Under the heading Symbol comes the passage: 'The Superior Man suppresses those who are evil and upholds the virtuous.' My interpretation (with the usual reservations about background and intuition) is thus:

The Text, Commentary and Symbol of Hexagram 5 all indicate that, as yet, no action should be taken against the alleged culprit, but that the search for conclusive proof should be diligently pursued, even at the cost of travelling a considerable distance, should that seem necessary. It is also made clear that hasty action at this time might do much harm and that the mind must be guarded against bewilderment (in this case, probably due to prejudice, rumours, accusations and so forth). The two moving lines emphasize that, however dangerous the current of events may seem or actually become, this danger must be met by relaxing and biding our time. The Text of Hexagram 14, in promising success to one already wealthy or powerful (or both), seems in this case to indicate that the success of the administration will not be impaired as a result of our patient inactivity. The Commentary on the Text demands firmness and strength—but against what? In the present context, this would seem to mean that we should resist any pressure brought upon us to dismiss the suspect without waiting for further proof. The passage derived from the hexagram's symbolism about suppressing the evil-minded and upholding the virtuous may indicate a need for zeal in refusing to allow ourselves to be led into acting unjustly. From all of this, I should conclude that the suspect is probably a maligned man, since the need for caution is stressed so often; that, in any case, the administration will weather any dangers arising from failure to dismiss him promptly; and that, unless and until his disloyalty is proved beyond all doubt, I must resist pressure to take punitive action.

It is true that we are still left in some doubt as to the man's guilt or innocence, since at best only the probability of his innocence has been established by the response; but, were the enquirer to express disappointment with this uncertain result, I should certainly chide him for underrating the *Book of Change* and seek to justify the response in these terms: 'Had the response ruled the suspect guilty, you would have been faced with the choice of punishing him and then feeling deeply contrite for having based so grave a decision upon a method of which scarcely one of your colleagues would have approved, or else of leaving him unpunished and then worrying acutely about his probable harmfulness to the interests of the administration you head. If, on the other hand, the response had ruled him innocent, though you might cease to worry about him, he would still remain an object of suspicion and dislike to his accusers and there would probably be times when you felt hesitant to trust him as fully as in the days before any accusation was whispered against him. Therefore the *I Ching* says in effect: "Wait for certain evidence before you take action, safe in the knowledge that your patience will in no way endanger the interests you serve." '

Case 3

A woman who still retains some affection for her husband is so worried by the lightness with which he takes his responsibilities that she has begun to contemplate divorcing him, both for her own sake and the children's. She frames her question simply: 'Shall I divorce him or not?' The reponse consists of Hexagram 11, T'ai, Peace. As there are no moving lines, no other hexagram is involved. The Text of Hexagram 11 reads: 'The mean decline; the great and the good approach—good fortune and success!' (If the reader has carefully read what was said in the foreword of this book about the terseness of the Chinese language he will be prepared to understand 'the mean, the great and the good' as being equally applicable to persons and to qualities; i.e., 'the mean' may signify evil people and persons of little worth in some contexts, evilness and worthlessness in others.) The Commentary on the Text powerfully stresses the divine nature of conjugal harmony and goes on to presage the decline of those whose moral worth is insignificant (or, alternatively, the decline of moral worthlessness). The symbolism of the hexagram stresses further the perfections of conjugal harmony.

How to interpret what is said about the mean declining and so on will depend upon which, if any, of those involved in the case at issue can rightfully be regarded as despicable. The husband? Perhaps! Yet if he were entirely lacking in good qualities, his wife would scarcely need to consult the *I Ching* before making up her mind to divorce him. Some woman or women who have seduced him away from her? Possibly! Or does 'mean' refer to certain qualities in her husband which, according to the response, are not likely to remain with him much longer? Again, perhaps. If the wife feels that it would be unjust to identify him with 'the mean', the Chinese sense of which is synonymous with despicable, then what is said about the mean declining must either signify that some unprincipled woman or women are about to lose their influence over him or else that he is about to rid himself of his more evil qualities. In either of these cases, divorce is not indicated. On the contrary, the heavy stress laid upon conjugal harmony is a clear indication that the marriage can be saved if the wife is sufficiently intelligent, magnanimous and ready to forgive the past. Indeed, the omen promises a degree of marital felicity reminiscent of the perfect union of heaven and earth.

Under different circumstances, the oracle would have to be interpreted in quite another sense. If the husband has consistently behaved so badly as to deserve being classed as despicable by his wife even at moments when she is calm and free from anger; then it appears that, not only is a divorce much to be desired, but that it will be followed by the approach of 'the great and the good', namely of a future husband with whom she can enjoy conjugal bliss as harmonious as the mating of heaven and earth! (However, if the woman is merely a little tired of her present husband's infidelity, she must not allow wishful thinking to lead her into the error of supposing that her best way to conjugal happiness necessarily lies through divorce and remarriage.)

The fact that two strongly conflicting interpretations can be put upon the same passages serves to underline the importance of taking into full consideration a host of background details absent from these examples and of giving proper scope to the work of intuition. Where both these matters receive adequate attention, there can be no room for doubt or conflicting opinions, for then it will be abundantly clear as to which of the alternatives applies.

In all the above cases, only the most simple form of interpretation has been attempted. In particular, very little weight has been given to the symbolism, which involves a detailed knowledge of the mutual influence of the component trigrams and of the compatibility or otherwise of the component lines. But as this knowledge cannot be acquired without long study and the guidance of an expert, it is safer to rely chiefly upon the texts and commentaries attached to the hexagrams and moving lines, for these provide the interpretations made by King Wên, Duke Chou and Confucius or, in any case, by men scarcely inferior to them in calibre as regards their understanding of the hexagrams and their component parts. To add or substitute our own interpretations based directly on the forms of the hexagrams would, for most of us, be rash, though we may one day find ourselves qualified to undertake at least a small amount of direct interpretation.

CHAPTER 6

A SUMMARY OF INSTRUCTIONS

This short chapter contains no new materials and can be omitted during the first reading of the book. It is intended as a concise guide for those who wish to refresh their memories just before undertaking an enquiry.

1. The *Book of Change* when not in use is left cleanly wrapped upon a suitably high shelf. The divining sticks in their special lidded receptacle are placed next to it.

2. Shortly before a consultation, the book is taken from its shelf and placed on a table facing south in the middle of the room, together with an incense-burner, the divining sticks, two small trays and some writing materials.

3. If the enquiry has not yet been precisely formulated, this should be done now. If necessary, it should contain time limits which will help to place the response in the required perspective.

4. Facing the table and with his back to the South, the enquirer prostrates himself thrice, lights a stick of incense and—with his mind fully concentrated on the question—mentally or verbally propounds it in the form previously decided upon. While doing so, he takes the divining sticks in his right hand and passes them three times through the incense smoke by describing clockwise circles with his wrist.

5. Returning one stick to the receptacle, he places the remaining forty-nine on a tray and, with a rapid motion of his right hand, divides them into two heaps.

6. To establish the first line of the answering hexagram, he performs the three stages of the first of six identical processes. (*a*) From the right heap, he takes one stick and places it between the last two fingers of his left hand. Then from the left heap he takes away the sticks, four by four, until only 1, 2, 3 or 4 remain. This small remainder he places in the next space between the fingers of his left hand. Next, he removes the sticks, four by four, from the right heap until only 1, 2, 3 or 4 remain (unless he prefers to calculate this remainder from the amount of the previous one with the help of the divining table, in which case,

he merely picks the correct number of sticks from the right heap). The single stick between the last two fingers of his left hand plus the two remainders will add up to a total of either five or nine. These five or nine sticks are placed in a heap on the second tray. (*b*) The forty-four or forty sticks remaining on the first tray are swept together in one heap and the enquirer proceeds as before, with the result that he ultimately obtains a total of four or eight sticks. These he places on the second tray at a little distance from the heap of five or nine already there. (*c*) With the sticks still remaining on the first tray (i.e. 40 or 36 or 32), he again proceeds as before and once more obtains a total of four or eight. Finally, the second tray will contain three heaps of sticks; the first, 5 or 9; the second, 4 or 8; the third 4 or 8. The divining table (see p. 64) will disclose what type of line is signified by the combination of numbers thus arrived at and he will draw it on a piece of paper as the bottom line of the answering hexagram.

7. To establish the remaining five lines of the hexagram, working from the bottom up, he places the forty-nine sticks together again and proceeds as in paragraph 6 above for each individual line.

8. When the hexagram has been established, if there are any moving lines, he draws a second hexagram identical with the first except that the moving Yang or Yin lines are replaced by Yin or Yang lines respectively, i.e. a closed moving line by an open line or an open moving line by a closed line. The response will be indicated by the Text and Commentary appended to the first hexagram, plus those appended to the moving lines (if any), plus those appended to the second hexagram (if there have been any moving lines to bring about its formation).

9. Interpretation of the response must be objective and therefore untainted by wishful thinking. It depends upon three factors: the wording of the appropriate Texts and Commentaries; the context supplied by the question; the enquirer's ability to supplement the obvious answer by his power of intuition.

10. After writing down his interpretation, if he has no further enquiries to make, he lights another stick of incense, performs three prostrations and replaces the book and the divining sticks on the shelf where they are usually kept.

11. None of these rules, except those governing the manipulation of the divining sticks is absolutely hard and fast. The rest can be modified according to circumstances, but modification should not be lightly undertaken.

A SUMMARY OF INSTRUCTIONS

NOTES ON THE SIGNIFICANCE OF CERTAIN FREQUENTLY USED PHRASES IN THE TEXTS AND COMMENTARIES

Sublime success—complete success resulting from heaven's accord with our aims.

Persistence in a righteous course brings reward—we may safely persist with our plans provided that they involve no harm to anyone who is not working against the public good.

No error or *no blame*—if results do not accord with our wishes, the fault is not ours; they are due to circumstances beyond our control.

Nothing brings advantage—we should desist.

It will be advantageous to cross the great river (or sea)—It is advisable to go on a long journey in connection with our plans.

It is advisable to see a great man—we shall greatly benefit if we approach someone of great wisdom and moral worth for advice or assistance.

It is of advantage to have in view a goal (or destination)—this is a time to advance provided that we have a clear objective, whether it is a place or something more abstract.

Persistence would bring misfortune—the only safe course is to give up our plan completely.

Fulfilment of what is willed—we shall gain our present objective, provided that it is a worthy one. (Note that the operative word is 'willed', not 'desired'. A desire may be good or bad. 'Will' in the sense of the *Book of Change* means something like 'a noble desire'.)

To advance—to go forward, either in the literal sense or in the sense of continuing to carry out our plans.

Shame—disgrace, either in the eyes of others or in our own eyes when we review our conduct impartially.

Regret—a consciousness that our troubles are due to our own conduct or lack of foresight, etc.

Superior Man or *great man* or *holy sage*—these seem to be used synonymously; they connote a man of the highest moral worth and of great wisdom; he is not a superman, for he is capable of error and, very occasionally, of conduct unworthy of a sage; but, when he errs, he is swiftly repentant and strives to make up for his error. In many passages where he is mentioned, perhaps in most of them, the implication is that the finest course for us to pursue is the one attributed to him in the passage concerned. Thus, 'the Superior Man does so and so' implies that it would be best for us to do the same, or at least to act in an equivalent manner within the context of our own sphere of activity.

PART TWO

THE BOOK OF CHANGE (TEXT AND COMMENTARIES)

HEXAGRAM 1[1]
CH'IEN[2] THE CREATIVE PRINCIPLE

Component trigrams:
Below: CH'IEN,[2] heaven, male, active, etc.
Above: CH'IEN, heaven, male, active, etc.

TEXT   The Creative Principle. Sublime Success! Persistence in a righteous course brings reward. 9 for the bottom place: the concealed dragon avoids action. 9 for the second place: the dragon is perceived in an open space; it is advantageous to visit a great man. 9 for the third place: the Superior Man busies himself the whole day through and evening finds him thoroughly alert. Disaster threatens—no error! 9 for the fourth place: leaping about on the brink of a chasm—no error! 9 for the fifth place: the dragon wings across the sky; it is advantageous to visit a great man. 9 for the top place: a wilful dragon —cause for regret! 9 for all six places: a brood of headless dragons— good fortune![3]

COMMENTARY ON THE TEXT   Vast indeed is the sublime Creative Principle, the Source of All, co-extensive with the heavens! It causes the clouds to come forth, the rain to bestow its bounty and all objects to flow into their respective forms. Its dazzling brilliance permeates all things from first to last; its activities symbolized by the component lines, reach full completion, each at the proper time. (The Superior Man), mounting them when the time is ripe, is carried heavenwards as though six dragons were his steeds! The Creative Principle functions through Change; accordingly, when we rectify our way of life by conjoining it with the universal harmony, our firm persistence is richly rewarded. The ruler, towering above the multitudes, brings peace to all the countries of the world.

SYMBOL   This hexagram symbolizes the power of the celestial forces in motion, wherewith the Superior Man labours unceasingly to strengthen his own character.

[Here follow some references to the individual lines; these have been inserted under the lines concerned.]

THE WÊN YEN COMMENTARY ON THE TEXT The sublime is above all, that which is imbued with virtue. Success implies the advent of everything auspicious. Reward refers to the bringing together of all that favours righteousness. Persistence in a righteous course is the proper way of ordering our affairs. The Superior Man fits himself for leadership by becoming the embodiment of human kindness. The advent of everything auspicious renders him capable of perfect conduct. His success in acquiring material satisfactions enables him to act with justice. His righteous persistence makes him fully capable of attaining his ends. The Superior Man never ceases to exercise these four virtues.[4] Hence it may be said of him: 'The Creative Principle ensures his sublime success; his persistence in a righteous course brings him reward.'

FURTHER COMMENTARIES Whatever it undertakes, the Creative Principle invariably carries to a successful conclusion. It possesses the inherent characteristic of rewarding right persistence.

From the very first, the Creative Principle has exercised its power of bestowing upon all under heaven the gift of beauty, while never boasting of benefits bestowed—what magnanimity!

Great indeed is the Creative Principle—firm, filled with power, unbiassed, righteous, pure, sublime! Its six component lines, when properly expounded, lead to an understanding of every aspect of creation. Leaping upon them when the time is ripe, we ride heavenwards upon the backs of six dragons. The clouds come forth; the rain bestows its bounty and the whole world is filled with peace!

The Lines

9 FOR THE BOTTOM PLACE The concealed dragon refrains from action. What does this signify? THE WÊN YEN COMMENTARY According to the Master,[5] this symbolizes someone dragon-like in his virtues who conceals his light, avoids all compromise with the world, makes no name for himself, withdraws from worldly life without regret, cares not that no one seeks him out, does what pleases him and avoids whatever he might rue. Firm as a rock, he can by no means be uprooted. Such a man may well be called a concealed dragon! FURTHER COMMENTARIES (*a*) The concealed dragon refraining

CH'IEN THE CREATIVE PRINCIPLE

from action implies that the life-sustaining force is still submerged. (*b*) This is indicated by the position of the line at the bottom of the hexagram. (*c*) A celestial dragon refraining from activity implies that the life-sustaining force lies hidden in the earth. (*d*) The activity of the Superior Man consists in accomplishing deeds of virtue. All day long he can be seen at work. Concealed means that his light is not yet seen, as his conduct has still to be perfected. That is his reason for refraining from activity.[6]

9 FOR THE SECOND PLACE   The dragon is perceived in an open space; it is advantageous to visit a great man. What does this signify? THE WÊN YEN COMMENTARY   According to the Master,[5] this signifies someone dragon-like in his virtue who rightly stands at the centre of things. In speech sincere, in action cautious, he holds evil at a distance and preserves his integrity. He does the world much good, but makes no show of it. His virtue is ample to endow him with great influence. Indeed, this passage concerning a dragon in the open and a great man refers to one so greatly endowed with virtue as to be worthy of exercising supreme sovereignty.

FURTHER COMMENTARIES   (*a*) The concept of a dragon appearing in the open suggests that the great man's deeds are everywhere distributed. (*b*) This passage indicates that the time for action has arrived.[6] (*c*) It also means that the whole world is civilized by the Superior Man's power. (*d*) The Superior Man studies in order to assemble facts, questions others to gain discrimination, makes forgiveness his life's motto and kindness the essence of his conduct. The passage about the dragon in the open and about going to see a great man was inspired by the virtues of such people.

9 FOR THE THIRD PLACE   The superior man busies himself the whole day through and evening finds him thoroughly alert. Trouble threatens, but he is not at fault. What does this signify? THE WÊN YEN COMMENTARY   According to the Master,[5] the superior man progresses in virtue and takes great pains with his work. By progressing in virtue, he achieves loyalty and integrity. By guarding his speech, he makes himself sincere and is thus able to ensure that his work will endure. Knowing what should be done, he does it and thereby fulfils the highest expectations. Understanding how to bring his tasks to fruition, he does so without departing from righteous conduct. Hence,

neither can a high position puff him up nor a low one cause him to repine. That is why he labours and labours, remaining thoroughly alert when circumstances so require. Thus, though danger may threaten, he is by no means at fault. FURTHER COMMENTARIES (*a*) Busying himself all day long implies that he goes over his work again and again. (*b*) It is said with reference to affairs of importance. (*c*) It also implies that he harmonizes his work with the needs of the times. (*d*) This line is a strong one, but not central (to a trigram). It is not high enough to correspond with heaven, nor low enough to correspond with earth; so hard work is required of him and alertness where necessary.[6] The danger in the current position involves no blame.

9 FOR THE FOURTH PLACE Leaping about on the brink of a chasm, he is not at fault. What does this signify? THE WÊN YEN COMMENTARY According to the Master,[5] neither rising nor falling endures for long; what matters is to avoid committing evil. Neither advance nor retreat can go on indefinitely; what matters is not to desert the others. The Superior Man progresses in virtue and takes pains with his work so that what he seeks to accomplish will reach fruition in good time—no blame to him. FURTHER COMMENTARIES (*a*) Though he be leaping about on the brink of a chasm, for him to advance would involve no fault. (*b*) This passage means that he is testing his powers. (*c*) It also means that the way followed by the Creative Principle is leading towards one of its great transformations. (*d*) The line is a strong one, but not central (to a trigram); it is not high enough to correspond with heaven or low enough to correspond with earth nor, despite its relatively central position (in the hexagram), central enough to correspond with man. Hence it suggests uncertainty and implies a situation of which the outcome is doubtful[6]—that is why he is not at fault.

9 FOR THE FIFTH PLACE The dragon wings across the sky; it is advantageous to visit a great man. What does this signify? THE WÊN YEN COMMENTARY According to the Master,[5] musical instruments which emit identical notes vibrate in response to each other. People of the same disposition seek each other out. Water flows where wetness lies; fire burns where things are parched. Like clouds trailing behind dragons and the wind which follows in a tiger's wake, all creatures follow with their gaze the advent of a holy sage. Whatever is of celestial origin feels affinity with what lies above; things of

CH'IEN THE CREATIVE PRINCIPLE

terrestrial origin feel their affinity with what lies below. Thus all things follow their own kind. FURTHER COMMENTARIES (*a*) This passage presages the emergence of a being who is truly great. (*b*) It also symbolizes the supreme position of the ruler. (*c*) It exemplifies accord with heaven's virtue. (*d*) The Superior Man (or 'great man' of the text) is one whose virtues bring him into accord with heaven and earth; his clarity of mind resembles that of the sun and moon; his actions are as well-ordered as the unfolding of the seasons; his joys and sorrows make him the equal of gods and demons. When he acts in advance of heaven's decree, heaven will surely support his action; if he awaits that decree and then acts, he follows the heaven-ordained sequence.[6] Yes, even heaven grants him full support—then how much more so men and how very much more so gods and demons!

9 FOR THE TOP PLACE   A wilful dragon has cause for regret. What does this signify? THE WÊN YEN COMMENTARY According to the Master,[5] a man of the highest capability who lacks a suitable appointment or who is granted a high post but with no people under his control, or one whose excellent assistants nevertheless fail to support him, can do nothing that will not cause him regret. FURTHER COMMENTARIES (*a*) This signifies that not for long will his cup be full.[7] (*b*) It suggests the approach of overpowering calamities. (*c*) It also implies that sooner or later all things reach their end. (*d*) Wilful suggests that he is one who knows how to advance but not how to retreat, how to amass but not how to relinquish, how to win but not how to lose.[6] Only a holy sage can know how to do all these things with perfect integrity—yes, only a holy sage!

9 FOR ALL SIX PLACES   (No text appears here. The commentaries refer to the last words of the main text: 'A brood of headless dragons appears; good fortune.') THE WÊN YEN COMMENTARY Nil. FURTHER COMMENTARIES (*a*) None of the Creative Principle's virtues can form a head.[8] (*b*) This hexagram, when all its component lines are moving lines, presages rule over the entire world. (*c*) These six moving lines indicate a breadth of understanding which embraces the whole pattern of the universe!

NOTES (1) The treatment given to the hexagram is in some ways unique, though hexagram 2 shares one of its peculiarities. It is the only hexagram for which details of the individual lines appear in the body of the main text. Moreover, the Wên Yen Commentary and several of the other commentaries appear only in connection with Hexagrams 1 and 2.

I have somewhat altered the order of the Chinese original, so that all that pertains to the main text is brought together and all that pertains to each line appears close to the line concerned. The rather haphazard order of the original is scarcely astonishing in view of the book's enormous antiquity. Quite possibly, parts of the complete Wên Yen and other commentaries were lost and the remnants attached to the appropriate hexagrams, namely 1 and 2. What is remarkable is the perfect order and relative completeness of surviving texts and commentaries throughout the whole of the rest of the book; there are relatively few obviously corrupt passages. (2) Ch'ien appears both as the name of a hexagram and as the name of a trigram, but I have translated it somewhat differently in each case. (3) These enigmatic references to dragons and so on are fully explained under the heading 'THE LINES'. In China, the dragon has always been regarded as a highly admirable creature of celestial origin. Dragons provide rain, make rivers run and rule the ocean. The European dragon is clearly of another species. (4) The four virtues are human kindness, perfect conduct, justice and wisdom. The first three are mentioned by name above; the fourth is implicit in 'fully capable of attaining his ends'. (5) Confucius. (6) From the point of view of divination, it is this sentence which best serves as a guide to action. (7) His cup of happiness and success. (8) Can take precedence over the others—see Note (4), in which the virtues are enumerated.

HEXAGRAM 2[1]
K'UN[2] THE PASSIVE PRINCIPLE

Component trigrams:
Below: K'UN, *earth, female, passive, etc.*
Above: K'UN, *earth, female, passive, etc.*

TEXT   The Passive Principle. Sublime success! Its omen is a mare, symbolizing advantage. The Superior Man has an objective and sets forth to gain it. At first he goes astray, but later finds his bearings. It is advantageous to gain friends in the west and the south, but friends in the east and the north will be lost to us. Peaceful and righteous persistence brings good fortune.

COMMENTARY ON THE TEXT   Exalted indeed is the sublime Passive Principle! Gladly it receives the celestial force (of the Creative Principle) into itself, wherefrom all things receive their birth. This Passive Principle contains a vast plenitude of objects and into it the celestial power (literally 'virtue') enters unhindered. It is an all-embracing, shining vessel brimming with multitudinous contents. The mare symbolizes

K'UN THE PASSIVE PRINCIPLE

those (passive, female) creatures which wander unfettered throughout its confines. Gentle and accommodating, how auspicious is this omen! The passage about the Superior Man setting forth to gain his object suggests that, though at first he will lose his way due to some confusion, ultimately his situation will improve and return to normal.[3] Finding friends in the south and west really means that we should make friends with people of our own kind. Our losing friends in the east and north points to a situation in which, ultimately, there will be cause for rejoicing. The good fortune resulting from peaceful persistence will be due to our accord with the terrestrial forces.

SYMBOL This hexagram symbolizes the passivity of the terrestrial forces. The Superior Man displays the highest virtue by embracing all things.

THE WÊN YEN COMMENTARY ON THE TEXT The Passive Principle, thanks to its exceeding softness, can act with tremendous power.[4] Silent, tranquil, its virtue is amorphous until, receiving into itself the subjective force, it becomes clearly defined. Embracing all that exists, it becomes bright and shines forth. Its essential characteristic is glad acceptance. After receiving the celestial power, it acts in harmony with the sequence of time.

(The rest of this commentary is attached to the individual lines concerned.)

The Lines

6 FOR THE BOTTOM PLACE Hoarfrost underfoot betokens the coming of solid ice. THE WÊN YEN COMMENTARY A household which accumulates good deeds will enjoy blessings in abundance, while one which piles up evils will inevitably face a host of sufferings. The assassination of a ruler by his minister or the crime of patricide does not result from the events of a single day and night. The causes have gradually accumulated and, though they should have been observed long before, were not noticed and put right in time. The passage about hoarfrost underfoot being followed by the forming of solid ice indicates a need for caution.[5] THE MAIN COMMENTARY This line indicates the approach of (winter's) dark power; following nature's sequence, the season of solid ice is at hand.

6 FOR THE SECOND PLACE   Straight and of broad capacity, though we do nothing, all our affairs prosper.   THE WÊN YEN COMMENTARY   Straightness denotes rectitude. Broadness denotes a capacity for righteousness. The Superior Man is reverent and thereby strengthens his inner self; his righteousness enables him to deal justly with the external world. With reference and righteousness established in our hearts, we shall never depart from moral excellence. Straight, of broad capacity and great—whatever we undertake is sure to prosper; no longer need we doubt the successful outcome of our affairs.[3]   THE MAIN COMMENTARY   The six in this place indicates a straightforward movement to occupy a spacious area. Though nothing is done, everything prospers—this is a glorious characteristic of the terrestrial forces.

6 FOR THE THIRD PLACE   Concealment of talent (or beauty) constitutes the right course. As to the undertaking of public affairs, though immediate success may not be achieved, their ultimate fruition is assured.   THE WÊN YEN COMMENTARY   The passive dark force has many beauties but keeps them hidden. In public service, we must not presume to settle affairs by ourselves; instead we should emulate the terrestrial forces and behave like a wife (to her husband) or like one who serves his king. They complete nothing; yet, in course of time, fruition comes of itself.[3]   THE MAIN COMMENTARY   Talent (beauty) now concealed will be unfolded when the time is ripe; once it is engaged in public affairs, this talent will become great and glorious.

6 FOR THE FOURTH PLACE   Taciturnity—no blame, no praise.   THE WÊN YEN COMMENTARY   The transformations caused by the celestial and terrestrial forces bring forth a rich profusion of plants and trees; but when those forces are inactive, the Superior Man avoids the limelight. This passage has the underlying meaning of 'Be extremely watchful'.   THE MAIN COMMENTARY   The passage means that, with proper caution, we shall escape trouble.[3]

6 FOR THE FIFTH PLACE   A yellow[5] jacket—sublime good fortune.   THE WÊN YEN COMMENTARY   The Superior Man, yellow (virtuous) within, seeks to grasp life's fundamental principles and is contented with his prosperous condition. The beauty lying within him permeates his whole being with joy and influences all his undertakings.[3] Such is

K'UN THE PASSIVE PRINCIPLE

supreme beauty! THE MAIN COMMENTARY   The passage refers to inner (spiritual or moral) beauty.

6 FOR THE TOP PLACE   Dragons contending in the wilderness shed black and yellow blood. THE WÊN YEN COMMENTARY   When the passive dark force seeks to vie with the creative light force, the lack of which is bitterly regretted,[6] a struggle is inevitable. That is why the dark force is called a dragon (normally a Yang symbol), even though it still belongs to its own (Yin) category and is therefore also symbolized by blood (a Yin symbol). In truth, the black and the yellow betoken an intermingling of the celestial and terrestrial forces,[7] with black symbolizing the former and yellow the latter. THE MAIN COMMENTARY   The dragons contend, for their stock of merit is exhausted.[7]

6 FOR ALL SIX PLACES   Unfaltering determination will place our affairs on a permanent basis.[3] THE WÊN YEN COMMENTARY   Nil. THE MAIN COMMENTARY   This indicates constancy as a means of attaining great ends.

NOTES   (1) This hexagram resembles the preceding one in that the Wên Yen Commentary is given only for these two. In the original, the Wên Yen Commentary on the lines follows immediately after that on the text; I have divided it up for convenience.   (2) The name of the hexagram and of the two component trigrams is the same, but I have translated it somewhat differently in each case.   (3) From the point of view of divination, it is this sentence which best serves as a guide to action.   (4) The power of softness is a favourite theme with Taoists; cf. the power of water over rock in the process of erosion.   (5) Yellow has always been an exalted colour in China, where its use for garments was long restricted to the Imperial Family. Here it clearly symbolizes virtue.   (6) That is to say, Yin, the passive dark force, sometimes longs to possess the qualities of the celestial light force, Yang, and struggles to obtain them.   (7) The two commentaries appear contradictory, at least to some extent. Unfortunately, in divination it is the main commentary (here unfavourable) which is usually followed.

HEXAGRAM 3
CHUN   DIFFICULTY¹

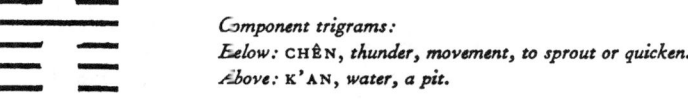

Component trigrams:
Below: CHÊN, *thunder, movement, to sprout or quicken.*
Above: K'AN, *water, a pit.*

TEXT   Difficulty followed by sublime success! Persistence in a righteous course brings reward; but do not seek some (new) goal (or destination); it is highly advantageous to consolidate the present position.

COMMENTARY ON THE TEXT   Difficulty! When the Strong (the celestial forces) and the Weak² (the terrestrial forces) first unite (to procreate something new), the birth that follows is not easy. Yet, to those struggling upward from the pit³ of adversity, determination to follow a righteous course promises great success. As when the universe was first created amidst the fury of thunder and rain with everything still primitive and obscure, this is a time to strive unceasingly for consolidation.

SYMBOL   This hexagram symbolizes lightning spewed forth by the clouds⁴—difficulty prevails! The Superior Man busies himself setting things in order.

The Lines

9 FOR THE BOTTOM PLACE   Uncertainty prevails. It is best to make no move, but to build up determination and to consolidate the position.
COMMENTARY   Despite prevailing uncertainty, the way of righteousness must be pursued with firm determination. Men in high places, by co-operating with those under their care, will thereby win (the) support (of the people).

6 FOR THE SECOND PLACE   He makes no more progress, covers no more distance, than a mounted man trotting to and fro. (His hesitation

CHUN DIFFICULTY

is due) not to an obstacle but to his wooing a girl who chastely repulses his advances and waits ten years before giving her consent.⁵ COMMENTARY The difficulties presaged by a six for the second place are revealed by this (weak) line's position just above a firm one. Waiting for ten years to receive the beloved's consent implies awaiting a gradual return to normal conditions.

6 FOR THE THIRD PLACE Pursuing a deer without a guide, the hunter finds himself lost in the forest. The Superior Man perceives that he must stay where he is, as going forward would lead to trouble. COMMENTARY His lack of caution in hunting the deer resulted from his being too set on capturing it. The Superior Man always desists when to advance would bring disaster.

6 FOR THE FOURTH PLACE Hesitating like a man trotting to and fro, he waits for marriage. Thenceforth, good fortune will prevail and every action prosper.⁶ COMMENTARY To pursue what we desire, that is wisdom.

9 FOR THE FIFTH PLACE Fertility cannot easily be brought about. Persistence in small things will bring good fortune; in greater matters, it will bring disaster. COMMENTARY This passage indicates that we have wrought insufficiently (for the public good).

6 FOR THE TOP PLACE (He hesitates) like a man trotting to and fro or like one shedding blood and tears. COMMENTARY How could a flow of blood and tears endure for long?⁷

NOTES (1) The fundamental idea of this hexagram is that of birth and growth amidst difficulty, as with a sprouting seed becoming a young plant and forcing its way through the earth. Our affairs, being still in their early stages, are vulnerable; we must not wander forth, but attend to them until they ripen; then, with proper care, the seed will bring forth a splendid tree. The upper trigram, a pit, suggests a need for caution; but, if we heed these omens, our success is assured. (2) The Strong and the Weak are suggested by the two component trigrams. (3) The upper trigram suggests this. (4) In this analogy, the upper trigram, water, stands for clouds and the lower, thunder, for lighting. (5) If the enquiry concerns matrimony, this passage may be taken to mean that the lady will not be in a hurry to consent; otherwise it indicates that willing delay will be well rewarded after a time. (6) This passage indicates that success can certainly be obtained, but only after a considerable period of waiting patiently. (7) In other words, our present troubles will pass away in time.

HEXAGRAM 4
MÊNG IMMATURITY, UNCULTIVATED GROWTH[1]

Component trigrams:
Below: K'AN, *water, a pit.*
Above: KÊN, *a mountain, hard, obstinate, perverse.*

TEXT Immaturity. Good fortune! I am not one to seek out uncultivated youths, but if such a youth seeks me out, I shall at first read and explain to him the omens. Yet should he ask me many times, just because of his importunity, I shall not explain anything more. (The omen indicates) a need for proper direction.

COMMENTARY ON THE TEXT Uncultivated growth! At the foot of the mountain lies a dangerous abyss.[2] To abide where danger lurks is youthful folly. Yet such rashness may bring good fortune—fortune to be utilized when the moment comes. The passage about not seeking out uncultivated youth and so on means that, should such a youth seek me out, at first I shall be inclined to respond by reading and explaining the omens to him, as the firm line in the middle (of the lower trigram) indicates. But, should he importune me several times, his very importunity would make me cease from further explanation, as this would indicate youthful boorishness. It is our sacred duty to correct the follies of youth through education.

SYMBOL This hexagram symbolizes a watery hole at the foot of a mountain[3] amidst uncultivated growth. The Superior Man by determined good conduct nourishes his virtue.[4]

The Lines

6 FOR THE BOTTOM PLACE To enlighten immature youth, it is advisable to apply discipline; even fetters may be required, but to use

MÊNG IMMATURITY, UNCULTIVATED GROWTH

them overmuch is harmful. COMMENTARY Though it is advisable to apply discipline, this must be done in accordance with just rules.

9 FOR THE SECOND PLACE Being gentle with the immature brings good fortune. Taking a wife brings good fortune. Sons will be capable of taking over the household affairs when the strong (young) and the weak (old) are in mutual harmony.

6 FOR THE THIRD PLACE Do not choose a wife who, on seeing a wealthy man, cannot contain herself. Nothing brings advantage.[5] COMMENTARY Do not take to wife one whose behaviour is disorderly.

6 FOR THE FOURTH PLACE Obstinacy and immaturity cause harm.[6] COMMENTARY They harm us by leading us astray from the right course.

6 FOR THE FIFTH PLACE Youthful innocence brings good fortune.[7] COMMENTARY This is because such conduct coincides with what is soft and gentle.

9 FOR THE TOP PLACE In dealing firmly with youthful immaturity, there is nothing to be gained from doing what is wrong.[8] Advantage lies in preventing wrong. COMMENTARY Preventing wrong has the advantage of bringing senior and junior into accord.[9]

NOTES (1) This hexagram suggests stubbornness (the upper trigram) issuing from the softness of the womb (the lower trigram). While it sometimes happens that youthful rashness succeeds where sober counsels fail, it is nevertheless the duty of the mature man to cultivate the minds of the young and to respond, within reason, to their requests for guidance. As an omen, this hexagram may be taken to imply a case in which a certain amount of rashness may lead to success, but in which older people are not absolved from the duty of guiding the young There is also a suggestion that the Book of Change itself, though fully responsive to those who make the right approach, will not brook importunity in the form of trivial questions or of seeking to reverse its judgements by further questioning. Whether the omen may be taken to mean that we should go ahead with some rash scheme or that it is time for us to restrain someone's youthful rashness will depend upon the nature of the enquiry, the people concerned in it and the particular moving lines involved in the response. (2) This is deduced from the position of the two trigrams. (3) A reference to the component trigrams. (4) The second sentence is deduced from the first; both are suggested by the component trigrams. (5) This line, besides furnishing a specific warning to those with marriage in view, means generally that this time is unpropitious from the point of view of the enquirer, whatever his question may concern. (6) This line may also be taken as a warning against a too idealistic or visionary attitude.

(7) Here the Chinese text suggests that we are dealing not with youthful folly but with the innocent misdemeanours of quite small children. (8) In other words, we must be very careful to avoid putting ourselves in the wrong by being unjust or too severe in correcting the faults of our juniors. (9) Improperly applied discipline may lead the young to hate those whom they are expected to love. Few young people gladly kiss the rod before punishment.

HEXAGRAM 5
HSÜ CALCULATED INACTION[1]

Component trigrams:
Below: CH'IEN, *heaven, male, active, etc.*
Above: K'AN, *water, a pit.*

TEXT Calculated inaction (or exhibiting the power to wait) and the confidence of others win brilliant success. Righteous persistence brings good fortune. It will be advantageous to cross the great river (or sea).

COMMENTARY ON THE TEXT To accord with the circumstances now prevailing, action must be avoided. Danger[2] lies ahead; but, with firmness and strength, we shall avoid failure. This implies not allowing ourselves to be bewildered. The first two sentences of the text are indicated by the fact that the ruling line of this hexagram (in this case, the fifth line) is the line of heaven, which acts with rectitude and attains its end. The passage about crossing water simply means that a journey at this time will be rewarding.

SYMBOL This hexagram symbolizes clouds rising to the zenith[3]—inactivity! The Superior Man will pass this time in feasting and enjoyment.

The Lines

9 FOR THE BOTTOM PLACE Stay on the outskirts avoiding action. Constancy preserves from harm. COMMENTARY Remaining on the outskirts means not rushing forward to undertake what is difficult

to perform. Constancy preserves from harm, suggests doing nothing out of the ordinary.

9 FOR THE SECOND PLACE Inactivity upon the river beach—some slight gossip may arise, but the final result will be good fortune. COMMENTARY The first sentence indicates a place with water flowing through the middle.[4] Though there be gossip, all will be well in the end.

9 FOR THE THIRD PLACE Inactivity amidst the mud[5]—this permits the approach of evil. COMMENTARY Remaining inactive in the midst of mud subjects us to external dangers, but the approaching evil will not harm us if we exercise proper care.[6]

6 FOR THE FOURTH PLACE Inactivity amidst blood—we shall emerge from the abyss. COMMENTARY To abstain from action amidst deeds of blood is to accord with the principle of allowing things to take their course.

9 FOR THE FIFTH LINE Inactivity amidst food and wine—righteous persistence will bring good fortune.[7] COMMENTARY This is indicated by the fact that the line is a firm one between two yielding lines.

6 FOR THE TOP PLACE Entering a pit. Three uninvited guests arrive; to honour them will ultimately bring good fortune. COMMENTARY When uninvited guests arrive, our treating them with honour brings good fortune. Although this is not customary, nothing is lost by it.[8]

NOTES (1) The significance of this hexagram is that inaction while awaiting the outcome of events will enable us to avoid a danger now threatening. Firmness, clarity of mind and success in winning the confidence of others are now demanded of us; with them, our undertakings will prosper. Moreover, this period of inaction is a good time in which to go on a journey or else for relaxation and enjoyment. (2) This danger is suggested by the upper trigram. (3) Clouds are symbolized by the upper trigram, the zenith by the lower. (4) Sitting on a river beach watching the water flow past symbolizes watching what is going forward without taking part. (5) This suggests a danger of our being so bogged down that we can neither fight nor flee. (6) We must not allow the mud to bog us down. (7) We may safely relax and enjoy ourselves, but we must preserve our determination to act when the time is ripe. (8) There is a Chinese proverb which runs: 'Being over-courteous excites no blame from others.'

HEXAGRAM 6
SUNG   CONFLICT[1]

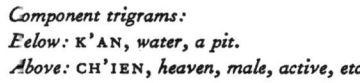

Component trigrams:
Below: K'AN, *water, a pit.*
Above: CH'IEN, *heaven, male, active, etc.*

TEXT   Conflict. Confidence accompanied by obstacles! With care, affairs can be made to prosper in their middle course, but the final outcome will be disaster. It is advantageous to visit a great man, but not to cross the great river (or sea).[2]

COMMENTARY ON THE TEXT   In this hexagram, the upper trigram indicates firmness; the lower, danger. When danger is met by firmness, conflict follows. What is said above about affairs prospering in their middle course if care is exercised is derived from the firm line in the middle (of the lower trigram). The final disaster occurs because the conflict is one which cannot be resolved. The advantage of going to see a great man is indicated by the firm line just mentioned. It would be unwise to cross the great river (go on any journey) as we should inevitably tumble into the watery abyss.[3]

SYMBOL   This hexagram symbolizes sky and water in opposition.[4] The Superior Man does not embark upon any affair until he has carefully planned the start.

The Lines

6 FOR THE BOTTOM PLACE   Provided that affairs are not pressed through to the end and that as little as possible is said about them, they will end propitiously.   COMMENTARY   Not pressing affairs through to the end implies not dragging on a dispute. Though little should be said, its purport should be clear.

9 FOR THE SECOND PLACE   As the conflict cannot be resolved, he

beats a hasty retreat. His clan, numbering three hundred households, also escapes harm.⁵ COMMENTARY This passage means that, if we pit ourselves against superior strength, we shall find ourselves bowed beneath the dint of conflict to the bitter end.

6 FOR THE THIRD PLACE He nourishes himself upon the ancient virtues. Right determination leads to initial trouble followed by good fortune. Were he to seek public office now, he would not be able to attain it. COMMENTARY The good fortune will result from obedience to superiors which stems from cherishing the ancient virtues.

9 FOR THE FOURTH PLACE Since the conflict cannot be resolved, it is best to retreat and submit to heaven's will. Peaceful determination brings good fortune. COMMENTARY Provided we submit to heaven's will, peaceful determination will enable us to win through.

9 FOR THE FIFTH PLACE Conflict followed by supreme good fortune. COMMENTARY This is indicated by the fitting position of the central line (of the upper trigram).

9 FOR THE TOP PLACE If a girdle of honour were bestowed upon him, he would be forced to strip it off thrice within one day. COMMENTARY Garments of honour obtained through strife do little credit to the wearer.⁶

NOTES (1) In general, this hexagram indicates that we have little chance of success in any conflict, dispute or lawsuit in which we are now engaged and that retreat is the best policy—unless line one or five is a moving line, in which case the position is more hopeful. (2) We can profit from the advice of someone truly wise, but a journey of any kind at this time would be disastrous. (3) Suggested by the lower trigram. (4) The component trigrams suggest two domes, that of the sky and that of the watery pit. (5) This sentence may have been taken from some ancient writing known to readers of the *Book of Change* at that time. In divination, unless it obviously has some bearing on the case, it may be disregarded, or else interpreted symbolically without paying much regard to the number three hundred. (6) In divination, garments of honour may be taken to symbolize any of the prizes obtained through a successful dispute.

HEXAGRAM 7
SHIH   THE ARMY[1]

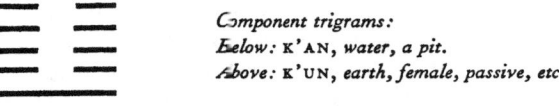

Component trigrams:
Below: K'AN, *water, a pit.*
Above: K'UN, *earth, female, passive, etc.*

TEXT   The Army. Persistence in a righteous course brings to those in authority good fortune and freedom from error.

COMMENTARY ON THE TEXT   This hexagram suggests a great host. Persistence is required for their governance. He who can govern people rightly is worthy to be a ruler. The firm line (in the lower trigram) is central and the others respond to it. Making progress with a highly dangerous task is a way of obtaining control of the realm and of winning the people's allegiance. When such good fortune is obtained, how can there be room for error?

SYMBOL   The hexagram symbolizes water surrounded by land.[2] The Superior Man nourishes the people and treats them with leniency.

The Lines

6 FOR THE BOTTOM PLACE   An army is built up through discipline; without it, corruption leading to disaster occurs.   COMMENTARY The disaster indicated in this passage results from a breakdown of discipline.

9 FOR THE SECOND PLACE   The general in the midst of his army enjoys good fortune and is free from error. Thrice he is honoured by the King.   COMMENTARY   It is because he is esteemed by the King that he enjoys good fortune and the protection of his army. Solicitous about the welfare of the empire, the King thrice awards him the command.

SHIH THE ARMY

6 FOR THE THIRD PLACE   The army carries waggon-loads of corpses—disaster!   COMMENTARY   This indicates a serious defeat.

6 FOR THE FOURTH PLACE   The army retreats and halts—no error!   COMMENTARY   No error is involved because retreating and halting are a normal part of military activity.

6 FOR THE FIFTH PLACE   Wild beasts roam the field. To avoid error, speech should be guarded. The eldest son is in command; the younger son carts away the corpses. Persistence would lead to calamity.[3]   COMMENTARY   The moving line in the centre (of the upper trigram) indicates that the elder son is in command. The younger son is put in charge of carrying away the corpses because he is unsuited to worthier employment.[4]

6 FOR THE TOP PLACE   The mandate is given to a great prince so that the work may go forward satisfactorily. A man of mean ability would be useless,[5] for he would merely spread disorder through the realm.

NOTES   (1) If the enquiry is not concerned with military affairs, we must interpret this hexagram symbolically in the sense that life is a battle.   (2) This is deduced from the component trigrams.   (3) What is said here about the elder and younger sons is not deduced in the ordinary way from either the component or the nuclear trigrams; for, while the lower nuclear trigram (lines 2, 3 and 4 from the bottom) is that of the elder son, the younger son is not represented by any of the four trigrams.   (4) In line with the symbolical interpretation usually accorded to this hexagram, this line may refer to the suitability or otherwise of a person required to fill an important post in any sort of organization or in carrying out some scheme.   (5) We cannot now rely on anyone of less than exceptional ability.

HEXAGRAM 8
PI UNITY, CO-ORDINATION[1]

Component trigrams:
Below: K'UN, *earth, female, passive, etc.*
Above: K'AN, *water, a pit.*

TEXT   Unity (or co-ordination). Good fortune! Further consultation of the oracle will provide an omen of great and lasting value. No error! Those whose hearts are troubled assemble. The laggards suffer disaster.

COMMENTARY ON THE TEXT   Unity (or co-ordination) brings good fortune by ensuring the support and willing obedience of subordinates. What is said about renewed consultation of the oracle is indicated by the strong line in the middle (of the upper trigram). Those in trouble will be drawn together because of the accord between those in command and those who obey. The laggards will suffer because their stock of Tao[2] is exhausted.

SYMBOL   The hexagram symbolizes water lying upon the land—co-ordination.[3] The ancient rulers strengthened the realm by being on affectionate terms with the feudal lords.[4]

The Lines

6 FOR THE BOTTOM PLACE   Where there is confidence, the work of unification is carried on faultlessly, for confidence is like a flowing bowl. There is a windfall yet to come.   COMMENTARY   Six for the bottom place here indicates unexpected good fortune.

6 FOR THE SECOND PLACE   Unification (or co-operation) should proceed from within our own circle. Righteous persistence will bring good fortune.   COMMENTARY   When unification (or co-operation)

PI UNITY, CO-ORDINATION

proceeds from within our own circle, the results will not be disappointing.

6 FOR THE THIRD PLACE He joins himself with evil-doers. COMMENTARY If we do this, how can we fail to suffer for it?

6 FOR THE FOURTH PLACE He co-operates with people beyond his immediate circle. Righteous persistence will bring good fortune. COMMENTARY Co-operation with such people and leading them into virtuous ways must be accomplished by working through their leaders.

9 FOR THE FIFTH PLACE Relying on his people's co-operation, the King pursues game which is enclosed on three sides, but loses the quarry ahead. This is because the local people were not warned.[5] Righteous persistence brings good fortune. COMMENTARY This good fortune is indicated by the central position of the ruling line [i.e. central to the upper trigram]. Leaving alone those difficult to catch and following where the chances seem good, the King nevertheless loses the game in front of him. This means that, although the local people were not warned, the ruler adopts a fair and liberal policy.[6]

6 FOR THE TOP PLACE Attempts to bring about unity when there is no one at the head result in disaster. COMMENTARY No one at the head means no one to complete the work of administration.[7]

NOTES (1) Just as the last hexagram deals ostensibly with military affairs, so does this one largely concern administration. For divination purposes, it should be regarded figuratively—unless a problem of administration is actually involved in the enquiry. (2) Here Tao means innate virtue and merit. (3) This is indicated by the nature of the component trigrams. It is by co-operation between the fertile earth and the water which irrigates it that growth is achieved. (4) This may suggest dealing kindly with immediate subordinates, but in certain rare cases it may be taken to mean that a friendly nobleman, if rightly approached, would prove helpful. (5) This would seem to suggest that our loss is not due to disloyalty but to our having failed to take people into our confidence. (6) The implication is that such a policy is required for the success of our plans. (7) This suggests a general lack of co-ordination due to poor leadership.

HEXAGRAM 9
HSIAO CH'U   THE LESSER NOURISHER[1]

Component trigrams:
Below: CH'IEN, *heaven, male, active, etc.*
Above: SUN, *wind, wood, bland, mild.*

TEXT   The Lesser Nourisher. Success! Dense clouds giving forth no rain approach from the western outskirts.

COMMENTARY ON THE TEXT   In this hexagram, a yielding line takes the ruling position and all the lines above and below correspond to it. This is called the Lesser Nourisher. Strong and yet gentle,[2] the firm line in the centre (of the lower trigram) indicates that our will be accomplished and that success will follow. The dense clouds giving forth no rain signify that our affairs are still going forward; what is said about their coming from the west[3] indicates that matters have not yet reached the point at which we may take action.

SYMBOL   This hexagram symbolizes wind blowing across the sky.[2] The Superior Man displays his scholarly accomplishments.

The Lines

9 FOR THE BOTTOM PLACE   How could returning to this path be blameworthy?   COMMENTARY   This passage assures us of good fortune.

9 FOR THE SECOND PLACE   Compelling ourselves to go back brings good fortune.   COMMENTARY   This is indicated by the central position of this line (in the lower trigram). The idea of not getting lost is also implied.

9 FOR THE THIRD PLACE   The chariot is separated from the spoked

HSIAO CH'U THE LESSER NOURISHER

wheel. Husband and wife stand glaring at each other. COMMENTARY Disorder reigns within the house.

6 FOR THE FOURTH PLACE   Owing to confidence, bloody and terrible deeds are avoided—no error. COMMENTARY   This means that the will of our superiors is identical with our own.

9 FOR THE FIFTH PLACE   Confidence is like a cord (to bind the hearts of others). With it we enrich our neighbours. COMMENTARY   This implies not getting rich on our own.

9 FOR THE TOP PLACE   The rains are falling and a time of rest has come. Virtue continues to increase. At this moment, persistence would bring serious trouble to women. Were the Superior Man to venture forth at the time of the full moon, he would be courting calamity.[4] COMMENTARY   The first sentence indicates that our stock of virtues is mounting; that about the Superior Man indicates that we may expect trouble.

NOTES (1) On the whole, this hexagram presages good for us. The wind blowing across the heavens does not have the nourishing virtues of rain, but it refreshes us and makes us feel better. Thus, if things are going reasonably well with us, we may expect an improvement, especially in the future when, presumably, the nourishing rain will fall. However, as lines three and six indicate, if we are in serious trouble, we must not expect much help from the rather mild good fortune that is blowing our way. The conception of something weak or yielding bringing great benefit has been greatly developed by the Taoists who, as though they were familiar with judo, recognize the strength to be found in softness and the dangerous weakness sometimes occasioned by too much strength. The name of this hexagram understood somewhat differently may also be taken to mean that the time is propitious for undertaking some additional activity or the care of the young. (2) A reference to the component trigrams. (3) The text implies western outskirts; however, those familiar with the way in which the *Book of Change* answers our enquiries will know better than to take every word literally. Moreover, the actual Chinese words which, on good advice from a Chinese expert, I have translated 'western outskirts' actually read 'to the west of us'; so it may be understood that some good fortune, which has yet to materialize fully, is to be found somewhere to the west of where we happen to be or is coming from that direction to where we are. (4) The commentary which follows this passage would seem to indicate that, in most cases, we need not take what is said about the time of the full moon too literally, but that we may expect trouble within a few days or weeks—i.e. at the time of the full moon or within the period between now and the night of the next full moon. Yet there are occasions when the *Book of Change* gives very literal answers, so it will be wise to avoid doing much out of doors on the night of the full moon.

HEXAGRAM 10
LÜ TREADING, CONDUCT[1]

Component trigrams:
Below: TUI, *a body of water, pool, marsh, joy.*
Above: CH'IEN, *heaven, male, active, etc.*

TEXT Though he treads upon the tiger's tail, it does not bite him. Success!

COMMENTARY ON THE TEXT In this hexagram, the mild stands upon the firm (a reference to the arrangement of the lower component trigram). The tiger does not bite the man who has trodden upon its tail because it is joyous and responds to heaven's will.[2] The man enjoys success. The firm central line (of the upper trigram) is well suited to its (commanding) position. Blamelessly setting foot in the place of the supreme ruler denotes glory.

SYMBOL This hexagram symbolizes a body of water lying open to the sky.[3] The Superior Man consults both high and low and thereby steadies the people's will.

The Lines

9 FOR THE BOTTOM PLACE Simple in his conduct, he goes forth— no error! COMMENTARY Conducting ourselves with simplicity while advancing suggests the ability to realize our desires without aid from others.

9 FOR THE SECOND PLACE The recluse treads his path peacefully. Righteous persistence will bring good fortune. COMMENTARY The recluse is a fortunate man because he cleaves to the middle path and does not allow himself to be confused.

6 FOR THE THIRD PLACE Though a man have but one eye, he can

LÜ TREADING, CONDUCT

still see; though he be lame, he can still walk; but he who treads upon the tiger's tail will get bitten⁴—disaster! The warrior undertakes things for his lord.⁵ COMMENTARY The one-eyed man does see, but not clearly; the lame man can walk, but not keep up with the others. The disaster suffered by the man who gets bitten is indicated by this line's unsuitable position. The warrior undertakes his lord's affairs because the latter is strong of will.

9 FOR THE FOURTH PLACE To tread (with impunity) upon a tiger's tail, breathless caution is required—good fortune in the end.⁶ COMMENTARY This breathless caution leads to good fortune because the ruler's will is carried out.

9 FOR THE FIFTH PLACE He treads delicately. Persistence could lead to trouble. COMMENTARY This trouble could arise despite the suitable position of the line.⁷

9 FOR THE TOP PLACE If they watch their step (or look to their conduct) and heed the omens, sublime good fortune will be theirs. COMMENTARY The sublime good fortune presaged by this top line takes the form of immense felicity.

NOTES (1) The general idea of this hexagram is that success can be won, but that the situation is dangerous enough to require extreme caution. The 'tiger' MAY not bite, but on the other hand, as lines three and five demonstrate, we cannot be certain of this. To consort with rulers and people in high places may be most beneficial; but, should we fail to please, they may make us regret our temerity. (2) The words 'joyous' and 'heaven's will' are derived from the component trigrams. (3) This is pictured by the component trigrams. In Hexagram 6, water in a pit lying beneath heaven symbolized conflict; it was as though the watery pit was trying to emulate heaven's dome; but here the flat stretch of water lying open to the sky has a favourable meaning, all the more so as the lower trigram has the secondary meaning of joy. Whereas K'an, the watery pit, always has an unpropitious significance, Tui is a favourable omen. (4) Here the significance of the line runs counter to the benign significance of the hexagram; in all such cases, it is the line which provides the main indication of what is going to happen with regard to the matter forming the subject of enquiry. (5) This is no time to stand up to our superiors (tread on the tiger's tail); it is a time for obedience. (6) This is an occasion for doing something dangerous, provided we are very cautious. (7) A firm line between two firm ones is usually an omen of strength and compatibility, but not in this case. Thus, even though we are quite certain our course is a right one and we therefore follow it boldly, trouble cannot be avoided; we should either walk delicately or refrain from the course altogether.

HEXAGRAM 11
T'AI   PEACE

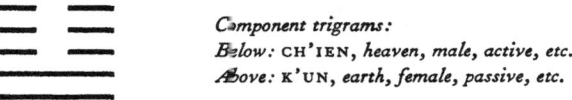

Component trigrams:
Below: CH'IEN, *heaven, male, active, etc.*
Above: K'UN, *earth, female, passive, etc.*

TEXT   Peace. The mean decline; the great and good approach—good fortune and success!

COMMENTARY ON THE TEXT   This hexagram indicates that the celestial and terrestrial forces have intercourse and all things are in communion with one another.[1] High and low mingle and are of one will. The active, bright principle (Yang) lies within; the passive, dark principle (Yin) lies without—strength lies within, glad acceptance without.[2] The Superior Man is at the centre of the things; those of low moral worth hover about the fringes. The way of the former waxes, that of the latter wanes.

SYMBOL   This hexagram symbolizes heaven and earth in communion.[2] It is as though a mighty ruler, by careful regulation of affairs, has brought to fruition the way of heaven and earth. In harmony with the sequence of their motions, he gives help to people on every hand.

The Lines

9 FOR THE BOTTOM PLACE   When grass is uprooted, what is attached to it is pulled up as well.[3] It is an auspicious time for advancing according to plan.   COMMENTARY   The favourable conditions promised in this passage are due to the fact that the mind[4] is outward looking (i.e. fixed upon the people's welfare).

9 FOR THE SECOND PLACE   Supporting the uncultivated, crossing the river without boats, not retreating despite the distance (from his

base), not abandoning his comrades, he still manages to steer a middle course. COMMENTARY This passage means that a middle course can be steered because the situation is so brilliantly clear.

9 FOR THE THIRD PLACE Every plain is followed by a slope; every going forth is followed by a return. Persistence under difficulty will not lead to error. Do not lose faith, for an eclipse is sometimes a blessing.[5] COMMENTARY 'Every going forth is followed by a return' is a law of the universe.

6 FOR THE FOURTH PLACE Running to and fro, kept from riches by those around him, he does not cease to put his trust in them.[6] COMMENTARY His running to and fro and his lack of riches are due to his idealism. He preserves his faith in others because in his heart of hearts he WANTS to trust them.

6 FOR THE FIFTH PLACE By giving his daughter in marriage, the Emperor attained felicity and extreme good fortune. COMMENTARY This was because of his impartiality in carrying out what he felt to be desirable.[7]

6 FOR THE TOP PLACE The wall has tumbled into the moat; do not put up a fight, but just maintain order in the village. Although this is the right course, blame cannot be avoided.[8] COMMENTARY This signifies a troubled destiny.

NOTES (1) In the following hexagram, Pi, where the trigrams symbolize heaven and earth in what would appear to be their normal positions, that arrangement is held to be disastrous; whereas here, where they seem to be upside down, everything is propitious. This may be because heaven above earth is held to imply that the two are existing separately without that intercourse which is the root of all growth; whereas here their intercourse is so absolute that heaven is actually supporting earth. (2) The component trigrams illustrate the kind of close intercourse just alluded to. This is surely the only way of depicting it under the circumstances, for any mingling of their component lines would produce quite different trigrams having no reference to heaven and earth. (3) This would seem to mean that we are likely to get what we seek plus something more. (4) This really means the mind of the Superior Man, whose duty it is to look after the people's welfare. If he is truly a Superior Man, when his mind is turned inward it is to meditate upon and eradicate his faults; when outward turned, it is concentrated upon his duty to the ruler (provided the king is worthy) and his care for the people. (5) The whole of this passage suggests present difficulties which we can surely overcome. (6) He runs to and fro in his anxiety to be of service, whether people reward his kindness or not. (7) This suggests a need for impartiality in conducting our affairs. (8) We shall be blamed for not being more aggressive even though circumstances more than warrant our failure to be so.

HEXAGRAM 12
P'I STAGNATION, OBSTRUCTION

Component trigrams:
Below: K'UN, *earth, female, passive, etc.*
Above: CH'IEN, *heaven, male, active, etc.*

TEXT Stagnation (obstruction) caused by evil-doers. Although the omen portends ill for the Superior Man, he must not slacken his righteous persistence. The great and the good decline; the mean approach.

COMMENTARY ON THE TEXT This passage indicates that the celestial and terrestrial forces are without intercourse and that everything is out of communion with everything else.[1] High and low do not mingle and the state boundaries within the empire have been obliterated. Yin, the dark principle lies within; Yang, the light principle, lies without—weakness[2] within, strength without. Mean men are at the centre of things, superior men at the fringes. The way of the mean waxes, that of the Superior Man wanes.

SYMBOL This hexagram symbolizes heaven and earth cut off from each other.[3] To conserve his stock of virtue, the Superior Man withdraws into himself and thus escapes from the evil influences around him. He declines all temptations of honour and riches.

The Lines

6 FOR THE BOTTOM PLACE When grass is uprooted, what is attached to it is pulled up as well.[4] Righteous persistence brings good fortune and success.[5] COMMENTARY The omen is favourable owing to continued loyalty to the ruler.[6]

6 FOR THE SECOND PLACE Because they (know how to) please the authorities, fortune now favours the mean, but the Superior Man

P'I STAGNATION, OBSTRUCTION

prefers to contend with (the causes) of stagnation (in the realm).[7] COMMENTARY He does so by not entangling himself with the masses.

6 FOR THE THIRD PLACE He conceals his shame. COMMENTARY This is indicated by the unsuitable position of the line.

9 FOR THE FOURTH PLACE Whatever is done in response to a command from on high cannot be a wrong.[8] His companions are also made illustrious and blessed.[9] COMMENTARY His blamelessness is due to the fact that those carrying out commands are obeying the ruler's will.

9 FOR THE FIFTH PLACE Stagnation (obstruction) is now coming to an end and fortune favours the Superior Man, but he must not forget the situation is so dangerous that collapse may yet occur. Accordingly, he must strengthen himself as mulberry trees are strengthened by tight bindings. COMMENTARY That fortune now favours the Superior Man is indicated by the suitable position of this line.[10]

9 FOR THE TOP PLACE Stagnation (obstruction) has now been overcome and is followed by great joy. COMMENTARY In the end it MUST be overcome. How could it endure forever?[11]

NOTES (1) When heaven and earth cease to co-operate, no growth is possible and stagnation results. (2) The trigram K'un, when in intercourse with heaven, has the auspicious meaning of glad acceptance; but, when separated from heaven, it represents weakness and darkness, etc. (3) To understand why the trigrams for heaven and earth arranged in what seems to be their natural positions have this unauspicious significance, see notes one and two on the preceding hexagram, T'ai. (4) See note three on the preceding trigram, T'ai. (5) Although this hexagram is ominous, the first line is auspicious. This sort of contradiction is common with bottom and top lines, which are often held to precede or follow after the main situation. (6) The ruler is now surrounded by evil men or men of mean attainments, but the Superior Man continues to help him. (7) He cares for the welfare of others more than for being in favour. (8) Yet, according to Confucius, if a ruler is wholly evil, he may be regarded as a bandit and removed. Short of that, however, obedience to authority had to be unquestioning. (9) Because they too were obedient. (10) A firm line with other firm lines to either side. (11) The process of change is continuous. This is the last line, which is held to have emerged from the evil symbolized by the hexagram as a whole.

HEXAGRAM 13

T'UNG JÊN LOVERS, BELOVED, FRIENDS, LIKE-MINDED PERSONS, UNIVERSAL BROTHERHOOD

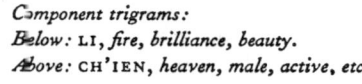

Component trigrams:
Below: LI, fire, brilliance, beauty.
Above: CH'IEN, heaven, male, active, etc.

TEXT Lovers (friends) in the open—success! It is advantageous to cross the great river (or sea).[1] The Superior Man will benefit if he does not slacken his righteous persistence.

COMMENTARY ON THE TEXT This hexagram indicates that someone weak comes to power, occupies the centre of the stage and responds to the creative force.[2] Such a one is called the beloved. What is described in the above text is the work of the creative principle, which has a strong refining influence. The central line (in the upper trigram), to which all the others respond, symbolizes the Superior Man; he alone can carry out the will of all the people of the earth.[3]

SYMBOL This hexagram symbolizes heaven (the sun) and fire representing a pair of lovers. The Superior Man treats everything in a manner proper to his kind.[4]

The Lines

9 FOR THE BOTTOM PLACE The beloved is at the gate—no harm! COMMENTARY Who would find it blameworthy to receive the beloved at the gate?[5]

6 FOR THE SECOND PLACE His beloved (betrothed) is of the same clan as himself—trouble! COMMENTARY Choosing a beloved from a man's own clan is a sure way to unhappiness.[6]

9 FOR THE THIRD PLACE   Concealing his weapons in the bushes, he climbs his high hill. For three years he enjoys no happiness.⁷ COMMENTARY   He conceals his weapons because the enemy is strong—but three years without joy! Who would follow such a course?

9 FOR THE FOURTH PLACE   He climbs his battlemented wall, for he is unable to attack—good fortune!⁸ COMMENTARY   Being unable to worst the enemy, he settles down on a fortified wall. His good fortune consists in being able to retain his sense of what is right even when encountering difficulty.

9 FOR THE FIFTH PLACE   The lovers begin by weeping and wailing, but they finish by laughing, for the crowd succeeds in bringing them together. COMMENTARY   This strong line which is central (to the upper trigram) indicates that they began by weeping.⁹ Fortunately a crowd of people encountered them and, somehow, the right thing was said (to bring them together again).

9 FOR THE TOP PLACE   Her beloved is in a distant frontier region—no regret!¹⁰ COMMENTARY   This is not what was desired.

NOTES   (1) To make any kind of journey.   (2) If the weak one implies a woman, the passage may be taken to mean that the ascendancy a woman gains over a man in love with her is a necessary part of the process of creation. If it refers to a ruler, it may mean that, though young or otherwise weak, he is well-meaning and responds to the will of heaven.   (3) In either of the cases mentioned in note two, a strong and gifted person must sooner or later take the helm and guide that weaker person, wife or ruler.   (4) An analogy (based on the component trigrams) between the sun and fire, which to some extent are of a kind.   (5) Meeting the beloved so publicly cannot give rise to scandal. This implies that there is no need for secrecy.   (6) This Chinese belief was so strongly held that, until recently, even unrelated people of the same surname could not marry.   (7) His cowardice was so great that he dared not seek home, wife or children for three years. The implication is that boldness at all costs is required.   (8) At first sight this case looks rather like that indicated by the third line, but here cowardice and concealment are replaced by courage modified by common sense and a desire to do his duty as best he can.   (9) A strong central line is usually auspicious, but not in this case where we are dealing with something so soft and tender as love.   (10) In Chinese history, it often happened that a man was drafted and sent far away to a frontier region from which he could not be expected to return for many years. In this case, his beloved (betrothed or wife) has enough wisdom to give up repining, since the case is a hopeless one. The implication is that we should not repine.

HEXAGRAM 14
TA YU   GREAT POSSESSIONS[1]

Component trigrams:
Below: CH'IEN, *heaven, male, active, etc.*
Above: LI, *fire, brilliance, beauty.*

TEXT   He who possesses much—supreme success!

COMMENTARY ON THE TEXT   Here, the yielding obtains a place of high honour and respect, for this yielding line (line 5) occupies the more important of the places central (to the component trigrams) and all the other lines accord with it.[2] Therefore is it called Great Possessions. Its virtues are firmness, strength and cultural achievement. Because it is responsive to heaven and performs all things at the proper time, it wins supreme success.

SYMBOL   This hexagram symbolizes fire in the heavens.[3] The Superior Man suppresses those who are evil and upholds the virtuous. Most gladly he accords with heaven and carries out its commands.

The Lines

9 FOR THE BOTTOM PLACE   Having no contact with evil, he is blameless; therefore, even if he is involved in trouble, he remains without fault.   COMMENTARY   This line means that we shall avoid any intercourse with evil.

9 FOR THE SECOND PLACE   There are large supply waggons.[4] If there is some desired goal (or destination), setting out (to attain it) will involve no error.   COMMENTARY   This line indicates that some place where supplies have been accumulated will escape from danger.

TA YÜ GREAT POSSESSIONS

9 FOR THE THIRD PLACE   A prince may win rewards from his emperor, but this is beyond an ordinary man's power. COMMENTARY This passage means that the little man would only harm himself in the attempt.[5]

9 FOR THE FOURTH PLACE   Pride is not involved—no error! COMMENTARY This passage implies the possession of very great discriminatory powers.[6]

6 FOR THE FIFTH PLACE   His sense of confidence enables him to be sociable and well respected. A dignified bearing is an asset (literally, good fortune). COMMENTARY His good fortune in winning the respect of others enables him to make changes without prior preparation.[7]

9 FOR THE TOP PLACE   Those under heaven's protection enjoy good fortune and success in everything.[8] COMMENTARY The great good fortune pressaged by this line is that of being specially protected by heaven.

NOTES (1) Ta Yü could also be translated 'The Great Possessor', meaning 'he who has much'.   (2) As so often, the fifth line is the ruling line of this hexagram. Though a yielding line, it is very firmly supported by four firm lines and capped by yet another.   (3) When the trigram for heaven is above, whatever is below may be separated from it; when it is below, it indicates fusion or intermixture with what is above. The significance here is that the splendour of a very great man lights up the heavens.   (4) Apparently we need not fear failure through lack of resources.   (5) This omen suggests that a great goal can be won only by someone very powerful or distinguished; others would be well advised not to attempt it.   (6) Such as the power to recognize how very little of our success is really due to our own merits.   (7) This means that we shall be trusted even if we act unexpectedly.   (8) The top line of a very favourable hexagram is sometimes taken to symbolize heaven. Whoever receives a nine for this place may expect the utmost success.

HEXAGRAM 15
CH'IEN MODESTY

Component trigrams:
Below: KÊN, *a mountain, hard, perverse, obstinate.*
Above: K'UN, *earth, female, passive, etc.*

TEXT Modesty brings success. The Superior Man is able to carry affairs through to completion.

COMMENTARY ON THE TEXT This hexagram presages success. It is heaven's way to pour down succour from above and to shed radiance; earth's way is to be lowly and work upwards. Heaven's way is to diminish what is already over-full and to augment what is modest; whereas earth's way is to transform the full and help the modest to flow smoothly. Demons and gods destroy the full but heap prosperity upon the modest. Man's way is to dislike the full and love the modest. Thus modesty receives reverence and glory; it is a lovely quality; nothing can climb above it. The Superior Man makes it his goal.

SYMBOL This hexagram symbolizes a mountain in the centre of the earth.[1] The Superior Man takes from where there is too much in order to augment what is too little. He weighs things and apportions them fairly.

The Lines

6 FOR THE BOTTOM PLACE The Superior Man, ever modest and retiring, fords the great river—good fortune![2] COMMENTARY This passage means that he shows humility in disciplining himself.

6 FOR THE SECOND PLACE Modestly crows the cock. Righteous persistence brings good fortune. COMMENTARY Good fortune in that the cry reaches the depths of our hearts.

CH'IEN MODESTY

9 FOR THE THIRD PLACE The Superior Man, exceedingly hard-working yet modest, brings his affairs to fruition—good fortune! COMMENTARY The people (most willingly) submit to him.

6 FOR THE FOURTH PLACE Everything will be propitious for those who cultivate modesty. COMMENTARY Because this involves no departure from what is right.

6 FOR THE FIFTH PLACE In treating his neighbours, he is modest about his wealth. If he now attacks (the rebels), everything will contribute to his success. COMMENTARY Such an attack is warranted if the purpose is to chastise those who do not submit (to virtuous laws).[3]

6 FOR THE TOP PLACE Modestly crows the cock. Now is the time to set armies marching to subdue the cities and the countries of the empire. COMMENTARY Because (the ruler's) will has yet to be carried out, it is proper to do so.[4]

NOTES (1) The component trigrams symbolize a mountain surrounded by flat earth, thus suggesting too much in one place and too little in others. (2) Any journey undertaken at this time will bring good fortune. (3) This is not an invitation to use force in any circumstances, but only if its use is directed at what is truly perverse or evil. (4) This omen can be taken to indicate that we can afford to go forward boldly with our plans, but only if their fruition will tally with the general good. 'The ruler's will' in this case is roughly synonymous with the public good.

HEXAGRAM 16
YÜ   REPOSE[1]

Component trigrams:
Below: K'UN, *earth, female, passive, etc.*
Above: CHÊN, *thunder, movement, to sprout or quicken.*

TEXT Repose profits those engaged in building up the country and sending forth armies.[2]

COMMENTARY ON THE TEXT In this hexagram, firmness meets with response[3] and whatever is willed can be accomplished. Action according to the law of righteousness begets repose (calm confidence); repose (calm confidence) stems from righteous action. Therefore, heaven and earth accord with this law, all the more so when it is necessary to build up a country and send forth armies. It is because heaven and earth act in accordance with it that the sun and moon stay in their courses and the four seasons keep to their appointed times. The holy sage, because, he, too, accords with it, seldom has to impose punishment and yet the people submit to him. The timely application of this hexagram is indeed supreme (in its value).

SYMBOL   This hexagram symbolizes thunder over the earth.³ The ancient rulers venerated heaven's gifts with solemn music and they sacrificed abundantly to the Supreme Lord (of Heaven) in order to be worthy of their ancestors.

The Lines

6 FOR THE BOTTOM PLACE   The crowing of the cock bespeaks repose—an evil omen!⁴   COMMENTARY   The evil mentioned in this passage is that which results from utter exhaustion of the will-power.

6 FOR THE SECOND PLACE   Unmoved as a rock; before the end of day,⁵ righteous persistence will bring good fortune.   COMMENTARY   This is indicated by the suitable position of this line which is central (to the lower trigram).

6 FOR THE THIRD PLACE   To gaze reposefully brings regret; tardy action brings regret.⁶   COMMENTARY   This is indicated by the line's unsuitable position.

9 FOR THE FOURTH PLACE   From repose, great results accrue. Harbour no doubts. Why should it be harmful to befriend this official?⁷   COMMENTARY   The first sentence indicates the fullest attainment of our will.

6 FOR THE FIFTH PLACE   Illness is presaged, but it will not last long or cause death.   COMMENTARY   Illness is indicated because this (yielding) line comes immediately above a firm one. Recovery rather than death is to be expected because this line is, nevertheless, central (to the upper trigram).

YÜ REPOSE

6 FOR THE TOP PLACE   Madcap repose.⁸ Fortunately a change takes place, so no blame is involved.   COMMENTARY   Since this is a top line, the state of madcap repose cannot possibly last long.

NOTES   (1) The usual meaning of this character is 'beforehand' or 'happiness'. In the English translation of Wilhem's version, it appears as 'enthusiasm'. 'Repose' was suggested by the Chinese experts who kindly vetted this manuscript. At first I felt hesitant about adopting it, until I realized that, where it is used favourably, it must be understood as the kind of mental repose which follows absolute confidence that the action now being taken is the right one. In lines one, three and six, however, it clearly means failure to act when action is essential; in line five, failure to act owing to incapacity.   (2) This means that perfect certainty as to the rightness of our cause is of great value under the conditions mentioned.   (3) The two component hexagrams suggest this symbol, which combines the energy of Chên with the passive and glad acceptance of K'un.   (4) A sleepy cockcrow is not likely to bring men leaping from their beds, yet the traditional role of the cock is to sound the call to renewed action.   (5) Unmoved as a rock because of the repose which results from absolute confidence in a decision already taken.   (6) This suggests inactivity prolonged beyond reasonable measure.   (7) The meaning of this terse question is not obvious; but the enquirer may find it apt in the context either of his question or of subsequent events.   (8) Madcap repose implies being tardy to the point of extreme rashness in the face of approaching danger or of a need to act.

HEXAGRAM 17
SUI   FOLLOWING, ACCORDING WITH

Component trigrams:
Below: CHÊN, *thunder, movement, to sprout or quicken.*
Above: TUI, *a body of water, pool, marsh, joy.*

TEXT   Following. Sublime success!¹ Righteous persistence brings reward—no error!

COMMENTARY ON THE TEXT   In this hexagram, the firm comes beneath the yielding; moreover, (the trigrams of) movement and joy² are conjoined—hence sublime success, the reward of our persistence and freedom from error. This implies that the whole universe accords with what the times dictate for it. Great indeed is this principle of according with the pulse of time.

SYMBOL   This hexagram symbolizes thunder rumbling within a swamp![3] When darkness falls, the Superior Man goes within and rests peacefully.

The Lines

9 FOR THE BOTTOM PLACE   Those in power undergo a change—righteous determination brings good fortune! Going forth from home and mingling with those outside will produce tangible results. COMMENTARY   The first sentence presages the good fortune derived from officials undergoing a change of heart and following what is right. The tangible results mentioned at the end of the passage imply that we shall not fail.

6 FOR THE SECOND PLACE   He belongs to (i.e. puts himself at the service of) the boy and thereby loses the adult.[4] COMMENTARY   This happens because he cannot be of service to both of them.

6 FOR THE THIRD PLACE   He belongs to (i.e. is of service to) the adult and loses the boy. By following the former, he gains what he desires. It is advisable to make no move but to remain determined. COMMENTARY   The first sentence implies that he is willing to give up what is inferior.

9 FOR THE FOURTH PLACE   Following someone with an ulterior motive—persisting in this course would bring misfortune. But, if as he goes his way he makes sincerity his beacon, what harm can come to him? COMMENTARY   Following others with ulterior motives is surely evil; whereas sincerity along the way produces brilliant results.

9 FOR THE FIFTH PLACE   Confidence is admirable[5]—good fortune! COMMENTARY   The good fortune is indicated by the suitable position of this line.

6 FOR THE TOP PLACE   He obtained people's allegiance and his followers clung to him. During the time he spent on the Western Mountain, the King made sacrifice. COMMENTARY   Our obtaining the allegiance of others indicates that those above us have exhausted (their merit).[6]

NOTES   (1) This sublime success comes, of course, only to those who follow what is right, namely the will of heaven or of those whose own will embodies it.   (2) In the Book of Change, joy is frequently associated with willing obedience to and glad acceptance of what is right. Movement and joy refer directly to the attributes of the two component trigrams. (3) The component hexagrams can be read as thunder and marsh, but also as movement and joy. It is not hard to see the connection between following and resting peacefully; for, once we have given our allegiance to others, we no longer have to worry about what should be done. (4) The implied meaning is that he rejects what is superior and follows what is inferior. (5) Confidence in the context of this hexagram implies perfect trust in those we follow. (6) This is in accord with the Confucian doctrine that rulers who consistently behave ill thereby forfeit the mandate of heaven and cease to deserve obedience. The implication is that we may have to take the initiative ourselves.

HEXAGRAM 18
KU DECAY

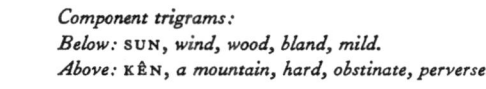

Component trigrams:
Below: SUN, *wind, wood, bland, mild.*
Above: KÊN, *a mountain, hard, obstinate, perverse.*

TEXT Decay augurs sublime success and the advantage of crossing the great river (or sea).¹ What has happened once will surely happen again (literally, 'three days before the commencement; three days after the commencement').²

COMMENTARY ON THE TEXT Here, the firm trigram is above the yielding, the gentleness is conjoined with the immovable.³ This implies sublime success⁴ and the right ordering of the world. The passage about crossing the great river suggests that there are good reasons for going forward. The rest of the text means that heaven's activities are such that every end is followed by a new beginning.

SYMBOL This hexagram symbolizes wind blowing at the foot of a mountain.⁵ The Superior Man, by stimulating people's hearts, nourishes their virtue.

The Lines

6 FOR THE BOTTOM PLACE Children exist to rectify the mistakes

wrought by their fathers; hence the departed are made free from blame—trouble ending in good fortune! COMMENTARY This implies assuming responsibility for their mistakes.

9 FOR THE SECOND PLACE Assuming responsibility for the mistakes of our mothers cannot be too serious. COMMENTARY At best a middle course is advisable.

9 FOR THE THIRD PLACE Making ourselves responsible for the mistakes of our fathers may involve some regret but not much blame. COMMENTARY This means that, in the end, we shall be free from blame.

6 FOR THE FOURTH PLACE Tolerating the mistakes of our fathers would occasion us regret in the course of time. COMMENTARY For, in that case, we should fail to rectify them.

6 FOR THE FIFTH PLACE Assuming responsibility for the mistakes of our fathers will win us praise. COMMENTARY Because to take them upon ourselves is a virtue.

9 FOR THE TOP PLACE He does not serve the King or the nobles—what he does is even loftier than that.[6] COMMENTARY This indicates that our own will can be our law.[7]

NOTES (1) I.e. of going on a journey or of going forward with one's plans. (2) It would have been hard to make sense of these words, were it not that the Confucian Commentary on the Text clearly explains them; hence the liberty I have taken with the Text. (3) A reference to the component trigrams. (4) Sublime success in that once decay is removed, a new strength is born. (5) Wind blowing at the base of a mountain is suggested by the component trigrams; in the analogy, the first is the activity of the Superior Man, the second is the normally inert man of the people. (6) In other words, if we directly serve the will of heaven; by doing so, we act as sages who may safely do whatever they feel is worth doing. (7) Provided we are acting from the loftiest motives.

HEXAGRAM 19
LIN APPROACH

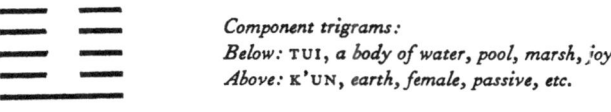

Component trigrams:
Below: TUI, *a body of water, pool, marsh, joy.*
Above: K'UN, *earth, female, passive, etc.*

TEXT   Approach. Sublime success! Righteous persistence brings reward. However, when the eighth month[1] is reached, misfortune will befall.

COMMENTARY ON THE TEXT   In this hexagram, the strong is well watered and grows large; joy and willing acceptance are conjoined.[2] The firm line central (to the lower trigram) finds response (from the other lines). Great success is won in rectifying things, which is the way of heaven. But that misfortune will follow in the eighth month indicates that this success will soon begin to wane.

SYMBOL   This hexagram symbolizes land rising above a marsh.[3] The Superior Man's teaching and his affection for his juniors are inexhaustible. Nothing hinders him in his care for the people.

The Lines

9 FOR THE BOTTOM PLACE   All approach[4]—righteous persistence will bring good fortune!   COMMENTARY   This is because what is willed is carried out in righteous ways.

9 FOR THE SECOND PLACE   All approach[4]—good fortune! Nothing is unfavourable.   COMMENTARY   This indicates that there is nevertheless some disobedience.

6 FOR THE THIRD PLACE   A willing approach, but there is nowhere towards which it would be advantageous to set out.[5] Feeling regret on that account involves no error.   COMMENTARY   The foregoing

is indicated by the unsuitable position of this line. However, if we grieve for it, we shall not be involved in error for long.[5]

6 FOR THE FOURTH PLACE   A perfect approach—no error! COMMENTARY   This is indicated by the suitable position of this line.

6 FOR THE FIFTH PLACE   A wise approach suited to a great prince —good fortune! COMMENTARY   This is a way of saying that we must keep to the middle path.[6]

6 FOR THE SIXTH PLACE   A magnanimous approach—good fortune, no error. COMMENTARY   This good fortune arises from concealing our will within our hearts.[7]

NOTES   (1) The eighth moon of the lunar calendar corresponds approximately to September.   (2) This is a reference to the component trigrams. The fertilizing effect of the water symbolizes rectification of the earth by the Superior Man's ministrations.   (3) The lower component trigram suggests the nourishment which the Superior Man gives joyfully to others. The upper trigram symbolizes the great bulk of those who benefit.   (4) All approach can be taken to mean that all things desirable are converging upon us.   (5) At present, there is no goal or destination towards which it would be profitable to move; however, if we sincerely regret this, it will not be long before we emerge from the rut.   (6) This is a reference to the central position of this line in the upper trigram.   (7) This would seem to mean that, for the present, we should gladly accord with others and carefully conceal our aims.

HEXAGRAM 20
KUAN   LOOKING DOWN[1]

Component trigrams:
Below: K'UN, *earth, female, passive, etc.*
Above: SUN, *wind, wood, bland, mild.*

TEXT   Looking down. The ablution has been performed, but not the sacrifice.[2] Sincerity inspires respect.

COMMENTARY ON THE TEXT   Looking down in its most important sense means that looking down which takes place from on high.

KUAN LOOKING DOWN

Willing acceptance and mildness are conjoined.[3] (The fifth line) is correctly centred for looking down upon the world. What is said in the foregoing text refers to those who look down upon their subjects[4] and transform them. They contemplate the sacred activities of heaven and note how the seasons unfold, each in its proper time. It is because the holy sage makes these matters the subject of his teaching that all the world accepts his dominion.

SYMBOL   This hexagram symbolizes wind blowing across the earth.[5] The ancient rulers visited the different regions to keep watch over their people and carefully instruct them.

The Lines

6 FOR THE BOTTOM PLACE   Looking at things in a childish way is not blameworthy in ordinary people, but in the Superior Man it is a misfortune.[5]   COMMENTARY   For such conduct is suited to people of inferior worth.

6 FOR THE SECOND PLACE   Watching through door-cracks is of advantage to women.   COMMENTARY   Nevertheless it is also shameful.[6]

6 FOR THE THIRD PLACE   By contemplating our own lives, (we learn to) advance or retreat (as required by circumstances).   COMMENTARY   This is the way to keep to the right path.

6 FOR THE FOURTH PLACE   Contemplating the conditions of a realm guides us as to whether we should become the ruler's guests.[7]   COMMENTARY   Those engaged in this way enjoy universal esteem.

9 FOR THE FIFTH PLACE   The Superior Man does no wrong in keeping a watch upon our lives.[8]   COMMENTARY   In this passage, 'our lives' means the lives of the people.

9 FOR THE TOP PLACE   Nor will it be an error for the Superior Man to contemplate his own life.   COMMENTARY   He contemplates his own life when troubled as to what course to take.

NOTES   (1) This word often means 'contemplation' and I have so translated it when the context so requires.   (2) This is generally understood to mean that the first step has been taken or that one has bound oneself to follow a certain course (as by entering the government service, for example), but that the main duties are yet to be performed. (3) A reference to the component trigrams. (4) Kuan never means look down in the sense of 'despise', but always in the sense of, 'heed', 'watch over' and so forth. The name of the Bodhisattva Avalokitesvara was later translated into Chinese as Kuan Shih-yin— She Who Looks Down upon the Cries (i.e. Sufferings) of the World. (5) It might be supposed that the Superior Man is incapable of such conduct; hence this passage must refer to one who is trying to be or who thinks himself a Superior Man. (6) If the enquirer or the one for whom the enquiry is being made is a woman, she will gain by keeping a secret watch, but it cannot be done honourably in this case. (7) In ancient China, many scholars, such as Confucius himself, wandered from kingdom to kingdom and princedom to princedom seeking a ruler wise and virtuous enough to profit by their teachings. It was by observing the splendours or miseries of each realm that they were able to form preliminary judgements and thus decide whether the ruler might be worth approaching or not. The implication is that we must not accept something as good without waiting to discover whether the alleged good qualities are genuine. (8) It is not wrong for us to be curious about the affairs of others if our motive is to be of more help to them.

HEXAGRAM 21
SHIH HÔ GNAWING[1]

Component trigrams:
Below: CHÊN, thunder, movement, to sprout or quicken.
Above: LI, fire, brilliance, beauty.

TEXT   Gnawing. Success! The time is favourable for legal processes.

COMMENTARY ON THE TEXT   When something is gripped between the jaws, we speak of gnawing and with this gnawing we associate success. The firm and the yielding are separate[2] and the two trigrams representing these qualities are movement and brilliance respectively. Thus thunder and lightning are brought together and emit brilliance.[3] The yielding obtains the central position and rises upwards (from the centre of the lower to the centre of the upper trigram). Although this arrangement is an unsuitable one, it favours the process of the law.[4]

SYMBOL   This hexagram symbolizes lightning[5] accompanied by thunder. The ancient rulers, after making their legal code perfectly clear to all, enforced the laws vigorously.

SHIH HÔ GNAWING

The Lines

9 FOR THE BOTTOM PLACE   Their feet are shackled so that they may not walk—no error is involved![6]   COMMENTARY   This method is used to prevent (evil-doers) from progressing (in their wickedness).

6 FOR THE SECOND PLACE   Gnawing flesh so that the nose is hidden in it—no error![7]   COMMENTARY   This is indicated by the position of the line (a yielding one) above a firm one.

6 FOR THE THIRD PLACE   Gnawing dried meat, he was poisoned, but not severely enough to indispose him for long—no error![8]   COMMENTARY   His being poisoned is indicated by the unsuitable position of this line.

9 FOR THE FOURTH PLACE   Gnawing dried meat on the bone, he found a metal arrow-head (embedded in it)—remaining determined in spite of difficulties will bring good fortune!   COMMENTARY   However, no ray of the good fortune here indicated is visible as yet.[9]

6 FOR THE FIFTH PLACE   While gnawing dried meat, he encountered a piece of gold (embedded in it)—unwavering determination now will bring down trouble, but no error is involved.[10]   COMMENTARY   That we shall not be to blame for the trouble is indicated by the suitable position of this line.

9 FOR THE TOP PLACE   He wears a wooden cangue which hides his ears—misfortune!   COMMENTARY   This implies dullness of hearing (or intellect).[11]

NOTES   (1) The concept of gnawing is suggested by the component trigrams, which are regarded (owing to the arrangement of their lines) as not commingling; they are as separate from each other as the upper and lower jaw when something tough is being gnawed.   (2) The firm and yielding lines more or less alternate; or the lower trigram can be regarded as filled with the power of thunderous force, while the upper trigram, representing beauty, is soft and yielding.   (3) I do not know what the ancient Chinese views on thunder and lightning were; it appears from this that they were regarded as two forces which, like steel and flint, emitted brilliance when brought into sharp contact with each other.   (4) A pair of trigrams both with yielding centres is not felt to be a good arrangement; that it nevertheless favours the process of the law may have been suggested to the writer of the Text by the fact that the weak lines (morally weak people?) are fully contained by the strong (prison walls, warders and so forth?)   (5) Li, the upper trigram, stands for lightning as well as for fire, beauty, etc.   (6) This line suggests that extreme

I

firmness would not be culpable at this time. (7) The meaning of this line is not at all obvious. The Chinese additional commentaries take it to mean that we may do a little harm to our own interests but that we shall not deserve blame for what happens. (8) This line presages trouble through no fault of ours which will not, however, incapacitate us for long. (9) Whatever good fortune is on its way to us is not visible as yet. In other words, the situation looks more gloomy than it is, so we must follow our course with firmness. (10) If we persist with our plans, trouble will arise; the only comfort we can take is that we shall not be to blame for it. (11) This suggests that, for the present, we should not put much trust in our own judgement.

HEXAGRAM 22
P'I ELEGANCE

Component trigrams:
Below: LI, *fire, brilliance, beauty.*
Above: KÊN, *a mountain, hard, obstinate, perverse.*

TEXT   Elegance. Success! Some small advantage can be derived from having a particular goal (or destination).[1]

COMMENTARY ON THE TEXT   That this hexagram presages success is indicated by the fact that the yielding lines adorn the firm. The last sentence of the text is derived from the fact that the individual firm top line (of the lower trigram) adorns the yielding lines. (This alternation of firm and yielding is) the very pattern of heaven itself.[2] Attaining to a certain level of cultural development and there coming to rest is man's pattern. By contemplating the pattern of heaven, we can examine the changes involved in time's unfolding; by contemplating that of man, we can successfully transform the world.

SYMBOL   This hexagram symbolizes fire at the foot of a mountain.[3] The Superior Man, desiring to ensure the enlightened functioning of the various departments of state, dare not make light decisions regarding legal matters.

P'I ELEGANCE

The Lines

9 FOR THE BOTTOM PLACE Elegantly shod, he leaves his carriage and proceeds on foot. COMMENTARY This means that he declines to make use of the carriage put at his disposal.[4]

6 FOR THE SECOND PLACE He adorns his beard. COMMENTARY He does so in order to be able to take part in the enjoyments of his superiors.[5]

9 FOR THE THIRD PLACE His adornments are such that he appears to glisten—righteous determination maintained up to the very end brings good fortune. COMMENTARY This implies that, to the very end, no one will thwart our purposes.

6 FOR THE FOURTH PLACE He so adorns himself as to seem white as snow. He is, as it were, a white steed. (What delays his progress is) not an obstacle but a matter of betrothal. COMMENTARY This ruling line indicates the existence of suspicion; however, as revealed by the last sentence, nothing blameworthy is involved.[6]

6 FOR THE FIFTH PLACE Elegantly he strolls amidst the garden of hillocks, but his silk girdle is of the poorest quality—disgrace followed ultimately by good fortune.[7] COMMENTARY This good fortune comes in the form of blessings.[8]

9 FOR THE TOP PLACE Simple elegance—no error! COMMENTARY This top line indicates the fulfilment of our will.

NOTES (1) The implication is that the advantage is not sufficient to make it worth while to seek that goal or destination unless no special difficulty or inconvenience is involved. (2) The arrangement of the lines in this hexagram is very similar to that in the previous one, but it is adjudged much more suitable. The general idea is that, like nature, we should conform to a regular and well ordered pattern of behaviour which, since we are human beings and not mere animals, involves a high degree of refinement. From the point of view of divination, it would seem that this is a time to watch carefully so as to learn how those involved in the situation think and behave, the better to influence them for the good when the opportunity arises. (3) The component trigrams, fire below mountain, suggest a brilliance which cannot be perceived from afar. The Chinese commentators go on to suggest that this symbolizes a firm and somewhat severe exterior which hides brilliance and the beauty within. For purposes of divination, this should be taken as a pattern for our comportment in the matter at issue. (4) This implies progressing in the way we know to be right and declining the help of those who are anxious to lead us from the path of rectitude. (5) There are times when it is wise to conform with the customs of our seniors, even if we attach little value to them. (6) It would seem that someone is suspected of loitering or hesitating for a somewhat sinister reason, but that his motive is in fact an honourable one. (7) The Chinese love landscape gardens. Here, obviously, someone improperly dressed is visiting a person of consequence and has to suffer for his carelessness. This should be taken figuratively to indicate a setback due to our own carelessness. Fortunately all ends well. (8) 'Blessings' implies good fortune which comes, as it were, by chance and not obviously as a result of our own merits or efforts.

HEXAGRAM 23
PO   PEELING OFF[1]

Component trigrams:
Below: K'UN, *earth, female, passive, etc.*
Above: KÊN, *a mountain, hard, obstinate, perverse.*

TEXT   Peeling off. At present, there is no goal (or destination) which can be sought with advantage.

COMMENTARY ON THE TEXT   Peeling off means just what it says. The weak succeed in altering the strong. No advantage is to be gained from seeking any goal (or destination), for this is a time when inferior men flourish. It is best to remain where we are and to accept the situation portended by this hexagram. The Superior Man respectfully contemplates the ebb and flow, the unending succession of repletion and depletion which constitutes the way of heaven.

SYMBOL   This hexagram symbolizes a mountain resting upon the earth.[2] The truly great shower generosity upon those under them to enable them to live in peace and comfort.

The Lines

6 FOR THE BOTTOM PLACE   He starts the peeling off at the foot of the bed. There is no steadfastness—misfortune! COMMENTARY This implies ridding ourselves of those below.[3]

6 FOR THE SECOND PLACE   He continues peeling off at the edge of

PO PEELING OFF

the bed. There is no steadfastness—misfortune! COMMENTARY This implies being left without friends.[3]

6 FOR THE THIRD PLACE He peels them (all) off—no error. COMMENTARY This implies losing contact with those above and below.[3]

6 FOR THE FOURTH PLACE He continues the peeling off at the mattress of his bed—misfortune![3] COMMENTARY This presages our being very close to a terrible misfortune.

6 FOR THE FIFTH PLACE A string of fishes symbolizing the high favour enjoyed by maids in the palace—everything is favourable.[4] COMMENTARY This implies that ultimately we shall be entirely free from blame.

9 FOR THE TOP PLACE The ripe fruit remains uneaten.[5] The Superior Man will acquire a carriage, whereas the mean man will lose his own house.[6] COMMENTARY The carriage symbolizes the support of the people. The mean wretch who loses his house is ultimately found useless for anything.

NOTES (1) Peeling off in the sense of getting rid of hindrances (or hinderers) one after another. The first four lines of this hexagram symbolize a process of ridding ourselves progressively of all those upon whom we are accustomed to rely, for the powers of darkness are in the ascendant and no one can be trusted. However, in the long run, virtue triumphs, as indicated by line five, and ultimately we are all the more esteemed for our steadfastness, as can be seen from line 6. (2) The upper and lower trigrams, mountain and earth, symbolize the Superior Man and the people in his care. (3) Because he finds them unworthy. What is said in the various lines about the foot, edge and mattress of the bed means that he is obliged to continue the peeling off process until he reaches those very close to himself; there is no one left whom he can trust to help him in his work of righteousness. (4) This line seems somewhat to contradict the omen provided by this unlucky hexagram. In such cases, what is said in the moving line must be regarded as specially apt for our particular circumstances; i.e. in spite of the wretched conditions prevailing, those who receive this moving line can pursue their goals without fear of failure. (5) Few care to accept advice or help, although the Superior Man will gladly give it them. (6) This line presages great good fortune for the truly virtuous; for, in the end, their virtue is widely recognized and men rally to their support. On the other hand, those who hitherto have managed to obtain good fortune through dishonest methods pursued at a time when virtue was under an eclipse will lose everything they have.

HEXAGRAM 24
FU   RETURN

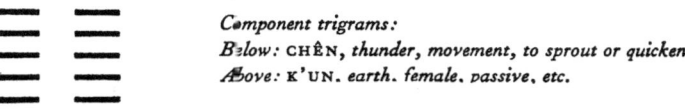

Component trigrams:
Below: CHÊN, *thunder, movement, to sprout or quicken.*
Above: K'UN, *earth, female, passive, etc.*

TEXT   Return. Success! All going forth and coming in is free from harm. Friends arrive and no error is involved. They return whence they came, spending seven days in all upon their coming and returning. It is favourable to have in view some goal (or destination).

COMMENTARY ON THE TEXT   This hexagram presages success because the firm returns (to the bottom of the hexagram from which it was absent in the previous hexagrams). Movement and willingness to move[1] are conjoined; this explains why going forth and coming in entail no harm. The next three sentences imply that this activity is in accord with the movements of heaven. It is favourable to have in view some goal (or destination) because strength is on the increase. It is in the return cycles that the very heart of the workings of heaven and earth becomes apparent.[2]

SYMBOL   This hexagram symbolizes thunder in the bowels of the earth.[3] The ancient rulers closed the passes during the solstices[4] and the merchants were unable to travel. Even the rulers abstained from touring their territories at those times.

The Lines

9 FOR THE BOTTOM PLACE   Returning from nearby—nothing much to regret and sublime good fortune! COMMENTARY   Turning back before having gone too far is a means of self-discipline.

6 FOR THE SECOND PLACE   A return blessed by heaven—good

FU RETURN

fortune! COMMENTARY This good fortune results from our treating others with loving-kindness.

6 FOR THE THIRD PLACE Frequent returns—trouble, but no error! COMMENTARY This means that we are in no way to blame for the trouble.

6 FOR THE FOURTH PLACE Setting forth in company, but returning alone.[5] COMMENTARY This solitary return is necessary if the path of righteousness is to be followed.

6 FOR THE FIFTH PLACE Returning for some high purpose—no regret! COMMENTARY This middle line (of the upper trigram) implies critical self-examination.

6 FOR THE TOP PLACE A confused return—misfortune! Disasters and injury threaten. Armies are set marching, but ultimately a great defeat takes place. Disaster is about to overtake the ruler and for at least ten years there can be no hope of putting things to right. COMMENTARY The misfortune described here is the result of deviation from the path of the Superior Man.[6]

NOTES (1) The trigram K'un, earth, often symbolizes willingness, glad acceptance and so forth. (2) For it is only when the whole series is completed that we can understand the reasons for many things (death, winter and so on) which, at the time, seemed unproductive, negative or positively evil. (3) The component trigrams in this position suggest thunder coming from under the earth; but the trigram or thunder also means to sprout or quicken; it is this concept of a quickening within the earth that makes this hexagram generally favourable. (4) The solstices were times for solemn sacrifice; it has always been the practice in China for people to return to their homes for the celebration of the great yearly festivals. Return in this sense is highly auspicious. (5) This suggests that our companions will try (or are trying) to lead us astray and that we must let them go forward alone. (6) The omen presages very serious trouble affecting many people besides ourselves as a result of deviation from the path of virtue.

HEXAGRAM 25
WU WANG   INTEGRITY, THE UNEXPECTED[1]

Component trigrams:
Below: CHÊN, *thunder, movement, to sprout or quicken.*
Above: CH'IEN, *heaven, male, active, etc.*

TEXT   Integrity. Sublime success! Righteous persistence brings reward. Those opposed to righteousness meet with injury. It is not favourable to have in view any goal (or destination).[2]

COMMENTARY ON THE TEXT   The firm enters this hexagram from without[3] and becomes lord (i.e. the ruling line) of that which lies within. Movement and strength are conjoined.[4] This firm central line (of the upper trigram) finds response (from all the remaining lines in the hexagram). Those who do what is right win great success, in accordance with the decrees of heaven. Those opposed to righteousness will suffer and have nowhere favourable to go; for, without integrity, what remains for them? What is the use of going anywhere (or seeking any goal) when heaven's decrees no longer afford protection?

SYMBOL   This hexagram symbolizes thunder rolling across the whole earth; from it, all things receive their integrity.[5] The ancient rulers gave abundant and timely nourishment to all.

The Lines

9 FOR THE BOTTOM PLACE   Moving onward with integrity brings good fortune.   COMMENTARY   What is willed comes to pass.

6 FOR THE SECOND PLACE   Do not calculate the size of the harvest while the ploughing is still in progress, nor gloat over the third year's crop while still planting the virgin ground. It is favourable to seek some object (or destination).   COMMENTARY   It is not meet to calculate profits at such an early stage, nor can we expect to become rich soon.

WU WANG INTEGRITY, THE UNEXPECTED

6 FOR THE THIRD PLACE   Unexpected calamity. Someone ropes an ox and leads it off—a gain to the passer-by but a loss to the farmer (who owns it)!   COMMENTARY   The former gains an ox at the cost of the owner's suffering.[6]

9 FOR THE FOURTH PLACE   Something can be accomplished by righteous persistence and no error is involved.   COMMENTARY   That is to say firmness will enable us to fulfil our aim.

9 FOR THE FIFTH PLACE   Unexpected illness, but it will be best not to treat it.   COMMENTARY   What this really means is that we should avoid applying untried remedies.[7]

9 FOR THE TOP PLACE   If it is unexpected, a journey now would be injurious. This is a time favourable for those with no destination in view.   COMMENTARY   That is to say, an unexpected journey now would plunge us into a state of dangerous exhaustion.

NOTES   (1) Wu Wang has two widely different meanings, both of which occur in what follows.   (2) Usually this sentence may be taken to have a wide application; but, in this case, what is said in the Commentary on the Text suggests that it applies only to the enemies of righteousness, though it does have a general application for those who receive a moving line for the sixth place.   (3) The hexagrams, taken together, are held to symbolize sixty-four stages in a process of unending movement. Thus a firm (or yielding) line not present in the previous hexagram may be said to have entered from outside.   (4) A reference to the component trigrams.   (5) The lower trigram is pictured as thunder, but it acts through its power to quicken growth.   (6) The calamity may be threatening us. Otherwise, the implication is that we cannot avoid gaining something at severe cost to others.   (7) The commentary suggests that the text contains an error and supplies what the commentator considered to be its correct meaning.

HEXAGRAM 26
TA CH'U   THE GREAT NOURISHER

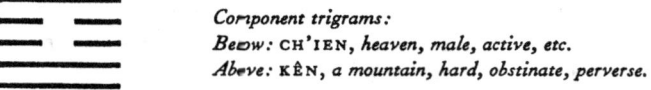

Component trigrams:
Below: CH'IEN, *heaven, male, active, etc.*
Above: KÊN, *a mountain, hard, obstinate, perverse.*

TEXT   The Great Nourisher favours righteous persistence. Good fortune results from not eating at home. It is a favourable time for crossing the great river (sea).[1]

COMMENTARY ON THE HEXAGRAM   This hexagram presages firmness, strength, magnanimity, truth, glory and brilliance, a daily renovation of our virtue. The firm ascends[2] and pays respect to the worthy. Ability to exercise restraint in the use of power is excellent indeed! Receiving good fortune as a result of not eating at home implies entertaining good people elsewhere.[3] The time is suitable for crossing the great river (or sea) because to do so now would be to accord with heaven's will.

SYMBOL   This hexagram symbolizes the sky (visible) amidst the mountain (peaks).[4] The Superior Man, acting from his profound knowledge of the words and conduct of the wise men of old, nourishes his virtue.

The Lines

9 FOR THE BOTTOM PLACE   Trouble threatens—it would be wise to bring activities to a halt. COMMENTARY   That is, no attempt should be made to avert the trouble.

9 FOR THE SECOND PLACE   A broken axle. COMMENTARY   This line, being central (to the lower trigram), indicates that we are not to blame.[5]

9 FOR THE THIRD PLACE   A fine steed galloping. Persistence under

TA CH'U THE GREAT NOURISHER

difficulties will win advantage. It is best to be occupied all day long with defensive measures. It is favourable to have a goal (or destination) in view. COMMENTARY For this line, which tops (the lower hexagram) presages the fulfilment of our will.

6 FOR THE FOURTH PLACE The headboard of a young ox[6]—sublime good fortune! COMMENTARY That is, good fortune in the form of happiness.

6 FOR THE FIFTH PLACE A gelded boar's tusk[7]—good fortune! COMMENTARY That is, good fortune in the form of blessings.[8]

9 FOR THE TOP PLACE Carrying (i.e. according with) heaven's way. COMMENTARY This implies great progress along the way of virtue.

NOTES (1) I.e. going on a long journey, perhaps abroad. (2) 'Ascends' may be taken to mean 'is in the ascent', for both of the component trigrams are topped by firm lines. (3) This is a time for going from home and giving concrete expression to our appreciation of what others have done for us or for the public good. (4) The arrangement of the component trigrams suggests glimpses of the sky among the peaks of the mountains. This points to something very far off and thereby indicates the advisability of setting out for some distant place. (5) A relatively serious hindrance threatens, but we are not to blame for it. (6) The symbol is a piece of wood, not unlike a cangue, used for the same purpose as a rope and nose-ring. The suggestion is that one who has not yet attained his full strength benefits from being restrained. (7) This is an emblem of opportunity. (8) I.e. good fortune apparently unconnected with our efforts or deserts.

HEXAGRAM 27
I (pronounced YEE) NOURISHMENT (literally JAWS)[1]

Component trigrams:
Below: CHÊN, thunder, movement, to sprout or quicken.
Above: KÊN, a mountain, hard, obstinate, perverse.

TEXT Nourishing. Righteous persistence brings good fortune. Watch people nourishing others and observe with what manner of things they seek to nourish themselves.[2]

COMMENTARY Persistence brings good fortune to those who nourish themselves on what is fitting. The rest of the passage means that we should observe what people give to nourish others and also what kind of things they choose for their own nourishment. The celestial and terrestrial forces give nourishment to all; the holy sage nourishes everybody from those who are truly worthy to the people as a whole. The timely application of this hexagram is of the highest importance.

SYMBOL This hexagram symbolizes thunder[3] rumbling at the foot of a mountain. The Superior Man is thoughtful in speech and frugal in his eating and drinking.

The Lines

9 FOR THE BOTTOM PLACE You released your sacred tortoise and stared at me with mouth agape[4]—misfortune! COMMENTARY Looking at me like that is hardly to be regarded as admirable behaviour.

6 FOR THE SECOND PLACE Nourishment on the mountain peak; he abandons normal ways to seek nourishment in the hills[5]—misfortune! COMMENTARY The misfortune is due to his having separated himself from his own kind.

6 FOR THE THIRD PLACE He is determined to relinquish nourishment[6]—misfortune! For ten years he performs no useful function and there is nowhere favourable for him to go. COMMENTARY Ten years because his ways are utterly perverse.

6 FOR THE FOURTH PLACE Nourishment on the mountain peak[7]— good fortune! He glares like a tiger stalking its prey so ardent is his look—no error! COMMENTARY The good fortune is due to light shed from above.

6 FOR THE FIFTH PLACE Normal ways are abandoned. Righteous persistence will bring good fortune to those who stay where they are.[8] The great river (or sea) must not be crossed.[8] COMMENTARY The good fortune attainable by such people consists in being able to obey their superiors most willingly.

9 FOR THE TOP PLACE Nourishment gives rise both to trouble and

I (pronounced YEE) NOURISHMENT (literally JAWS)

good fortune.⁹ It is favourable to cross the great river (or sea).¹⁰
COMMENTARY   The first sentence means that (in any case) we shall enjoy great blessings.¹¹

NOTES   (1) The form of this hexagram readily brings to mind the concept of wide open jaws, but the word nourishment must not be taken only in a literal sense; for we are concerned here with all those things which men seek both for their own advantage and for giving succour or assistance to others.   (2) For this will teach us a lot about their characters.   (3) The lower trigram, thunder, also represents the power of quickening growth; hence its place in a hexagram concerned with nourishment.   (4) The shells of tortoises were used for divination. Here, the implication seems to be that someone abandons his sacred duty in his greed (symbolized by 'mouth agape') to obtain what he wants from the person to whom 'me' refers. It may be that contemporaries of the authors of the *I Ching* were familiar with a story to which this sentence pertains.   (5) From ancient times, there has been a large body of opinion in China that Taoists and other mystics leading the life of a recluse are odd people who have abandoned their duties to family, state and mankind. However, the *Book of Change*, revered by both Taoists and Confucians, is not likely to be guilty of bias; indeed, in the fourth place, 'nourishment on the mountain' brings good fortune. Perhaps the implication is that those who withdraw from ordinary life more on account of their oddity than because of any genuine desire for spiritual guidance waste their talents and their time.   (6) Such extreme eccentricity can only end in barrenness. Those familiar with Buddhism will recollect that the Lord Buddha abandoned nourishment on the advice of his teachers and then came to regret this fruitless method of self-discipline.   (7) This line, like the second line, suggests a recluse; but in this case he is well qualified for the spiritual life and obviously gains the fruit of his endeavour. His tigerish glance calls to mind a Master of Zen or, rather, a Taoist sage who has reached a similar stage of enlightenment.   (8) In such abnormal times, it is best to stay at home.   (9) Our quest for the necessities of mind and body brings mixed results. (10) I.e. to go on a long journey.   (11) 'Blessings' means good fortune apparently unconnected with our merits or endeavours.

HEXAGRAM 28
TA KUO   EXCESS

Component trigrams:
Below: SUN, *wind, wood, bland, mild.*
Above: TUI, *a body of water, pool, marsh, joy.*

TEXT   Excess! The ridgepole sags.¹ It is favourable to have some goal (or destination) in view. Success!

COMMENTARY ON THE TEXT   This hexagram indicates something

altogether too large (or else excessive in some other way). The sagging of the ridgepole results from its weakness at both ends. The firm line in the centre (of the lower trigram) is unsuitably situated, for there are too many (firm lines). Nevertheless, the gentle and the joyful act as one,² so it is good to have in view a goal (or destination); success will follow! The timely application of this hexagram is of vast importance.

SYMBOL   This hexagram symbolizes a forest submerged in a great body of water.³ The Superior Man, though standing alone, is free from fear; he feels no discontent in withdrawing from the world.

The Lines

6 FOR THE BOTTOM PLACE   For mats, use white rushes⁴—no error! COMMENTARY   The reference to rush mats is derived from the position of this yielding line below (so many firm ones). (A further commentary explains that they symbolize treating things with gentleness).

9 FOR THE SECOND PLACE   The withered willow tree puts forth new shoots—an old man takes to wife a young girl. Everything is favourable. COMMENTARY   He weds her because they have been overmuch together.⁵

9 FOR THE THIRD PLACE   The ridgepole sags—misfortune! COMMENTARY   That is to say the misfortune of being without adequate support.

9 FOR THE FOURTH PLACE   The ridgepole is upheld—good fortune! Were it otherwise, there would be cause for blame. COMMENTARY   Good fortune in the sense that it does not fall.⁶

9 FOR THE FIFTH PLACE   The withered willow tree puts forth blossom—an old woman takes a vigorous (young) husband; no blame, no praise!⁷ COMMENTARY   How can such blossom endure for long? From another point of view, both of them should feel ashamed.⁸

6 FOR THE TOP PLACE   While he was fording the river, the water rose above his head—misfortune, but he was not at fault. COM-

TA KUO EXCESS

MENTARY   This presages a misfortune for which we cannot possibly be blamed.

NOTES   (1) A glance at the hexagram will show that it is too heavy in the middle and too weak at the ends. A number of firm lines is generally auspicious, but there can be too much of a good thing! (2) A reference to the component trigrams. (3) This is suggested by the component trigrams. Water is necessary for the nourishment of the trees, but too much of it can cause serious damage. (4) White rushes are less common than ordinary ones and probably make more beautiful mats. The implication may be that, if we decide to do things rather nicely, we might just as well go a little further and do them as charmingly as possible. (5) For an old man to wed a young girl may not be ideal in all circumstances; but if his association with her has already given rise to gossip, it is probably the best thing he can do. From his point of view, it is in any case a matter for satisfaction, so it is taken here to symbolize favourable circumstances. Some commentaries suggest another implication, namely that the old man is able to take on tasks normally difficult for the elderly. (6) This would seem to be good fortune of a negative kind; not so much good fortune as the failure of expected bad fortune to materialize. (7) No blame, in that there is no prohibition against such marriages; no praise, in that they are generally considered far more unsuitable than when the husband is much older than his wife. This implication for us is set forth in note eight. (8) The question of blaming or praising such a marriage is in any case of little importance, since it can scarcely be destined to endure for long. The second sentence of the commentary perhaps reveals that, for once, Confucius was inclined to disagree with his beloved mentor, the *Book of Change*, and to be taken aback by the words 'no blame'. From the point of view of divination, lines of this sort do not always indicate marriage; this line could mean that we shall do or have done something rather unusual of which the results will be more or less negative.

HEXAGRAM 29
K'AN   THE ABYSS

Component trigrams:
Below: K'AN, *water, a pit.*
Above: K'AN, *water, a pit.*

TEXT   Abyss upon abyss—grave danger! All will be well if confidence is maintained and a sharp hold kept upon the mind; activities so conducted will win esteem.

COMMENTARY ON THE TEXT   Abyss upon abyss; this involves grave danger; but, like water flowing without ever spilling over, he traverses the abysses without ever losing confidence (in his ability to succeed). That his keeping a sharp hold on his mind will enable him to win through is indicated by the firm line in the middle (of the lower trigram). That his activities will win esteem implies that his pursuit of a goal (or destination) will bring tangible results. None can escape from dangers sent from heaven, but earthly dangers are (nothing worse than) mountains, rivers, hills and precipices.[1] Kings and princes use dangerous devices to protect their realms.[2] The timely application of this hexagram is of vast importance.

SYMBOL   This hexagram symbolizes water flowing on and on and abyss upon abyss.[3] The Superior Man acts in accordance with the immutable virtues and spends much of his time instructing others in the conduct of affairs.

The Lines

6 FOR THE BOTTOM PLACE   Abyss upon abyss! In one of them, he tumbles into a cranny—misfortune!   COMMENTARY   Namely the misfortune of getting lost upon the way.

9 FOR THE SECOND PLACE   Danger lurks within the abyss; only in small matters can he obtain what he desires.   COMMENTARY   Though he obtain these trifles, he remains within the abyss.[4]

6 FOR THE THIRD PLACE   Abyss upon abyss rears up and the danger is acute. He falls into a cranny and there is nothing he can do to help himself.   COMMENTARY   This presages our ultimate failure to accomplish anything at all.

6 FOR THE FOURTH PLACE   A flagon of wine and a bamboo food-basket—both. These objects were handed to him through a hole (in the rock). To the very end he remains free from blame.[5]   COMMENTARY   This passage is suggested by the nature of the line, which forms a border between yielding and firm.

9 FOR THE FIFTH PLACE   The abyss is not filled to the brim; (the flowing water) maintains its level—no error!   COMMENTARY   This is because the line, being central (to the upper trigram), indicates (a level) that is not too high.[6]

K'AN THE ABYSS 145

6 FOR THE TOP PLACE   Bound with black ropes and imprisoned amidst thorns, for three years he fails to obtain (what he seeks).⁷
COMMENTARY   The line indicates that we lose our way and suffer misfortune for three years.

NOTES   (1) I.e. they are dangers which can be surmounted with confidence and skill. (2) These are another form of earthly danger which it is possible to surmount.   (3) The trigram K'an is usually inauspicious; here it occurs in duplicate as the upper and the lower trigram; thus, the implication is that we are beset by grave dangers from which, if we can escape them at all, the utmost skill and confidence will be required to extricate ourselves. (4) Whatever small successes we may win will not have any effect in lessening the danger that threatens.   (5) The terrible trouble in which we find ourselves occurs through no fault of ours; others are able to help us to some extent—but it looks as though their help may serve only to prolong our agony.   (6) The danger threatening whoever receives a moving line for the fifth place is relatively less serious than for many of the others whose enquiries are answered by this unfortunate hexagram.   (7) This situation is far from cheerful, but not as hopeless as the situation of those who receive moving lines in the second and third places.

HEXAGRAM 30
LI   FLAMING BEAUTY

Component trigrams:
Below: LI, *fire, brilliance, beauty.*
Above: LI, *fire, brilliance, beauty.*

TEXT   Flaming Beauty. Righteous persistence brings reward. Success! Rearing cows—good fortune!¹

COMMENTARY ON THE TEXT   This hexagram implies dependence. The sun and moon depend from the heavens; the myriad kinds of plant life depend from the earth. Immense clarity (of mind) depending upon what is right can transform and perfect the world.² The yielding lines, being dependent, are suitably centred between firm lines (in both trigrams); that is why the hexagram presages success and why (the symbol) rearing cows is used to denote good fortune.

SYMBOL   This hexagram symbolizes fire rising in two tongues of
K

brilliant flame.³ The Superior Man, by perpetuating the brilliance (of the ancients), illumines every quarter of the earth.

The Lines

9 FOR THE BOTTOM PLACE   Approaching with reverent steps, he pays them his respects—no error. COMMENTARY   He walks reverently expressly to avoid blame.⁴

6 FOR THE SECOND PLACE   Yellow sunlight—sublime good fortune! COMMENTARY   The good fortune of being able to keep to a middle path.⁵

9 FOR THE THIRD PLACE   In the light of the setting sun, young men do not beat upon their cooking pots or sing; the old sigh piteously—misfortune! COMMENTARY   Sunset beauty—how can it endure for long?⁶

9 FOR THE FOURTH PLACE   How sudden its coming! Then (with) flamelike (swiftness) it is dead and cast away.⁷ COMMENTARY   Its coming was sudden and there was no place for it.

6 FOR THE FIFTH PLACE   His tears streamed forth as though to extinguish his piteous sighs—good fortune!⁸ COMMENTARY   This good fortune stems from the rulers.⁹

9 FOR THE TOP PLACE   The King went forth to set things to rights and, blessed (by heaven with victory), he destroyed the leader (of the rebels); but he did not chastise the (rebel) followers—no error! COMMENTARY   The King acted thus in order to rectify the affairs of the various states (comprising his realm).¹⁰

NOTES   (1) Cows are gentle creatures which require looking after; hence this sentence means that good fortune can be gained from looking after those in need of help.   (2) In other words, we should make ourselves as completely dependent on the principle of righteousness as natural objects are dependent upon nature; in this way, we are sure to be successful.   (3) Here, both the component trigrams are the same. As Li is in itself an auspicious trigram, its duplication makes the hexagram unusually auspicious.   (4) This suggests a rather delicate situation in which we should avoid any appearance of lacking respect for others.   (5) This is suggested by the position of the line, which is central to the lower trigram. The middle path, the golden mean, is praised by Taoists, Confucians and Buddhists alike. It has always been regarded by traditionally minded Chinese as the principle upon which conduct should be based. Extremes of any kind have no place in Chinese philosophy, which is thus more humanistic than many of the philosophies of India and the Middle East. (6) This passage suggests that our present happiness or success is not destined to endure; we must prepare for a setback. (7) Apparently we may expect some unlooked for good fortune, but of a kind that will have passed away before we have had time to enjoy it. (8) Bitter regret serves us in good stead. (9) For purposes of divination, we may take it that 'rulers' means anyone with authority over us. (10) This passage implies that we may be compelled to resort to forceful measures but that we should avoid chastising those who have been led to do harm by others.

HEXAGRAM 31
HSIEN   ATTRACTION, SENSATION

Component trigrams:
Below: KÊN, *a mountain, hard, obstinate, perverse.*
Above: TUI, *a body of water, pool, marsh, joy.*

TEXT   Attraction. Success! Righteous persistence brings reward. Taking a wife will result in good fortune.

COMMENTARY ON THE TEXT   Attraction involves stimulation. The yielding is above, the firm below.[1] Though they are opposite in character, a mutually responsive feeling enables them to be together. The stubborn and the joyous are conjoined,[2] with the man below the girl[3]—hence all the good things promised in the Text. The myriad objects owe their existence to the mutual stimulation subsisting between heaven and earth. Similarly, the holy sage stimulates men's hearts and the whole world is thenceforth at peace. The inner nature of everything in heaven and earth can be gauged by observing what it is that stimulates each of them.[4]

SYMBOL   This hexagram symbolizes a lake[5] situated upon a mountain. In dealing with men, the Superior Man shows himself to be entirely void (of selfishness).

The Lines

6 FOR THE BOTTOM PLACE   Sensation in the toe.   COMMENTARY   This implies that the will is fastened upon external matters.

6 FOR THE SECOND PLACE   Sensation in the legs—misfortune![6] Good fortune comes to those who do not venture forth.   COMMENTARY   Despite these predictions, if we gladly accord with others, we shall come to no harm.[7]

HSIEN ATTRACTION, SENSATION

9 FOR THE THIRD PLACE   Sensation in the thighs. He cleaves so closely to his wife (handmaiden, etc.) that for him to continue in this manner would be shameful.   COMMENTARY   Sensation in the thighs also denotes restlessness; while being guided by the will of a wife (or subordinate) involves clinging to what is inferior.

9 FOR THE FOURTH PLACE   Righteous persistence brings good fortune and regret vanishes; but only friends and immediate followers will waste their thoughts on one who dithers irresolutely to and fro.   COMMENTARY   Persistence rewarded and the vanishing of regret both result from our not having incited anyone to evildoing, but this irresolute conduct scarcely indicates clarity of mind (on our part).[8]

9 FOR THE FIFTH PLACE   Sensation in the fleshy covering of the spinal column—no regret.   COMMENTARY   This betokens inability to impose our will as yet.

6 FOR THE TOP PLACE   Sensation in the jaws and the tongue.   COMMENTARY   This is a way of saying that we open wide our mouths and talk (too much).

NOTES   (1) This is a reference to the component trigrams, whose position is auspicious, for the firm can easily support the weak.   (2) Another reference to the component trigrams.   (3) I doubt if this should be regarded as shedding light upon the ancient Chinese concept of the most acceptable position for intercourse; it is more likely to mean that the girl is able to depend upon the man as a plant depends upon the earth for its nourishment.   (4) Men reveal their characters to those who observe what things cause them pleasure or pain.   (5) The upper hexagram, Tui, denotes a marsh rather than a lake full of clear water, but I have avoided translating it as marsh because it has none of the derogatory significance possessed by the English word. The mountain lake or marsh suggests a wild, open place which provides a suitable symbol for the voidness referred to just below.   (6) I.e. misfortune if we yield to the urge to exercise our legs by going somewhere else.   (7) This means that, even if we do not stay at home—obviously the best course for us at this time—no harm will result provided that we accord with the wishes of others.   (8) This suggests the rather negative good fortune of having a clear conscience; apparently we have little reason for self-congratulation, since our rather spineless conduct alienates everyone who is not bound to us by ties of blood or friendship.

HEXAGRAM 32
HÊNG   THE LONG ENDURING

Component trigrams:
Below: SUN, *wind, wood, bland, mild.*
Above: CHÊN, *thunder, movement, to sprout or quicken.*

TEXT   The Long Enduring. Success and freedom from error! Righteous persistence brings reward. It is favourable to have in view some goal (or destination).

COMMENTARY   The name of this hexagram implies that which continues long. The firm is above and the yielding below.¹ Thunder and wind conjoined—mildness coupled with activity.¹ The mutual responsiveness of the firm and yielding makes for endurance. Success, freedom from error and the reward to be won from being firmly determined all indicate long continuance along our present way. The way followed by heaven and earth endures for so long as to be endless. It is favourable to have some goal (or destination) in mind, since every end is succeeded by a new beginning.² Supported by heaven, the sun and moon can shine for age upon age; the four seasons, with their ceaseless transformations, are able to produce their effects for aeons. The holy sage continues upon his way so steadfastly that he succeeds in transforming the world. The inner nature of everything in heaven and earth can be judged from contemplating whatever it is that makes them continue (to be as they are).

SYMBOL   This hexagram symbolizes thunder accompanied by wind.³ The Superior Man stands so firmly that he cannot be uprooted.

The Lines

6 FOR THE BOTTOM PLACE   To ensure his continuance, he digs a hole for himself. This sort of determination brings misfortune, for he

HÊNG THE LONG ENDURING

is unable to go anywhere. COMMENTARY Misfortune caused by trying to achieve enduring results at the very beginning.

9 FOR THE SECOND PLACE Regret vanishes. COMMENTARY The line implies ability to remain upon the middle path.[4]

9 FOR THE THIRD PLACE He is not consistently virtuous and therefore meets with disgrace. To continue thus would be shameful. COMMENTARY Because, then, no one could endure him.[5]

9 FOR THE FOURTH PLACE No game in the field. COMMENTARY How can one who remains long out of place[6] hope to gain his quarry?

6 FOR THE FIFTH PLACE Making a virtue of (marital) constancy[7] is a type of persistence which brings good fortune to women, but it is harmful to men. COMMENTARY A woman follows one lord for the whole of her life, but men have to hold to their public duties. For them to subordinate themselves to women would bring shame upon them.

6 FOR THE TOP PLACE Prolonged violent exercise—misfortune![8] COMMENTARY The prolonged violent exercise signified by this line is completely void of worthwhile results.

NOTES (1) A reference to the component trigrams. (2) This suggests that the time has come to strike out after a goal that is new to us. (3) The component trigrams stand for thunder and wind. This might be regarded as a bad combination; but here the stress is upon ability to endure under any circumstances whatever. (4) I.e. to avoid extremes and cleave to the golden mean. This is suggested by the position of the line which is central to the lower trigram. (5) We can bear with an evil man more easily than with one who is liable to behave so inconsistently that we never know what to expect of him. (6) A reference to the unsuitable position of this line. An example of what is implied is furnished by people whose talents and interests incline them towards a profession quite different from the one in which they are employed; with the best will in the world, they cannot to justice to themselves. (7) Here 'constancy' is used in the limited sense of devotion to husband or wife and willingness to submit absolutely to his or her judgement. (8) This implies violent activity directed to wrong ends and therefore barren of result.

HEXAGRAM 33
TUN YIELDING, WITHDRAWAL[1]

Component trigrams:
Below: KÊN, *a mountain, hard, obstinate, perverse.*
Above: CH'IEN, *heaven, male, active, etc.*

TEXT Yielding. Success! Persistence in small things wins advantage.

COMMENTARY ON THE TEXT The success indicated here is precisely that sort which results from yielding. The firm (fifth) line is the ruling line and wins response from the rest; its activities accord with the times. Persistence in small things brings advantage in the sense that (plants) grow well when properly watered.[2] The timely application of this hexagram is of vast importance.

SYMBOL This hexagram symbolizes mountains beneath the sky.[3] The Superior Man, by keeping his distance from men of inferior character, avoids having to display wrath and preserves his dignity.

The Lines

6 FOR THE BOTTOM PLACE Withdrawal to the hindermost point—trouble! It is useless to seek any goal (or destination) at such a time. COMMENTARY To withdraw to the hindermost point causes trouble, but if you refrain from moving (back so far) what misfortune can overtake you?

6 FOR THE SECOND PLACE He bound it with thongs of yellow oxhide and no one could untie it. COMMENTARY This symbolizes a powerful will.

9 FOR THE THIRD PLACE Yielding under constraint results in ills and trouble, but there is good fortune in store for those who are supporting servants and concubines. COMMENTARY The evils referred to here are those attendant on extreme fatigue. Though

TUN YIELDING, WITHDRAWAL 153

supporting servants or concubines brings good fortune, it does not lead to achieving anything of consequence.⁴

9 FOR THE FOURTH PLACE Withdrawal for good reasons—for the Superior Man, good fortune; for people of mean attainments, misfortune! COMMENTARY For when, quite rightly, the Superior Man withdraws, lesser men are bound to suffer.

9 FOR THE FIFTH PLACE An admirably carried out withdrawal. Persistence in a righteous course brings good fortune. COMMENTARY This good fortune results from a withdrawal carried out as a result of rectifying our aims.⁵

9 FOR THE TOP PLACE A 'sleek' withdrawal⁶—everything is favourable! COMMENTARY In this case, there cannot be the smallest doubt.⁷

NOTES (1) Much of the teaching of the *Book of Change* is concerned with the wisdom of restraint or withdrawal as the best way of achieving our goal under certain circumstances; so this hexagram is not necessarily unfavourable to the wise. (2) This is not a time when we can hope to achieve much; but attention to small matters will stand us in good stead later. (3) The component trigrams, symbolizing mountain and sky, indicate withdrawal to a solitary place when circumstances are unfavourable. (4) Seemingly, Confucius, always inclined to be austere, does not altogether approve of this type of good fortune. (5) I.e. revising them in the light of unfavourable circumstances. (6) The Chinese commentators suggest that this means going to live in retirement. They add that the phrase also implies excellent health. (7) I.e. not the smallest doubt as to the wisdom of withdrawal.

HEXAGRAM 34
TA CHUANG   THE POWER OF THE GREAT¹

Component trigrams:
Below: CH'IEN, *heaven, active, male, etc.*
Above: CHÊN, *thunder, movement, to sprout or quicken.*

TEXT The Power of the Great. Persistence in a righteous course brings reward.

COMMENTARY ON THE TEXT   TA CHUANG   (literally Great

Power) here means the Power of the Great. The firm wields power by reason of its active nature. Right persistence is rewarded because (as indicated by the arrangement of the hexagram) great and right are (in this context) synonymous. Righteousness and greatness combined lead to understanding of the inner nature of everything in heaven and earth.

SYMBOL   This hexagram symbolizes thunder in the sky.[2] The Superior Man never takes a step involving impropriety.

The Lines

9 FOR THE BOTTOM PLACE   Power in the toes.[3] To advance now would bring misfortune, but confidence remains.   COMMENTARY   The confidence symbolized by power in the toes is soon exhausted.

9 FOR THE SECOND PLACE   Persistence in a righteous course brings good fortune.   COMMENTARY   This is indicated by the line's central position (in the lower trigram).

9 FOR THE THIRD PLACE   Inferior men use their power where (under the circumstances prevailing) the Superior Man refrains from using his. Persistence now would bring serious consequences, as when a goat butts against a hedge and gets its horns entangled.   COMMENTARY   This means that inferior men use their power and the Superior Man (is likely to be) tricked.

9 FOR THE FOURTH PLACE   Righteous persistence brings good fortune and regret vanishes. The hedge falls apart and he is no longer entangled. There is great power in the cart axle.[4]   COMMENTARY   Once the hedge has fallen apart, he can get up and go forward.

6 FOR THE FIFTH PLACE   He sacrifices a goat too lightly—no regret![5]   COMMENTARY   This is indicated by the line's unsuitable position.

6 FOR THE TOP PLACE   A goat butts against a hedge and can move neither backward nor forward; it can get nowhere.[6] Yet at this time, difficulty presages good fortune.[7]   COMMENTARY   Inability to retire or advance is hardly conducive to good fortune; but our very

TA CHUANG THE POWER OF THE GREAT

difficulties will generate it; the ignoble circumstances (in which we find ourselves) will not endure for long.

NOTES (1) This hexagram with a solid group of firm lines topped by a small number of yielding ones obviously signifies strength—in this case the power to succeed in spite of difficulties. Much of what follows concerns goats—a symbol presumably suggested by the form of the hexagram, namely a solid body distinguished by a pair of horns—the yielding lines at the top. (2) The combination of trigrams meaning thunder and sky suggests something of the awe-inspiring quality of the truly great. (3) I.e. power of a rather low or limited kind. (4) A powerful axle indicates that the time is favourable for an advance towards our goal. (5) I.e. he resorts too easily to force, which is not advisable. (6) 'It can get nowhere' is a rendering of a phrase which, taken symbolically, means that this is not a time to advance towards our goal (or destination). (7) The implication is that the shame we feel at finding ourselves prisoners of circumstances will drive us to make an effort powerful enough to release us.

HEXAGRAM 35
CHIN   PROGRESS

Component trigrams:
Below: K'UN, *earth, female, passive, etc.*
Above: LI, *fire, brilliance, beauty.*

TEXT   Progress. The richly endowed prince receives royal favours in the form of numerous steeds and is granted audience three times in a single day![1]

COMMENTARY ON THE TEXT   The character CHIN is identical with (a more commonly used character meaning) progress. The earth is radiant with beauty, for glad acceptance conjoined with beauty[1] sheds a brilliant light. The yielding advances and ascends (to the fifth and ruling place of the hexagram). Hence the imagery of a splendid prince, royal steeds and frequent audiences.

SYMBOL   This hexagram symbolizes fire blazing from the earth.[2] The Superior Man reflects in his person the glory of (heaven's) virtue.

The Lines

6 FOR THE BOTTOM PLACE Where progress seems likely to be cut short, righteous persistence brings good fortune. To respond to lack of confidence with liberality entails no error. COMMENTARY Progress likely to be cut short refers to a single-handed attempt to do what is right. Such liberality entails no blame where commands (from the ruler) have not yet been received.[3]

6 FOR THE SECOND PLACE Where progress is being made sorrowfully, righteous persistence brings good fortune. A little happiness is received, thanks to the Queen Mother.[4] COMMENTARY What is said regarding happiness is implied by the position of this line which is central (to the lower trigram).

6 FOR THE THIRD PLACE All are in accord—regret vanishes! COMMENTARY This implies unanimous determination to press upwards.

9 FOR THE FOURTH PLACE Squirrel-like progress[5]—persistence would have serious consequences. COMMENTARY Because the position of this line is unsuitable.

6 FOR THE FIFTH PLACE Regret vanishes. Care not for loss or gain. To seek some goal (or destination) now would bring good fortune; everything is favourable. COMMENTARY If, without regard for loss or gain, we just press forward, our actions will be blessed.

9 FOR THE TOP PLACE He advances as with lowered horns, intent solely upon subduing the cities (of his enemies). Whether his affairs go awry or prosper, he is not in error, but for him to persist thus would involve him in ignominy. COMMENTARY Solely to subdue the cities? The way is not yet clear![6]

NOTES (1) This passage indicates great merit richly rewarded. (2) A reference to the component trigrams. (3) In a literal sense, this means that there is no harm in an official being liberal, even to those who have withheld their confidence from him, until he has received specific orders as to what he must do. For purposes of divination, it can be taken to mean that we can safely be generous even to people inclined to mistrust us, until those whom we obey have given us a clear ruling in the matter. (4) Queen Mother is one of the names given, in this case, to the fifth or ruling line of the hexagram which, as the central line of the upper hexagram and a Yin line, nicely balances this central line of the lower hexagram, also a Yin line. In divination, we must take it that a little happiness will

CHIN PROGRESS 157

come to us regardless of our endeavours or merits, as though by chance; or else that we shall receive some small assistance from a person in authority, probably a woman. (5) This implies trying to rise too high and advance too quickly, thus exposing ourselves to unnecessary risk. (6) A king may sometimes be compelled to chastise rebellious subjects, but to be concerned with their punishment to the exclusion of all else is not a sign of enlightenment. The implication is that, if we are compelled to use forceful measures, we should not be too intent upon another's downfall, but exert pressure only for as long as is absolutely necessary.

HEXAGRAM 36
MING I (pronounced MING YEE) DARKENING OF THE LIGHT. INJURY

Component trigrams:
Below: LI, *fire, brilliance, beauty.*
Above: K'UN, *earth, female, passive, etc.*

TEXT Darkening of the Light. Righteous persistence in the face of difficulty brings reward.

COMMENTARY ON THE TEXT Entering into the earth, the light is extinguished.¹ A man who clothed his inner being with refinement and intelligence and who displayed gentleness and willing acceptance in his outward conduct, the better to meet adversity—such as King Wên! Determination to win advantage from difficulty involves concealing brilliance (of mind and character). A man who, despite the troubles locked within his heart, unfalteringly fixed his will upon righteousness —such was Prince Chi!²

SYMBOL This hexagram symbolizes light hidden within the earth.³ In governing the people, the Superior Man, though taking care to conceal (his light), nevertheless shines.

The Lines

9 FOR THE BOTTOM PLACE Failure of the light during his progress

through the sky caused him to lower his wings. When busy with affairs, the Superior Man may go without food for three days on end, so intent is he on reaching his goal; but his lord will have something to say about this.⁴ COMMENTARY It is the duty of the Superior Man to go without food for three days if his activities require this of him.⁵

6 FOR THE SECOND PLACE Though injured in the left thigh, he made use of a horse in relieving distress—good fortune! COMMENTARY This good fortune results from compliance with laws and regulations.⁵

9 FOR THE THIRD PLACE Wounded while on a military expedition in the south, he still managed to capture the rebel leader. Persistence amounting to madness should be avoided.⁶ COMMENTARY His willingness to undertake the expedition in the south symbolizes determination to achieve great results.

6 FOR THE FOURTH PLACE It is as though he had penetrated someone's left side and perceived a darkened heart (as clearly as if that heart had been abstracted) from its dwelling-place.⁷ COMMENTARY This is a way of saying that he saw clearly into the other's heart.

6 FOR THE FIFTH PLACE Prince Chi suffered injury, but his persistence along a righteous course was rewarded. COMMENTARY Prince Chi's persistence was rewarded in the sense that his was a light which can never be extinguished.

6 FOR THE TOP PLACE Nothing to lighten the darkness! Having once climbed to heaven, he later descended into the earth.⁸ COMMENTARY That he had once climbed to heaven means that, at one time, he illumined the four quarters of the empire; his descent into the earth means that he transgressed divine law.

NOTES (1) As when the sun goes down. (2) The implication is that we should seek to emulate these ancient heroes by steadfastness in the face of immeasurable difficulties. (3) The relative positions of the two component hexagrams suggest light hidden in the earth. (4) This sort of conduct is much admired by the Chinese. We are reminded of the Emperor Yü who, when in the previous reign he was charged with the duty of flood control, often passed the door of his old home without so much as stopping to greet his family. Confucius himself is said to have gone for several days without food. The implication is that, when we are working for the public good, we must put aside all selfish considerations. It does not matter if our superiors or other people criticize what they consider to be our madness in so doing. (5) The implication would seem to be that, when charged with emergency duties, we must persist in carrying them out at all costs. (6) Though his intentions were good and though he happened to succeed in this case, he was nevertheless behaving with excessive zeal amounting almost to madness. The idea is that, while it is a most excellent thing to fight against adversity, we should not go so far as to endanger our lives unnecessarily. (7) The Chinese text for this line is so far from clear as to suggest that it is corrupt. My interpretation must be regarded as no more than an intelligent guess. The actual text runs something like this: 'Into left side, obtain light-darkened heart—or heart of light-darkening—outside the gates and courtyards (of home).' Fortunately, the commentary on this line explains the general meaning, so the matter is not of great importance. (8) If we have once risen to great heights, it is doubly shameful to sink low.

HEXAGRAM 37
CHIA JÊN   THE FAMILY[1]

Component trigrams:
Below: LI, *fire, brilliance, beauty.*
Above: SUN, *wind, wood, bland, mild.*

TEXT   The Family. Women's persistence brings reward.[2]

COMMENTARY ON THE TEXT   Women's appropriate place is within; men's, without. When men and women keep to their proper places they act in accord with heaven's great norm.[3] Among the members of a family are the dignified master and mistress whom we term Father and Mother. When Father, mother, sons, elder and younger brothers all act in a manner suited to their various positions within the family, when husbands play their proper role and wives are truly wifely, the way of that family runs straight.[4] It is by the proper regulation of each family that the whole world is stabilized.

SYMBOL   This hexagram symbolizes wind rising from fire.[5] The Superior Man's speech is full of substance and he behaves with constancy.

The Lines

9 FOR THE BOTTOM PLACE   The family dwelling stands within an enclosure—regret vanishes.   COMMENTARY   The first part of this passage symbolizes determination which has never swerved.

6 FOR THE SECOND PLACE   (This is a time when) nothing can be brought to completion; however, within the household, righteous persistence brings good fortune.[6]   COMMENTARY   Namely, good fortune arising from compliance and gentleness.

9 FOR THE THIRD PLACE   When members of the family speak sharply (to one another), the (mutual) regret and the serious situation which follow may lead to good fortune; but, if the women and children take to tittering, misfortune is assured.[7]   COMMENTARY   Because sharp words do not cause much harm, but the tittering of women and children leads to the destruction of good order within the family.

6 FOR THE FOURTH PLACE   A well-to-do household—great good fortune!   COMMENTARY   This good fortune is indicated by the position of the line which symbolizes cheerful acceptance.

9 FOR THE FIFTH PLACE   The King draws near to his 'family' (i.e. the nation)—no cause for worry; good fortune!   COMMENTARY   This means that the ruler and his people meet together with love in their hearts.[8]

9 FOR THE TOP PLACE   His sincerity (and/or confidence) is such as to make him appear awe-inspiring—good fortune in the end!   COMMENTARY   He will enjoy good fortune because he subjects himself (frequently) to self-examination.

NOTES   (1) The arrangement of this hexagram suggests a harmonious family, in the Chinese traditional sense, for the women (Yin lines) are all within, surrounded by their menfolk (Yang lines), some of whom stand guarding the family from those without. (2) Women who receive this hexagram in response to their enquiries may take it as a fortunate omen; not so men, unless they also receive a moving line which promises good fortune; otherwise, for them, the omen is rather negative.   (3) Modern people, especially Americans, may be inclined to scorn this piece of wisdom; yet, if they think in Chinese terms, that is by putting family happiness above individual happiness (or its pursuit), they may appreciate it. It is certain that the family discord and broken marriages are rarer in those ages and those parts of the world where family harmony is cherished above most

CHIA JÊN THE FAMILY

else. (4) The classical Chinese notion of behaviour proper to parents, children, brothers and sisters, husbands and wives was not a one-sided one; for the senior in each pair, though he enjoyed certain privileges over juniors or his womenfolk, was expected to be punctilious about fulfilling his obligations to them. (5) A reference to the component trigrams. (6) This omen is unfavourable, except as regards household matters. (7) An occasional scolding may not do much harm, but constant mockery of parents or husband will cause irreparable damage to family accord. The former, if followed by regret and by the threat of an unwanted quarrel or separation, may bring people to their senses and make them mutually more considerate than hitherto. (8) This may be interpreted to mean that we enjoy the affection of our superiors or bestow affection on our juniors and those in our charge.

HEXAGRAM 38
K'UEI   THE ESTRANGED, OPPOSITES[1]

Component trigrams:
Below: TUI, a body of water, pool, marsh, joy.
Above: LI, fire, brilliance, beauty.

TEXT   The Estranged—good fortune in small matters.[2]

COMMENTARY ON THE TEXT   In this hexagram, fire moves upwards, the water moves downwards.[3] (It is as though they were) two women living under one roof whose wishes do not accord. But, when joy and beauty are conjoined[3]—what radiance! The yielding (Yin principle) advances and ascends to the middle (of the upper trigram); it responds to the firm (Yang principle)—hence good fortune in things small. Though heaven and earth lie apart, they are at one in their activity. Men and women are opposites, but their desire is for union. Everything has its own separateness and accomplishes its purpose according to its kind. The timely application of this hexagram is of the greatest value.

SYMBOL   This hexagram symbolizes fire above and a marshy lake below.[3] The Superior Man achieves difference through unity.[4]

L

The Lines

9 FOR THE BOTTOM PLACE   Regret vanishes! Do not follow the straying horse, for it will return of its own accord.[5] Though he allows evil men to visit him, he remains without error. COMMENTARY That is to say, his very purpose in receiving them is to avoid error.[6]

9 FOR THE SECOND PLACE   He encountered his lord in a narrow lane—no error![7] COMMENTARY He was not in error for he had not strayed from his path.

6 FOR THE THIRD PLACE   He watched them dragging at his axle and striking his oxen. As for himself, his topknot and nose were sliced off—not much of a beginning, but there was an end (to his troubles).[8] COMMENTARY The first part of this passage is indicated by the unsuitable position of the line. That, despite this poor beginning, there is an end (to his troubles—or ours—) can be deduced from this line's meeting with a firm one (immediately above it).

9 FOR THE FOURTH PLACE   After suffering estrangement and loneliness, she met an admirable husband and mutual confidence grew between them[9]—unpleasantness, but no error! COMMENTARY What is said about mutual confidence and freedom from error indicates the fulfilment of what is willed.

6 FOR THE FIFTH PLACE   Regret vanishes! The head of the clan bites through the flesh (or meat). What is there to prevent him proceeding (with his plans)?[10] COMMENTARY What is said about his biting through the flesh indicates that to proceed (with current plans) will result in blessings.[11]

9 FOR THE TOP PLACE   (Wandering) estranged and lonely, he saw a boar covered with mud and a waggon loaded with demons. First he stretched his bow, but then put it aside. It is not an obstacle but a matter of betrothal (which causes delay or hesitation). If rain is encountered during the conduct of affairs, good fortune will ensue.[12] COMMENTARY The last sentence implies the dispersal of all doubt.[13]

NOTES (1) It is the different nature of the component trigrams which indicates the meaning given to this hexagram. (2) The implication is that we should not try to proceed with great matters, unless encouraged to do so by a favourable moving line. (3) A reference to the component trigrams, which imply a union between the sexes. In

K'UEI THE ESTRANGED, OPPOSITES 163

the context of opposites, two people of the same sex cannot get along, whereas a mating of the sexes brings joy. (4) That is to say, he applies the same moral principles in all his dealings, though his methods must must differ according to the nature of each task. (5) This must be interpreted in the light of its bearing on our problems. (6) We must expect to encounter unlikeable people whom it would be impolitic or dangerous to ignore. (7) Chinese lanes can be VERY narrow. It is probable that he inconvenienced his lord, who was doubtless approaching with a group of retainers. The implications are that we are not to blame, any inconvenience we cause will not be deliberate. (8) This is a frighteningly inauspicious line. We must expect severe trouble; the only comfort we can take is the knowledge that it will not be permanent. (9) For those to whom the literal interpretation does not apply, the last six words of the commentary are all that matter. (10) This just means that all will go well with our plans. The head of the clan is our mind; the flesh is the difficulty we shall succeed in overcoming. (11) I.e. unexpected good fortune. (12) The first two sentences imply that we shall meet with unpleasant and frightening things; that, at first, we shall think to fend them off, but then decide to let them be. The sentence about betrothal means only that there will be some delay or hesitation for very good reasons. The last sentence may or may not mean exactly what it says. If we decide that it is not to be taken literally, then we must take it to mean that a slight setback on the way is a good omen. (13) Coupling this commentary with what is said about rain, we may suppose that, if rain (or an unexpected setback) occurs, then we shall no longer have any reason to doubt the successful outcome of our plans.

HEXAGRAM 39
CHIEN   TROUBLE

Component trigrams:
Below: KÊN, *a mountain, hard, obstinate, perverse.*
Above: K'AN, *water, a pit.*

TEXT   Trouble. The west and the south are favourable, but not the east and the north.¹ It is advisable to see a great man.² Persistence in a righteous course brings good fortune.

COMMENTARY ON THE TEXT   This hexagram implies difficulties. Danger lies ahead. To perceive danger and succeed in averting it—that is wisdom indeed! The west and south are favoured; for, proceeding in those directions, we shall be able to steer a middle course. The east and north are not favoured; the path leading to them peters out.¹ By going to see a great man, we shall achieve solid results. (The fifth line) being in the proper place (for a Yang line in such a case as this) indicates that righteous persistence will bring good fortune of a sort whereby the empire can be put to rights.[3] The timely application of this hexagram is of the greatest value.

SYMBOL   This hexagram symbolizes water upon a mountain.[4] The Superior Man cultivates virtue by bringing about a revolution within himself.

The Lines

6 FOR THE BOTTOM LINE   Going involves trouble; coming wins praise.   COMMENTARY   This passage stresses the advantage of waiting (for some time).

6 FOR THE SECOND PLACE   The King's minister[5] meets with difficulty upon difficulty, but through no fault of his.   COMMENTARY   This indicates that we shall be free from blame to the very end (or in the end).

9 FOR THE THIRD PLACE   To proceed would lead to trouble; therefore turn back!   COMMENTARY   This passage presages happiness for the women of the family (literally, happiness for those within).[6]

6 FOR THE FOURTH PLACE   To proceed would lead to trouble, whereas those coming will forge useful connections.   COMMENTARY   Because this line is suitably placed and possesses solidity.

9 FOR THE FIFTH PLACE   In the midst of severe trouble, friends (or a friend) arrive.   COMMENTARY   This is indicated by the line's central position (in the upper trigram).

6 FOR THE TOP PLACE   To proceed would lead to trouble; coming will produce excellent results. It is advisable to see a great man.[7]   COMMENTARY   The first sentence points to directing the will inwards. The other sentence is an injunction to submit ourselves to someone truly noble.

NOTES   (1) That is to say, if we try to forward our plans by proceeding in either of those directions, we shall get bogged down or lost. It could also mean that we should be driven to unvirtuous conduct.   (2) We should seek advice from someone of lofty moral stature and profound wisdom. (3) Good fortune that will enable us to be of immense service to our community, to our country or to the world. (4) A reference to the component trigrams. (5) This may be interpreted as someone engaged in public service or as the right-hand man of someone in high authority. (6) This could also be translated 'internal happiness', but I think the above rendering is what the author intended.

HEXAGRAM 40
HSIEH RELEASE

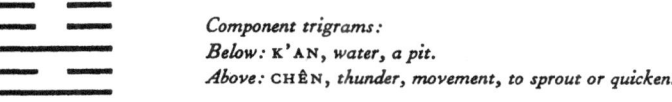

Component trigrams:
Below: K'AN, *water, a pit.*
Above: CHÊN, *thunder, movement, to sprout or quicken.*

TEXT   Release. The west and south are favourable. Those with nothing to gain from going forward will win good fortune by turning back;[1] those who do have much to gain from going forward must hasten to be sure of doing well.

COMMENTARY ON THE TEXT   This hexagram implies activity in the face of danger;[2] for it is activity by which danger is averted that brings release. West and south are favoured in the sense that those who go in those directions now will win the hearts of many. Returning brings good fortune and makes it possible to steer a middle course. If those with good reason to go forward hasten to their goal, they will be assured of concrete results. Heaven and earth find release in thunder and rain, whose action causes the seed pods of fruit-bearing shrubs and every kind of plant and tree to burst asunder. The timely application of this hexagram is of vast importance.

SYMBOL   This hexagram symbolizes thunder and rain[2] bringing release. The Superior Man tends to forgive wrongs and deals leniently with crimes.

The Lines

6 FOR THE BOTTOM PLACE   No error!   COMMENTARY   The con-

junction of yielding and firm (namely, lines one and two) implies freedom from error.

9 FOR THE SECOND PLACE With (one) yellow arrow, he killed three foxes in the field.³ Righteous persistence will bring good fortune. COMMENTARY The good fortune of being able to steer a middle course.

6 FOR THE THIRD PLACE (Travelling with both) luggage-bearers and a carriage,⁴ he attracted the attention of robbers. To persist would bring misfortune. COMMENTARY Moreover, his using both of them was shameful. If I (were to act thus and) bring robbers down on me, who (but myself) would be to blame?

9 FOR THE FOURTH PLACE A fumbled release.⁵ Put your trust in the friend(s) who will come. COMMENTARY A fumbled release is indicated by the unsuitable position of this line.

6 FOR THE FIFTH PLACE Only the Superior Man brings release. Good fortune! It is up to lesser men to put their trust in him.⁶ COMMENTARY But when the Superior Man offers them release, they take to their heels.⁷

6 FOR THE TOP PLACE The prince shot an arrow and killed a hawk perching on a high wall. Everything is favourable! COMMENTARY This means that he was able to liberate himself from perverse men.

NOTES (1) This is not a time to stay where we are. If we have no good reason to advance, it is best to retreat. (2) A reference to the component trigrams, which suggests that a certain amount of forceful action is required. (3) Three birds with one stone. (4) This could mean that someone bearing luggage on his back rides in a carriage. In any case, the Chinese additional commentaries explain that the passage refers to those who usurp privileges to which they are not entitled by rank or merit. (5) 'A fumbled release' is the result of my attempt to make something of three Chinese words—'release' and 'thumb' (or 'big toe') joined by a grammatical particle with various possible meanings. Whether my guess is right or not, the commentary on the line makes it clear that the omen is not a fortunate one. Happily, an awkward situation will be relieved by the arrival of a friend (or friends). (6) This could also mean 'He has confidence in lesser men'. (7) Perhaps this means that true release involves release from selfishness—a lesson which men of little merit have no desire to learn!

HEXAGRAM 41
SUN LOSS, REDUCTION[1]

Component trigrams:
Below: TUI, a body of water, pool, marsh, joy.
Above: KÊN, a mountain, hard, obstinate, perverse.

TEXT   Loss accompanied by confidence—sublime good fortune and no error! It is favourable to have in view some goal (or destination). If there is doubt as to what to use for the sacrifice, two small bowls will suffice.[2]

COMMENTARY ON THE TEXT   Loss is below, but gain is above[3] and the way leads upwards. What is said in the Text, including making use of two small bowls for the sacrifice, implies utilizing whatever lies to hand. There are times when it is meet to decrease the strong and augment the weak. Loss and gain, filling and emptying—each occurs at the proper time.

SYMBOL   This hexagram symbolizes a marshy lake at the foot of a mountain.[3] The Superior Man keeps his anger under control and is moderate in his desires.

The Lines

9 FOR THE BOTTOM PAGE   To hurry away when work is done is not wrong, but first consider whether such a hasty departure will harm the work.   COMMENTARY   Moreover, the approval of our superiors must first be obtained.

9 FOR THE SECOND PLACE   Persistence in a righteous course brings reward, but to advance (or go anywhere) now would bring misfortune. (This is) not (a time for) decreasing but (for) augmenting.   COMMENTARY   The central position of this line (in the lower trigram) indicates that persistence will be rewarded by the fulfilment of what is willed.

6 FOR THE THIRD PLACE   If three set forth together now, one will be lost on the way; whereas one man going forth alone will find company.   COMMENTARY   It is well to travel alone now, as three would give rise to suspicion.

6 FOR THE FOURTH PLACE   He reduced the number of ills besetting him and thus hastened the arrival of happiness—no error!   COMMENTARY   A reduction of troubles is in itself a cause for happiness.

6 FOR THE FIFTH PLACE   There was one who enriched him to the extent of ten PÊNG of tortoise shells[4] (2,100 of them) and who would accept no refusal—sublime good fortune!   COMMENTARY   Good fortune coming from those above.

9 FOR THE TOP PLACE   Gain which causes no loss to others involves no error. Persistence in a righteous course brings good fortune. It is favourable to have in view some goal (or destination). He obtains followers but not a family (or home).[5]   COMMENTARY   The first sentence presages the complete fulfilment of what is willed.

NOTES   (1) This is, on the whole, a favourable hexagram, in that loss now is timely—see the last sentence of the Commentary on the Text.   (2) See Commentary on the Text.   (3) A reference to the component trigrams. Tui, mountain, as something both solid and lofty, stands for gain, augmentation and so on.   (4) Tortoise shells were used for divination and must have been quite valuable, so 2,100 of them must have been equal to a small fortune.   (5) From the point of view of divination, this suggests that it is not a good time for marrying, founding a home, etc., but a very good one for hiring servants or employees, etc.

HEXAGRAM 42
I (pronounced YEE)   GAIN

Component trigrams:
Below: CHÊN, *thunder, movement, to sprout or quicken.*
Above: SUN, *wind, wood, bland, mild.*

TEXT   Gain. It is favourable to have in view some goal (or destination) and to cross the great river (or sea).[1]

I GAIN

COMMENTARY ON THE TEXT In this hexagram, loss is above and gain below.² The people's joy is boundless. When those above exhibit no pride to the ones below them, their virtue is brightly illumined. It is favourable to have an objective, for the route, being central and straight, leads to great blessings.³ What is said about crossing the great river means that (when you find) a wooden⁴ (causeway or boat) you may cross. Gain now proceeds actively and smoothly; each day unhindered progress can be made. Heaven bestows its gifts and earth brings forth its fruits; increase is occuring everywhere. However, each gainful activity must be undertaken at the proper time.

SYMBOL This hexagram symbolizes wind and thunder.⁵ The Superior Man, seeing what is good, imitates it; seeing what is bad, he corrects it.

The Lines

9 FOR THE BOTTOM PLACE The time is favourable for undertaking great works—sublime good fortune and no error! COMMENTARY What is said about sublime good fortune and freedom from error means that those below do not complain of having too much to do.⁶

6 FOR THE SECOND PLACE There was one who enriched him to the extent of ten PÊNG or tortoise shells (2,100 of them) and who would accept no refusal⁷—unwavering persistence in a righteous course brings good fortune! The King sacrificed to the Supreme Lord (of Heaven)⁸—good fortune! COMMENTARY The one who enriched him came from elsewhere.

6 FOR THE THIRD PLACE He used an unfortunate means to gain something; but, as he acted in all sincerity, he was not to blame. Walking up the centre (of the hall) to report to the Prince,⁹ he carried his jade tablet of office.¹⁰ COMMENTARY His gaining something by an unfortunate means (may lead to the supposition that such means are) a matter of course.

6 FOR THE FOURTH PLACE He walked up the centre (of the hall)⁹ and informed the Prince of his fealty.¹¹ It is favourable to be entrusted with the task of removing the capital.¹² COMMENTARY He reported his fealty so as to be of use in carrying out the Prince's will.¹³

9 FOR THE FIFTH PLACE   Be confident (or sincere) and kind, but refrain from asking questions and you will enjoy sublime good fortune. Faithfulness (or sincerity) and confidence are virtues proper to us.
COMMENTARY   The whole of this passage presages the fulfilment of what is willed.

9 FOR THE TOP PLACE   He did not (attempt to) benefit them and someone struck him for his inconstancy of heart—misfortune!
COMMENTARY   His not benefiting them indicates prejudice: his being struck presages (that we incur the wrath of) people outside our own circle.

NOTES   (1) To travel far.   (2) A reference to the component trigrams, perhaps implying that those above willingly deprive themselves in order that those below may benefit.   (3) 'Blessings' indicates unexpected good fortune.   (4) The text clearly indicates something wooden, but it is not clear what it is.   (5) Another reference to the component trigrams.   (6) This suggests that others will now work for us gladly.   (7) See Note 4 to the previous hexagram.   (8) From the point of view of divination, this can be taken to mean that we are about to benefit either from our earlier devotions or from some sacrifice either to moral principles or to the public good.   (9) This passage is suggested by the fact that line three is one of the two central lines, not of the component trigrams, but of the hexagram as a whole. The same applies to line four.   (10) The additional Chinese commentaries declared that the jade tablet is a symbol of our being able to give an assurance of our faithfulness.   (11) This implies convincing our superiors that we can be trusted.   (12) To be entrusted with a task that would never be given to men of mean ability or lacking in virtue.   (13) This implies that we should persuade our superiors of our fitness for some difficult task.

HEXAGRAM 43
KUAI   RESOLUTION

Component trigrams:
Below: CH'IEN, *heaven, active, male, etc.*
Above: TUI, *a body of water, pool, marsh, joy.*

TEXT   Resolution. When a proclamation is made at the court of the King, frankness in revealing the true state of affairs is dangerous.[1] In making announcements to the people of his own city, it is not fitting

KUAI RESOLUTION

for the ruler to carry arms.² It is favourable to have in view some goal (or destination).

COMMENTARY ON THE TEXT   Resolution implies determination. That is to say, the strong determine the affairs of the weak, combining strength with cheerfulness and resolution with peacefulness.³ The proclamation at the King's court is indicated by the single yielding line above five firm ones. The danger of speaking frankly is nevertheless a glorious danger. Bearing arms while making announcements to the people of his own city would forfeit their respect. Its being favourable to have an objective is indicated by the fact that the firm, after prospering exceedingly (there are five firm lines) comes to an end at the top.

SYMBOL   This hexagram symbolizes a marshy lake being drawn (sucked) towards the sky.³ The Superior Man distributes his emoluments to those below; dwelling in virtue, he renounces them.

The Lines

9 FOR THE BOTTOM PLACE   To set out with a great show of strength, advance, but win no success is shameful.⁴ COMMENTARY This illustrates the shame involved in taking on something and then failing.

9 FOR THE SECOND PLACE   Though disturbed by cries in the night, he who is armed knows no fear.⁵ COMMENTARY   Being armed and fearless is indicated by the central position of this line.

9 FOR THE THIRD PLACE   Strength in the cheekbones⁶—misfortune! The Superior Man is firmly determined; but if, while walking alone in the rain, he is irked by the mud, he is not to be blamed for that.⁷ COMMENTARY   The resolutely determined Superior Man is blameless to the end.

9 FOR THE FOURTH PLACE   His haunches have been flayed and he walks falteringly, though he could put an end to this shame by allowing himself to be dragged along like a sheep.⁸ Moreover, he puts no faith in the words of others. COMMENTARY   Walking falteringly (or hesitatingly) is indicated by the unsuitable position of this line. Having no faith in the words of others shows lack of intelligence.

9 FOR THE FIFTH PLACE With the tenacity of spinach clinging to the earth,⁹ he blamelessly steers a middle course. COMMENTARY Yes, blamelessly but not brilliantly!¹⁰

6 FOR THE TOP PLACE In the end, misfortune will come without warning. COMMENTARY This unheralded misfortune will be due to our failure to persist to the end.

NOTES (1) In vital matters, frankness may prove dangerous. (2) It is better to repose trust in our own people. (3) A reference to the component trigrams. (4) That is, we should not voluntarily and somewhat boastfully take on a difficult task, unless we are sure of success. (5) It is well to be forearmed. (6) Making a parade of our strength. (7) Nothing must deflect us, but a little grumbling at unpleasantness is in order. (8) Having recently suffered, we advance with hesitation and are unwilling to accept useful but rather humiliating assistance. (9) That is, weak but determined. (10) In this situation, we can do well enough, but not very well.

HEXAGRAM 44
KOU CONTACT (SEXUAL INTERCOURSE, MEETING, ETC.)

Component trigrams:
Below: SUN, wind, wood, bland, mild.
Above: CH'IEN, heaven, active, male, etc.

TEXT Contact. Women wield the power. Do not marry.¹

COMMENTARY ON THE TEXT In this hexagram, the yielding encounters the firm. A marriage made now would not endure for long. From the intercourse of heaven and earth, all things have their being. When strength is controlled and rightly used, everything in the world goes well. The timely application of this hexagram is of vast importance.

SYMBOL This hexagram symbolizes wind blowing across the face of the earth.² When the ruler issues commands, he has them proclaimed in every corner of the world.

KOU CONTACT

The Lines

6 FOR THE BOTTOM PLACE   The chariot wheel is held with a metal brake. Persistence in a righteous course brings good fortune. Those with a goal (or destination) in view will witness misfortune. However, even a lean pig is able to wiggle its trotters.[3]   COMMENTARY   The first sentence implies that the weak have to be dragged.

9 FOR THE SECOND PLACE   There is fish in the bag—no error! But it is of no advantage to the guests.[4]   COMMENTARY   This implies that we are not dutiful to our guests.

9 FOR THE THIRD PLACE   His haunches have been flayed and he walks totteringly—trouble, but no great error!   COMMENTARY   His walking totteringly implies being able to walk without being dragged.[5]

9 FOR THE FOURTH PLACE   No fish in the bag—this gives rise to misfortune.   COMMENTARY   Misfortune in the sense of being remote from the people.

9 FOR THE FIFTH PLACE   The medlar leaves wrapping the melon hide its beauty.[6] Something falls from heaven.   COMMENTARY   This line denotes beauty, for it is central and suitably placed. Something falling from heaven means that what is willed is consonant with heaven's decrees.

9 FOR THE SIXTH PLACE   It rubs against things with its horns—regret, but no error![7]   COMMENTARY   Regret owing to the complete exhaustion of our powers.

NOTES   (1) At this time marriage would be unfortunate; the husband would almost surely be henpecked.   (2) A reference to the component trigrams; the Chinese text actually says: 'there is wind below heaven'—heaven being the upper trigram.   (3) This whole passage suggests that we find ourselves weak or hampered in some way, but that persistence will enable us to emerge from the difficulty. Close to our goal (or destination), we shall witness (but not necessarily suffer) misfortune. Despite the weakness of our present position, we shall manage to progress if we take sufficient pains.   (4) There is a danger that we shall fail to share an advantage with people who have a right to expect a share.   (5) Despite rather severe trouble, for which we are not much to blame, we shall manage to get along somehow.   (6) This is more or less equivalent to hiding our light under a bushel.   (7) We shall regret our inability to progress, even though we are not at fault.

HEXAGRAM 45
TS'UI GATHERING TOGETHER, ASSEMBLING

Component trigrams:
Below: K'UN, *earth, female, passive, etc.*
Above: TUI, *a body of water, pool, marsh, joy.*

TEXT   Gathering Together—success! The King approaches the temple. It is advisable to see a great man, which will ensure success. Persistence in a righteous course brings reward. Great sacrifices are offered[1]—good fortune! It is favourable to have in view a goal (or destination).

COMMENTARY ON THE TEXT   This hexagram implies assembling. Willing acceptance is conjoined with joy.[2] A firm line (the fifth) occupies the central position (in the upper trigram) and wins response from the other lines—hence the implication of assembling. The King approached the temple in order to fulfil his filial duties and devote himself to (public) prosperity.[3] That it is advisable to see a great man and that persistence will be rewarded both imply assembling together for the purpose of putting things right. The last two sentences of the Text imply that (our actions will) accord with the will of heaven.[4] By observing what each gathers to itself, it is possible to understand the inner nature of all things in heaven and earth.

SYMBOL   This hexagram symbolizes a marshy lake rising above the earth.[5] The Superior Man gathers together his weapons in order to provide against the unforeseen.[6]

The Lines

6 FOR THE BOTTOM PLACE   When sincerity (or confidence) does not remain until the last, dispersal and assembling will alternate. There was a cry, but one (reassuring) clasp of the hand made him ready to

TS'UI GATHERING TOGETHER, ASSEMBLING

laugh[7]—no cause for anxiety. Advancing now will entail no error. COMMENTARY Alternating dispersal and assembly betoken indecision.

6 FOR THE SECOND PLACE Being drawn into something brings good fortune and no error is involved. Be confident and win advantage from making a sacrifice. COMMENTARY The first sentence is indicated by the constant nature of this line, which is central (to the lower trigram).

6 FOR THE THIRD PLACE A mournful gathering it would seem. There is no objective which would be favourable; yet to advance would involve no error, only slight regret.[8] COMMENTARY Advancing entails no error for what lies beyond (literally, 'above') is gentle.

9 FOR THE FOURTH PLACE Great good fortune and no error! COMMENTARY Because the line, though a firm one, is not in the ruling position.

9 FOR THE FIFTH PLACE On account of his high position, he gathers people together—no error! Yet he cannot secure the confidence of the people; therefore, he should exalt his virtue and prolong his persistence, so that he need no longer feel regret.[9] COMMENTARY It is only on account of his high position that he is able to assemble the people; his will is not strong enough (to achieve remarkable results from this).

6 FOR THE TOP PLACE Sighs and lamentations, but no error.[10] COMMENTARY For this top line presages distress.

NOTES (1) These were religious sacrifices, but they may be taken to mean that the time has come for us to make important sacrifices of another sort. (2) A reference to the component trigrams. (3) This suggests propitious circumstances for us. (4) So we need not hesitate to advance. (5) Another reference to the component trigrams. (6) This is a time when foresight is required of us, too. (7) Perhaps we shall experience an unnecessary fright. (8) Obviously we had better not advance now, unless our reasons for doing so are so important that we are willing to suffer a certain amount of regret. (9) All this is said of a minister; applied to ourselves, it suggests that we need people's confidence now and should strive hard to deserve it. (10) We shall be afflicted by distress, but through no fault of our own.

HEXAGRAM 46
SHÊNG   ASCENDING, PROMOTION

Component trigrams:
Below: SUN, *wind, wood, bland, mild.*
Above: K'UN, *earth, female, passive, etc.*

TEXT   Ascending. Supreme success! It is essential to see a great man, so as to banish anxiety. Progressing towards the south brings good fortune.

COMMENTARY ON THE TEXT   At the proper time, the weak ascend.[1] Gentleness and willing acceptance are conjoined.[2] A firm line is central (to the lower trigram) and wins response; hence great success is foretold. What is said about the freedom from anxiety to be gained from visiting a great man indicates that in this way blessings[3] will be attained. Going south brings good fortune in the sense that it will lead to the fulfilment of what is willed.

SYMBOL   This hexagram symbolizes trees growing upwards from the earth.[2] The Superior Man most willingly accords with virtuous ways; starting from small things, he accumulates a great heap (of merit).

The Lines

6 FOR THE BOTTOM PLACE   Certainty of promotion—great good fortune!   COMMENTARY   This is because the will of our superiors accords with our own.

9 FOR THE SECOND PLACE   Full of faith, he performed the summer sacrifice.[4]   COMMENTARY   The faith (or confidence) indicated by this line leads to great happiness.

9 FOR THE THIRD PLACE   He was promoted (to office) in a larger

CITY. COMMENTARY This line indicates that we cause no doubts (to arise in the minds of others).

6 FOR THE FOURTH PLACE The King sacrificed on Mount Chi—good fortune and no error!⁴ COMMENTARY This indicates our willing compliance (with duty, tradition, circumstances, etc.)

6 FOR THE FIFTH PLACE Righteous persistence brings good fortune, but the ascent must be made step by step.⁵ COMMENTARY Acting thus will lead to the fulfilment of what we will.

6 FOR THE TOP PLACE A night ascent—advantage lies in unremitting persistence. COMMENTARY But the night ascent will lead to loss, not to wealth.⁶

NOTES (1) Though our present position may be far from strong, attention to timing will assure us of success. (2) A reference to the component lines. (3) Unexpected or apparently unearned good fortune. (4) This suggests that faith in spiritual matters or ancient traditions will serve us well. (5) This is no time for rushing forward, but for patient plodding. (6) Taking the text and commentary of this line together, we may assume that righteous persistence will win some advantage for us as a result of rather blind progress, even though we are bound to suffer materially.

HEXAGRAM 47
K'UN   ADVERSITY, WEARINESS

Component trigrams:
Below: K'AN, *water, a pit.*
Above: TUI, *a body of water, pool, marsh, joy.*

TEXT Adversity leading to success thanks to persistence in a righteous course; good fortune for the truly great¹ and freedom from error! Though words be spoken, they will not inspire confidence.

COMMENTARY ON THE TEXT The adversity is caused by something which lies hidden. Danger and joy are conjoined.² He who attains success in spite of difficulty is indeed a Superior Man (and thus one of the truly great). That righteous persistence will bring good fortune to such a man is indicated by the firm line in the middle (of the upper trigram). Since what is said will not be believed, it would be a waste of effort to talk.

SYMBOL   This hexagram symbolizes a marsh in which no water (appears).[3] The Superior Man risks his life to carry out his will.

The Lines

6 FOR THE BOTTOM PLACE   With dried branches entangling the lower part of his body, he enters a gloomy valley. For three years he encounters no one.[4]   COMMENTARY   What is said about entering a gloomy valley indicates darkness that will not be dispelled.

9 FOR THE SECOND PLACE   Difficulties arise through indulgence in food and drink. A vermilion sash-wearer (man of very high rank) appears; it is advisable to utilize this opportunity to offer sacrifice.[5] Advancing brings misfortune, though no error is involved.   COMMENTARY   Part of this passage indicates that the difficulties arising from our gluttony may nevertheless be productive of blessings.

6 FOR THE THIRD PLACE   Faced by rock-like difficulties and (with naught) to lean upon (but) thistles and briars, he entered his dwelling but could not find his wife—misfortune![6]   COMMENTARY   His leaning upon thistles and briars is indicated by the firm line just below this one. His not finding his wife symbolizes bad luck.

9 FOR THE FOURTH PLACE   A slow arrival. Trouble in a golden carriage.[7] Shame, but not for long.   COMMENTARY   The tardy arrival implies that our will-power is at a low ebb. However, though the line is not suitably placed, it does not stand alone.[8]

9 FOR THE FIFTH PLACE   His nose and feet are chopped off owing to difficulties with a vermilion sash-wearer (man of high rank), but joy may come in time. It is advisable to offer sacrifice.[9]   COMMENTARY   His injuries signify that what we will now will not come to pass. That joy may come in time is suggested by the correct position of this line in the centre (of the upper trigram). It is advisable to offer sacrifice in order to ensure this good fortune.

K'UN ADVERSITY, WEARINESS

6 FOR THE TOP PLACE Entangled with creepers and tottering uneasily, he voices regret for his actions. Provided regret is felt, to advance will bring good fortune.[10] COMMENTARY The entangling creepers are indicated by the unsuitable position of this line. When our actions have been regrettable, feeling regret is a means to obtain good fortune.

NOTES (1) Here, as so often in the *Book of Change*, 'great' refers to high moral qualities. This hexagram is of evil omen for most people, but success can be won through tremendous persistence in doing what is right. (2) A reference to the component trigrams. (3) Usually the symbology can be understood very easily from the meanings attached to the component trigrams. This case is a little more difficult. Tui means a marsh; K'an, a pit. Presumably, the water of the marsh has been sucked into the pit or pits lying below; hence its dryness. (4) Whoever receives this line must resign himself to failure. (5) An imaginative reconstruction of the story lying behind this passage is that a man wasting the last of his substance in riotous living receives at his table an important guest and, by making a sacrifice to him or through his good offices, dispels his misfortune. If we are suffering owing to our own extravagance, the time has come to emulate the hero of this tale. (6) This line may be taken to presage insuperable difficulties; the word 'wife' does not necessarily have any special application to our case, as can be seen from the commentary on the line. (7) Trouble in a golden carriage coupled with shame suggests that we get into difficulty through our presumption, or through placing too much confidence in someone of much higher station than ourselves. (8) At least we may hope for a little aid from others. (9) It is very sure that we shall have to suffer bitterly. The joy to come is less certain, but may be assured by our making a suitable sacrifice. (10) We shall certainly suffer, but sincere regret will stand us in good stead.

HEXAGRAM 48
CHING   A WELL

Component trigrams:
Below: SUN, *wind, wood, bland, mild.*
Above: K'AN, *water, a pit.*

TEXT   A Well. A city may be moved, but not a well.[1] A well suffers from no decrease and no increase; but often, when the people come to draw water there, the rope is too short or the pitcher gets broken before reaching the water[2]—misfortune!

COMMENTARY ON THE TEXT   Where (the pitchers are put) into the water to draw it up—such is a well. That a well gives nourishment without suffering depletion and that a city may be moved, but not a well, are both implied by the firm line in the centre (of the upper trigram). The rope's being too short indicates failure to achieve results; the breaking of the pitcher presages a positive misfortune.

SYMBOL   This hexagram symbolizes water over wood.[3] The Superior Man encourages the people with advice and assistance.

The Lines

6 FOR THE BOTTOM PLACE   The muddy water at the well bottom is undrinkable; an old well attracts no animals. COMMENTARY   The first clause signifies that our affairs take a downward trend; the second, that it is time to give up.

9 FOR THE SECOND PLACE   Perch dart from the water in the well hole; the pitcher is worn out and leaks.[4] COMMENTARY   This is indicated by the failure of this line to win response (from the other lines).

9 FOR THE THIRD PLACE   The well has been cleaned out; to my heart's sorrow, no one drinks from it, though it could well be used to supply drinking water.[5] The King is wise and it is possible for the people to share his good fortune.[5] COMMENTARY   The first sentence implies activities which call forth pity; the second, that we should accept our good fortune.

6 FOR THE FOURTH PLACE   The well is being tiled—no error! COMMENTARY   For it is under repair.[6]

9 FOR THE FIFTH PLACE   The well is cool; its water tastes like water from an icy spring.[7] COMMENTARY   This is indicated by the suitable position of this line, which is central (to the upper trigram).

6 FOR THE TOP PLACE   The well-rope lies unconcealed—confidence and supreme good fortune! COMMENTARY   The supreme good fortune presaged here is in the nature of a great achievement.

CHING A WELL

NOTES (1) The building of a city depends upon ourselves; but wells cannot be moved to places where nature supplies no water. The implication is that our activities are limited by natural conditions. (2) What we desire is there for the taking, but we may not succeed in getting it. (3) A reference to the component trigrams. Wood may signify the bottom of a bucket or the wooden lining of an ancient well. (4) We are doubly unfortunate in that natural conditions (signified by fish in the water) and our own ineptitude or misfortune combine to ensure our failure. (5) If we fail now, it is not for lack of opportunity but because we do not make use of opportunity. (6) We are likely to suffer a necessary delay, but the situation is hopeful. (7) All goes well with us.

HEXAGRAM 49
KÔ REVOLUTION[1], LEATHER, SKIN

Component trigrams:
Below: LI, *fire, brilliance, beauty.*
Above: TUI, *a body of water, pool, marsh, joy.*

TEXT Revolution. Not before the day of its completion will men have faith in it—sublime success! Determination in a righteous course brings reward; regret vanishes!

COMMENTARY ON THE TEXT In this hexagram, water and fire extinguish each other,[2] behaving like two women who live together but whose wills conflict—such is the nature of revolution. That faith is not reposed in it until the day of its completion means that revolution must come first, whereafter public faith in it will be established. A civilized and enlightened attitude brings joy; great success makes it possible to put all things to rights. Upon the achievement of a necessary [or proper] revolution, regret vanishes. The renovating activities of the celestial and terrestrial forces produce the progress of the four seasons. T'ang and Wu[3] rebelled in accordance with Heaven ('s decree) and the people responded to them. The timely application of this hexagram is of vast importance.

SYMBOL This hexagram symbolizes fire rising from a marshy lake.[2] The Superior Man regulates the calendar and thus ensures that men are clear about times and seasons.

The Lines

9 FOR THE BOTTOM PLACE   For strength, use yellow oxhide. COMMENTARY   (Such aids to strength are necessary, for) this line cannot suit itself to its position.[4]

6 FOR THE SECOND PLACE   On the day the revolution is completed, to advance brings good fortune and is free from error.[5] COMMENTARY   This line presages great blessings.[6]

9 FOR THE THIRD PLACE   To advance now would bring misfortune and persistence would lead to (further) troubles. When talk of revolution has thrice arisen, then act with confidence.[7] COMMENTARY   What else could we do (under the circumstances)?

9 FOR THE FOURTH PLACE   Regret vanishes and confidence is established. A change of government brings good fortune.[8] COMMENTARY   Good fortune in the sense that people will put their faith in our objectives.

9 FOR THE FIFTH PLACE   The great man accomplishes the change like a tiger;[9] he is so confident that he does not need to employ divination. COMMENTARY   His accomplishing the change 'like a tiger' means in a brilliantly civilized manner.

6 FOR THE TOP PLACE   The Superior Man brings about the change like a leopard[9] and lesser men promptly switch their allegiance. To advance now brings misfortune. Righteous persistence brings good fortune to those who remain where they are. COMMENTARY   The Superior Man brings about the change 'like a leopard' means that he does so in a manner that is exceedingly graceful. That lesser men promptly switch their allegiance means that they readily accept his lead.

NOTES   (1) Very often, this means renovation, as of character, etc. But it may also mean exactly what it says; Confucius, though he regarded loyalty to the ruler as one of the highest virtues, recognized that evil men forfeit their right to rule by their excesses, and it is probable that this notion antedates him by many centuries.   (2) A reference to the component trigrams.   (3) Two greatly admired historical figures.   (4) We cannot adapt ourselves to the present situation; we must increase our strength so as to be able to combat it.   (5) We must not advance further until certain major changes have been completed.   (6) Unexpected good fortune.   (7) We must make very sure that a rumoured change will occur before we take further action.   (8) Taken out of its political context, this may presage a great change in some other walk of life.   (9) 'Like a tiger' and 'like a leopard' do not have any connotation of fierceness. The striped skin of the former and the spotted hide of the latter symbolize brilliance and beauty respectively.

HEXAGRAM 50
TING A SACRIFICIAL VESSEL

Component trigrams:
Below: SUN, wind, wood, bland, mild.
Above: LI, fire, brilliance, beauty.

TEXT   A Sacrificial Vessel—supreme success!

COMMENTARY ON THE TEXT   The TING is symbolical (of the peace and beauty presaged by the combination of the two component trigrams). Wood and fire combine to cook (the sacrifice).[1] The holy sage cooks in performing sacrificial ceremonies to the Supreme Lord (of Heaven); he cooks more lavishly to nourish the holy and the virtuous.[2] By their peaceful employment, eyesight and hearing are sharpened. The yielding enters and ascends (to the fifth place) where it responds to the firm—hence supreme success.

SYMBOL   This hexagram symbolizes fire upon wood.[1] The Superior Man, taking his stance as righteousness requires, adheres firmly to heaven's decrees.

The Lines

6 FOR THE BOTTOM PLACE   To rid it of decaying remnants of meat, the vessel is turned upside down.[3] It is not shameful to take a concubine for the sake of bearing sons.[4]   COMMENTARY   There is nothing improper about up-ending a sacrificial vessel to rid it of decaying matter. Such actions are necessary in the pursuit of what is noble.

9 FOR THE SECOND PLACE   The TING possesses solidity. My enemies are in difficulty and there is nothing they can do to me—good fortune!   COMMENTARY   The first sentence indicates a need for caution. 'My enemies are in trouble' indicates that I shall remain blameless to the end.

9 FOR THE THIRD PLACE The handles of the TING have been detached, so it is difficult to move it.⁵ The fat of the pheasant is not eaten.⁶ Suddenly rain comes, regret wanes and, ultimately, there is good fortune. COMMENTARY What is said about the handles of the TING implies our failure in carrying out our duty.

9 FOR THE FOURTH PLACE The legs of the TING snap. The prince's food is overturned and his person soiled—misfortune.⁸ COMMENTARY The prince's food is overturned—how is it possible to continue enjoying his confidence?

6 FOR THE FIFTH PLACE The TING has yellow handles with golden rings attached⁹—righteous persistence brings reward! COMMENTARY What is said here about the TING is indicated by the central position of this line (in the upper trigram) which implies solid worth.

9 FOR THE TOP PLACE The TING has jade handles¹⁰—great good fortune! Everything is now favourable. COMMENTARY The first part of the passage is indicated by this top line—a firm line which meets the yielding (fifth) harmoniously.

NOTES (1) A reference to the component trigrams, indicating that our duties are (or should be) carried out gently and gracefully. (2) It is proper to fulfil our religious (and or formal) obligations, but we should expend far more money and energy on our duties towards our fellow man than upon ceremonies. (3) Some actions, though highly improper in themselves, may be properly performed if circumstances so require; a merely ritualistic conception of right and wrong is not desirable. (4) This is added as an example, immediately acceptable to a traditionally minded Chinese of something improper in itself which becomes proper when the motive is acceptable. (5) A delay due to some remissness on our part. (6) Because of our remissness an opportunity goes to waste. (7) An omen of good fortune, of Heaven's nourishing powers. (8) Through gross carelessness an opportunity to advance our interests is not only lost but transformed into an occasion of trouble. (9) The faults described in the last two notes have now been put right; the position is even better than before they were committed. (10) A further improvement on the progress indicated in the preceding note.

CHÊN THUNDER 185

HEXAGRAM 51
CHÊN THUNDER[1]

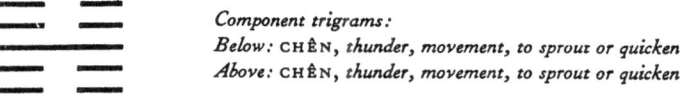

Component trigrams:
Below: CHÊN, *thunder, movement, to sprout or quicken.*
Above: CHÊN, *thunder, movement, to sprout or quicken.*

TEXT Thunder—success! Thunder comes with a terrible noise, laughing and shouting in awesome glee and frightening people for a hundred miles around. The sacrificial wine is not spilt.[2]

COMMENTARY ON THE TEXT Thunder indicates success; its terrible roar is frightening, but this leads to happiness.[3] It laughs and shouts in fearful glee, yet afterwards everything is in order. It frightens people for a hundred miles round, startling those afar and terrifying those close at hand. That the sacrificial wine is not spilt indicates that someone now appears who is capable of guarding the temple of the ancestors and the shrines of the harvest gods, one qualified to be the leader of the sacrifices.[4]

SYMBOL This hexagram symbolizes continuous thunder. The Superior Man in fear and trembling seeks to improve himself.

The Lines

9 FOR THE BOTTOM PLACE Thunder comes with a mighty roar which changes to noisy glee—good fortune! COMMENTARY Its frightening roar causes fear which leads to happiness;[3] its noisy glee is followed by good order.

6 FOR THE SECOND PLACE Thunder approaches—trouble is at hand! Sadly he lets go of his valuables and (fleeing) sets foot among the nine hills.[5] He should not search for them; in seven days he will regain them. COMMENTARY That the approach of thunder presages trouble is indicated by the position of this yielding line over a firm one.

6 FOR THE THIRD PLACE   Thunderous impetuosity—to emulate it at this time will not give rise to harm.[6]   COMMENTARY   Thunderous impetuosity is indicated by the unsuitable position of this line.

9 FOR THE FOURTH PLACE   After the thunderstorm, the paths are muddy.   COMMENTARY   This implies muddled thinking.

6 FOR THE FIFTH PLACE   Thunder comes and goes alternately—trouble is at hand! Careful thought will avert loss, but there are affairs needing attention.   COMMENTARY   The first sentence implies that danger threatens our activities. That affairs need our attention is indicated by this central line (of the upper trigram). There will be no important losses.

6 FOR THE TOP PLACE   Thunder brings disorder and people stare about them in terror. Advancing at this time brings misfortune. The thunder affects not ourselves but our neighbours—no error.[7] A marriage causes gossip.   COMMENTARY   That thunder brings disorder is indicated by the failure of the middle line (of the upper trigram) to win (supremacy over this top line). Although misfortune arises, we are not to blame. Fear of our neighbours makes us cautious.

NOTES   (1) This hexagram, like the trigrams of which it is composed, symbolizes not just thunder, but the powerful natural forces which lead to the growth and fruition of everything. Such forces, though terrifying in their manifestations, are beneficial in their results—except when their activity is untimely.   (2) This suggests that the holder of sacrificial vessel is not easily alarmed, or else that he is very wise and able to distinguish between the apparently dangerous and the really dangerous.   (3) Fear is often a good mentor; by causing us to change our ways, it leads to happiness.   (4) The ancient Chinese took these matters seriously. In modern parlance, we should say that someone appears who is capable of looking after and protecting those principles and objects which excite our deepest reverence.   (5) The Chinese additional commentaries in my possession explain how 'the nine hills' is derived from the form of the hexagram, but they do not explain the symbolical significance of this phrase.   (6) The Superior Man usually acts calmly and carefully, but there are times when impetuosity serves a good purpose or, at the very least, does no particular harm.   (7) We are not to blame for the trouble afflicting them; but, as the commentary on this line indicates, they may think we are to blame and plan reprisals.

HEXAGRAM 52
KÊN DESISTING, STILLING[1]

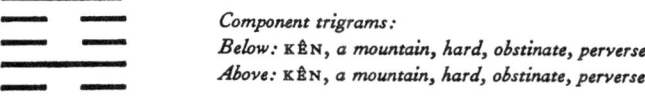

Component trigrams:
Below: KÊN, *a mountain, hard, obstinate, perverse.*
Above: KÊN, *a mountain, hard, obstinate, perverse.*

TEXT   Keeping the back so still as to seem virtually bodiless, or walking in the courtyard without noticing the people there involves no error![2]

COMMENTARY ON THE TEXT   Desisting means coming to a stop. When it is time to stop, then stop; when the time comes for action, then act! By choosing activity and stillness, each at the proper time, a man achieves glorious progress. The stillness imaged by this hexagram means stillness in its proper place. The upper and lower trigrams, being mutually opposed, do not go well together; hence the wording of the Text.

SYMBOL   This hexagram symbolizes two mountains conjoined.[3] The Superior Man takes thought in order to avoid having to move from his position.

The Lines

6 FOR THE BOTTOM PLACE   Stilling the toes[4]—no error. Unwavering persistence in a righteous course brings advantage.   COMMENTARY   This passage is implied by the position of this line, which is not out of order.

6 FOR THE SECOND PLACE   Stilling the calves.[5] His heart is sad because he is unable to save his followers.   COMMENTARY   He cannot save them because he failed to retire and wait.

9 FOR THE THIRD PLACE   Stilling the loins and stiffening the spine

—his heart is suffocated by trouble.⁶ COMMENTARY If the loins are stilled, there is a danger that the heart will suffocate.

6 FOR THE FOURTH PLACE Stilling the body⁷—no error! COMMENTARY Stilling the body means stilling the whole self.

6 FOR THE FIFTH PLACE Stilling the jaws. Since his words are well ordered, he ceases to have (cause for) regret. COMMENTARY This is indicated by the suitable position of this line, which is central (to the upper trigram).

9 FOR THE TOP PLACE The highest form of stillness—good fortune! COMMENTARY He achieves this in order to win greater benefit in the end.

NOTES (1) The prime Taoist concept that very often the best form of action is to refrain from action appears to antedate the founder of Taoism, for Lao-tzû was a contemporary of Confucius who regarded the *Book of Change* as an exceedingly ancient work. All that is said in connection with this hexagram points to the advantage of stillness when circumstances so dictate. (2) I am tempted to agree with Dr Wilhelm's suggestion that this may refer to the practice of meditation, that inward turning of the mind, which plays such a vital part in the eastern religions. The back is kept straight, but not stiff, and the mind seeks to attain a state that is above both sensory perception and conceptual thought —a state of voidness. (3) A reference to the component trigrams, whose combination suggests a rock-like stillness. (4) This suggests the simplest kind of stillness, namely staying where we are. (5) Perhaps the implication is that the mind's injunction to be still reached the calves but was delayed there, so that the feet continued moving until it was too late. In other words, we are too late in deciding to stay where we are, although circumstances make this most desirable. (6) I should have found this difficult to interpret, were it not for the guidance given in the commentary on the following line about 'the whole self'. Elsewhere in the *Book of Change*, it is made clear that the loins sometimes symbolize sexual desire. To force oneself to continence when the mind is not ready for it is exceedingly dangerous and may lead to mental and emotional disarrangement. What is required is a stilling of the WHOLE self, a cessation of desire itself. (7) See note six.

HEXAGRAM 53
CHIEN GRADUAL PROGRESS

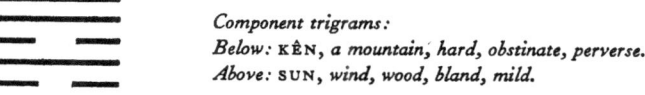

Component trigrams:
Below: KÊN, *a mountain, hard, obstinate, perverse.*
Above: SUN, *wind, wood, bland, mild.*

TEXT Gradual Progress. The marriage of a maiden brings good fortune. Persistence in a righteous course brings reward.

COMMENTARY ON THE TEXT This hexagram signifies a gradual advance and good fortune for maidens who marry now. Progress made now leads to a commanding position,[1] hence this advance achieves concrete results. By making progress in righteousness, a man becomes capable of ruling the country. (Such a man is symbolized by the ruling fifth line) which is firm and central (to the upper trigram). From the conjoining of stubbornness and gentleness[2] inexhaustible activity arises.

SYMBOL This hexagram symbolizes a tree upon a mountain.[2] The Superior Man, abiding in holiness and virtue, inclines the people towards goodness.

The Lines

6 FOR THE BOTTOM PLACE The wild goose[3] moves gradually towards the river bank. The younger son is in trouble. There is talk, but no error. COMMENTARY 'The younger son is in trouble' is just a way of saying that there is trouble for which we are not to blame.

6 FOR THE SECOND PLACE The wild goose[3] moves gradually towards the rock. Eating and drinking happily—good fortune! COMMENTARY Good fortune in the form of delicate and plentiful food.

9 FOR THE THIRD PLACE   The wild goose³ moves gradually towards the dry land. The husband goes forth and does not return. The wife is pregnant, but the child's birth is delayed—misfortune! This is an auspicious time for chastizing evil-doers.   COMMENTARY   The husband's failure to return symbolizes separation from our normal companions. The delayed childbirth symbolizes our going astray. The final sentence indicates willingness to take precautions for mutual protection.

6 FOR THE FOURTH PLACE   The wild goose³ moves gradually towards a tree and may find a suitable branch (on which to perch)—no error!   COMMENTARY   Its finding a suitable branch augurs willing acceptance and gentleness.

9 FOR THE FIFTH PLACE   The wild goose³ moves gradually towards the hillock. In the end, the results will be incomparable—good fortune!   COMMENTARY   Good fortune in the form of complete fulfilment of our desires.

9 FOR THE TOP PLACE   The wild goose³ moves gradually towards the mainland. Its feathers can be used for ritual purposes—good fortune!   COMMENTARY   The sentence about the feathers indicates that now disorder cannot prevail.⁴

NOTES   (1) A reference to the fifth or ruling line.   (2) A reference to the component trigrams.   (3) The additional Chinese commentaries explain that the wild goose is a bird which moves towards the sun. Now, a commonly used Chinese term for the sun is YANG, namely the male principle. So the bird obviously betokens a maiden seeking a husband. Its movement from river bank to rock, dry land, a tree, a hillock and the mainland (which is said in one commentary to mean peninsula) signifies gradual movement in an unchanging direction. From the point of view of divination, this is the best course for us, even if marriage is not our objective. Regarding marriage: the first line betokens gossip, although the marriage is not unsuitable; the second, a materially successful marriage; the third, an unfortunate marriage; the fourth, marriage to someone exceedingly kind and thoughtful; the fifth, a blissful marriage; the six, marriage to a public figure who bears some reasponsibility for good order within the realm and who succeeds in his task.   (4) The traditional Chinese conception of good government, good order within the family and so on, allots an important role to ritual because of its efficacy in making people inclined to regard their duties with solemnity and because it helps to make everything seem orderly.

HEXAGRAM 54
KUEI MEI THE MARRIAGEABLE MAIDEN[1]

Component trigrams:
Below: TUI, *a body of water, pool, marsh, joy.*
Above: CHÊN, *thunder, movement, to sprout or quicken.*

TEXT The Marriageable Maiden. Advance brings misfortune. No goal (or destination) is now favourable.

COMMENTARY ON THE TEXT This hexagram symbolizes a great principle of heaven and earth; for, if they had no intercourse, none of the myriad objects would come into existence. The Marriageable Maiden also signifies man's end and man's beginning.[2] Joy and movement conjoined[3]—such is a maiden's marrying. That going forward brings misfortune is indicated by the unsuitable position (of the third and fourth lines). That no goal is now favourable is indicated by the fact that yielding lines surmount the firm ones.

SYMBOL This hexagram symbolizes thunder over a pool.[3] The Superior Man knows that, to achieve an enduring end, he must be aware of his mistakes at the beginning.

The Lines

9 FOR THE BOTTOM PLACE The maiden marries and becomes a concubine. The lame can walk—to advance brings good fortune![4]
COMMENTARY What is described in the first sentence was due to her constancy; the second sentence presages mutual support.

9 FOR THE SECOND PLACE The one-eyed man can see. Righteous persistence brings advantage to the recluse.[5] COMMENTARY The second sentence indicates that, as yet, no change occurs in the ordinary course of events.

6 FOR THE THIRD PLACE   From being a servant, the marriageable maiden becomes a concubine.[6]   COMMENTARY   Her former state is indicated by the unsuitable position of this line.

9 FOR THE FOURTH PLACE   The maiden stays unwed beyond the proper time, but the day comes when she makes a late marriage.   COMMENTARY   Her firm desire to postpone her marriage indicates that we should wait before taking action.

6 FOR THE FIFTH PLACE   The Emperor's second marriageable daughter wore regal garments less splendid than those of her bridesmaid.[7] Close upon the full moon comes good fortune!   COMMENTARY   The first sentence means that, though we may be of only middle rank, we should behave with true nobility.

6 FOR THE TOP PLACE   A woman holds a basket with nothing inside; a man stabs a sheep without drawing blood. No goal (or destination) is favourable now.   COMMENTARY   This top line implies absence of solid worth, hence the symbol of holding an empty basket.

NOTES   (1) This hexagram is, on the whole, a most unfortunate omen. Wherever the moving lines do indicate a degree of success, it is usually qualified and not much to be desired. According to the family arrangement of trigrams, the lower trigram stands for the youngest daughter and the upper trigram for the eldest son. Because not much good fortune is signified, the hexagram is named after the former, rather than the latter. We must not suppose that it deals only with marriage. What is said about the maiden symbolizes in some way or other what we may expect for ourselves within the context of our enquiry.   (2) For it is she who gives birth to the new generation before the present one reaches its end.   (3) A reference to the component trigrams.   (4) Some advance is indicated, but not a very splendid one. To become a concubine is doubtless better than remaining single; to walk with a limp is better than not walking at all—neither is greatly to be desired.   (5) It is not unusual for a one-eyed man to see, more or less, or for a recluse to benefit from persistence in his meditations and devotions; neither of them symbolizes anything at all remarkable.   (6) Again, a small advance is made, but nothing very satisfying is won.   (7) The implication is that the princess showed better taste than her maid in not dressing too grandly. We must be on our guard against ostentation.

FÊNG ABUNDANCE

HEXAGRAM 55
FÊNG ABUNDANCE[1]

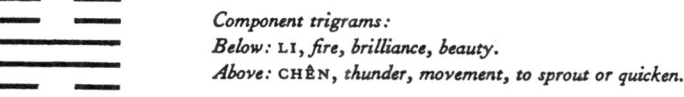

Component trigrams:
Below: LI, *fire, brilliance, beauty.*
Above: CHÊN, *thunder, movement, to sprout or quicken.*

TEXT   Abundance—success! The King inspires them.[2] Do not be sad; it is fitting (to be like) the sun at its zenith.

COMMENTARY ON THE TEXT   This hexagram signifies great quantity. Brilliance is conjoined with movement[3]—hence abundance. That the King inspires his people signifies that they hold him in great respect. Abstaining from sadness and being like the sun at its zenith signifies letting our light shine before the whole world. After reaching its zenith, the sun begins to set; even a full moon may suffer an eclipse. The ebb and flow, the filling and emptying of all that is in heaven and earth occur at the proper times for them; how much more so is this true of men and how very much more so of spirits and of the gods!

SYMBOL   This hexagram symbolizes thunder and lightning occurring simultaneously.[3] The Superior Man decides law suits and inflicts (the necessary) penalties.

The Lines

9 FOR THE BOTTOM PLACE   On meeting a prince of equal rank, though (he accepts his hospitality for) ten days, he is not at fault—progress is made in winning respect!   COMMENTARY   Though he may do so for ten days, were he to exceed that time, he would invite calamity upon himself.[4]

6 FOR THE SECOND PLACE   So great is the obstruction that the midday sun appears to him as a tiny star. To advance now would be to invite mistrust and various ills. However, confidence seems to be on the

increase—good fortune! COMMENTARY Increasing confidence reposed in us implies that presently people's trust will help us to accomplish our will.

9 FOR THE THIRD PLACE So copious is the rain that, even at midday, there is obscurity. He breaks his right forearm—no error! COMMENTARY The abundant rain implies that there is nothing great we can accomplish now. His breaking his right forearm indicates uselessness up to the very end.[5]

9 FOR THE FOURTH PLACE So great is the obstruction that the midday sun appears to him as a tiny star. Meeting a prince of equal rank—good fortune! COMMENTARY The extent of the obstruction is indicated by the unsuitable position of this line. His seeing only a tiny star at midday implies nothing wherewith to lighten the darkness (surrounding us). His good fortune in meeting a prince of equal rank indicates that action can now be taken.[6]

6 FOR THE FIFTH PLACE The variegated beauty (of the sky after a storm) now appears. Blessings[7] and fame are won—good fortune! COMMENTARY Here, good fortune connotes the blessings already mentioned.

6 FOR THE TOP PLACE There is abundance in his dwelling and a wall around his house; yet, peering through the gate, he sees no one. For three years, he sees nobody—misfortune! COMMENTARY Such is the abundance in his dwelling that he seems to be hovering on the border of the skies. He sees no one, for he has deliberately hidden himself.[8]

NOTES (1) Abundance in itself is often good; but it is generally followed by the waning of what was previously abundant; moreover, as we shall see, there can be abundance of darkness, or anything else unpleasant. (2) This may be taken as an auspicious omen. (3) A reference to the component trigrams. (4) It is all very well to accept the hospitality of our equals, but accepting too much of it will ultimately lead to trouble. (5) It is not clear whether the omen refers to our own uselessness for the task we have set ourselves or to that of someone on whom we have been depending. We must interpret the line in the context of our enquiry. (6) We are obstructed by ignorance or stupidity and should not act until someone ready to help us appears. (7) Unexpected or seemingly unmerited good fortune. (8) The whole of this refers to someone who has done very well for himself but who, out of snobbery or for a similar reason, refuses to share his good fortune and therefore remains alone and miserable amidst his splendid possessions.

HEXAGRAM 56
LÜ THE TRAVELLER

Component trigrams:
Below: KÊN, *a mountain, hard, obstinate, perverse.*
Above: LI, *fire, brilliance, beauty.*

TEXT   The Traveller—success in small matters. Persistence with regard to travelling brings good fortune.

COMMENTARY ON THE TEXT   This hexagram presages success in small things, for a yielding line gains the centre (of the upper trigram) and freely accords with the firm lines to either side. Stubbornness and beauty conjoined[1] make for success in small matters and ensure good fortune to determined travellers. The timely application of this hexagram is of vast importance.

SYMBOL   This hexagram symbolizes fire upon a mountain.[1] The Superior Man employs wise caution in administering punishments and does not suffer the cases (brought before him) to be delayed.

The Lines

6 FOR THE BOTTOM PLACE   Trifling with unimportant matters, the traveller draws upon himself calamity. COMMENTARY   The calamity attendant upon having no will of our own.

6 FOR THE SECOND PLACE   The traveller reaches an inn with his valuables still nestling safely in the bosom of his robe.[2] He gains the loyalty of a young servant. COMMENTARY   The latter sentence implies an assurance that there will be no trouble to the very end.

9 FOR THE THIRD PLACE   Owing to the traveller ('s lack of caution), the inn is burnt down and he no longer enjoys the young servant's loyalty. Persistence now would lead to trouble.[3] COMMENTARY

By causing the inn to burn down, he injures the young servant. The implication is that, travelling on a downward path, our sense of duty and fitness is impaired.

9 FOR THE FOURTH PLACE   The traveller reaches a place where he obtains the money needed for his expenses, yet laments that there is no joy in his heart.[4]   COMMENTARY   His wandering to that place is indicated by the unsuitable position of this line; his obtaining money for expenses brings him no joy.

6 FOR THE FIFTH PLACE   While pheasant shooting, he loses an arrow. In the end he wins praise and attains to office.[5]   COMMENTARY   Both of these are bestowed from above.

9 FOR THE TOP PLACE   A bird manages to burn its own nest. At first the traveller laughs, but then (has cause to) shout and weep.[6] A cow is lost through carelessness—misfortune!   COMMENTARY   The top of this hexagram signifies burning.[7] The loss of a cow through carelessness means that no news will ever be obtained of something we have lost (or are about to lose).

NOTES   (1) A reference to the component trigrams.   (2) This implies that we need fear no loss upon our journey.   (3) Our carelessness leads us into such difficulties that it would be folly to proceed with our plans.   (4) Were we to travel or continue to travel now, though material difficulties would not arise, we should not experience any happiness.   (5) The whole of this passage indicates that, after suffering a small loss, we shall receive considerable benefits from those above us.   (6) Presumably, someone's carelessness causes him misfortune which excites our mirth—until we discover that we ourselves are deeply involved in the resulting loss.   (7) A reference to the upper component trigram.

HEXAGRAM 57
SUN WILLING SUBMISSION, GENTLENESS, PENETRATION[1]

Component trigrams:
Below: SUN, *wind, wood, bland, mild.*
Above: SUN, *wind, wood, bland, mild.*

TEXT   Willing Submission—success in small matters. It is advantageous to have in view a goal (or destination) and to visit a great man.

COMMENTARY ON THE TEXT   In carrying out the will of heaven, the utmost submissiveness is required. The firm penetrates the middle (of both trigrams) and is correctly placed; this augurs the fulfilment of what is willed. Success in small matters and the rest of what is said in the Text are derived from the fact that the yielding lines all accord with the firm.

SYMBOL   This hexagram symbolizes a favourable wind.[2] The Superior Man performs his allotted tasks in consonance with heaven's (or the sovereign's) will.

The Lines

6 FOR THE BOTTOM PLACE   Advancing and retreating; the righteous persistence of the warriors brings advantage. COMMENTARY   The first three words imply that we have doubts about our own intentions. The rest of the passage suggests a will firmly under control.[3]

9 FOR THE SECOND PLACE   Crawling below the bed.[4] He employs the services of a disorderly rabble of diviners and wizards—good fortune and no error![5] COMMENTARY   Good fortune, despite the disorderly crowding is indicated by the position of this line, which is central (to the lower trigram).

9 FOR THE THIRD PLACE   Repeated submission—shame!   COMMENTARY   Shame resulting from the exhaustion of our will-power.

6 FOR THE FOURTH PLACE   Regret vanishes! Three kinds (of game) are caught in the field.   COMMENTARY   The second sentence augurs concrete results.

9 FOR THE FIFTH PLACE   Persistence in a righteous course brings reward; regret vanishes, and everything is favourable! A poor beginning, but a good end![5] The three days before and the three days after a change (now due to occur) are especially propitious.[6]   COMMENTARY   That we shall enjoy good fortune is indicated by the correct position of this line in the centre (of the upper trigram).

9 FOR THE TOP PLACE   Crawling below the bed.[4] He loses what is required for his travelling expenses—persistence brings misfortune!   COMMENTARY   Crawling below the bed—this top line indicates exhaustion (of all possibilities). Losing his travelling expenses presages certain misfortune!

NOTES   (1) This is a reasonably auspicious hexagram; it augurs a certain amount of success for those who submit to circumstances—unless a moving line indicating the contrary is received. This is not a time for resistance but for submission.   (2) The component trigrams combine the concepts of wind and blandness—hence a favourable wind.   (3) Probably the implication is that we are now too hesitant and that we should benefit from acquiring the strong determination exhibited by soldiers in combat.   (4) This symbolizes exaggerated submission, servile humility, etc. Apparently, we have been guilty of this fault.   (5) This could be taken to refer to the lines of the hexagram up to this point, for this one is much more favourable than those preceding it. Or it may be taken to mean that affairs which begin by going ill with us will later take a change greatly for the better.   (6) It would be well to identify the important change presaged here, so that we can make good use of the six auspicious days to prosecute our plans.

HEXAGRAM 58
TUI JOY

Component trigrams:
Below: TUI, a body of water, pool, marsh, joy.
Above: TUI, a body of water, pool, marsh, joy.

TEXT   Joy—success! Persistence in a righteous course brings reward.

COMMENTARY ON THE TEXT   This hexagram signifies gladness. (In each trigram), the firm is central, the yielding are to either side of it. (To seek) gladness through righteous persistence is the way to accord with heaven and to respond to men. When joyously led, the people forget their burdens; in wrestling joyously with difficulties, they even forget that they must die. Joy's greatest quality is the encouragement it affords the people.

SYMBOL   This hexagram symbolizes two bodies of water conjoined.[1] The Superior Man joins his friends in discussions and in practising (the various arts and virtues).

The Lines

9 FOR THE BOTTOM PLACE   Harmonious joy—good fortune! COMMENTARY   This indicates our being able to act without being troubled by doubts.

9 FOR THE SECOND PLACE   Confident joy—good fortune and absence of regret! COMMENTARY   This implies exerting our will with complete confidence.

6 FOR THE THIRD PLACE   Coming joy—misfortune![2] COMMENTARY   Misfortune is indicated by the unsuitable position of this line.

9 FOR THE FOURTH PLACE   Calculating (future) joys, he is restless and suffers from various small ills, yet he is happy.   COMMENTARY   There will be happiness (in spite of all this foolish anxiety) because blessings[3] will be received.

9 FOR THE FIFTH PLACE   Faith in what is disintegrating leads to trouble.[4]   COMMENTARY   However, this line is suited to its position (hence the trouble will hardly amount to much).

6 FOR THE TOP PLACE   Joy in the form of allurement.[5]   COMMENTARY   This sort of joy is experienced by the unenlightened.

NOTES   (1) A reference to the component trigrams.   (2) The relation between the misfortune indicated by this line and coming joy is not very clear. Interpreting it rather loosely, the passage can be taken to mean that we shall suffer misfortune at a time when we are expecting something which would afford us happiness; in other words, the expected joy may not materialize.   (3) Unexpected or seemingly unmerited happiness.   (4) Presumably, we put our trust in the continuance of something which, perhaps unknown to us, is already beginning to crumble away.   (5) This suggests the superficial joy offered by attractions that would make no appeal to the Superior Man.

HEXAGRAM 59
HUAN   SCATTERING, DISINTEGRATION, DISPERSAL

Component trigrams:
Below: KʼAN, *water, a pit.*
Above: SUN, *wind, wood, bland, mild.*

TEXT   Scattering—success! The King has approached his temple.[1] It is advantageous to cross the great river (or sea).[2] Persistence in a righteous course brings reward.

COMMENTARY ON THE TEXT   This hexagram presages success, for the firm (line two) approaches and is not exhausted. The yielding (line four) obtains a place outside (the lower trigram)[3] and the line above it responds to it. The King (line 5) has approached his temple and is to

HUAN SCATTERING, DISINTEGRATION

be found in its centre (i.e. the centre of the upper trigram). The advantage of crossing the great river (or sea) is that concrete results are obtained from mounting upon wood.[4]

SYMBOL   This hexagram symbolizes wind blowing across the face of the waters.[5] The kings of old built temples[6] in which to sacrifice to the Supreme Lord (of Heaven).

The Lines

6 FOR THE BOTTOM PLACE   Helping others with the strength of a horse—good fortune! COMMENTARY   This good fortune results from willing accord with others.

9 FOR THE SECOND PLACE   When disintegration is in process, hasten to the altar[7] and regret will vanish. COMMENTARY   This line indicates that we shall obtain what we desire.

6 FOR THE THIRD PLACE   Self (-centred) thoughts are dispersed—no regret! COMMENTARY   This indicates that the will is fixed upon something external (to our own well-being).

6 FOR THE FOURTH PLACE   He disperses his group of companions[8]—sublime good fortune! Dispersion leads to accumulation, but this is not something that ordinary people understand.[9] COMMENTARY   In this context, sublime good fortune connotes glory.

9 FOR THE FIFTH PLACE   Scattering perspiration,[10] he issues his royal command. The King disperses (the treasures in) his palace [among the people]—no blame. COMMENTARY   That his doing so was not culpable is indicated by the correct position of this ruilng line.

9 FOR THE TOP PLACE   Dispersing blood (i.e. fending off injury or violence[11]), he keeps it at a distance—no blame! COMMENTARY   This means keeping evil at a distance.

NOTES   (1) An omen of safety. See note six. (2) I.e., to go on a long journey. (3) The lower trigram, K'an, signifies danger, trouble and so forth; it is well to be outside it, as is the case with the top three lines. (4) Wood is one of the meanings attached to the upper trigram. Here, no doubt, a boat or ship is implied. (5) A reference to the component trigrams. (6) A temple is a place of safety from the ills of the world. The symbolism here is that the upper trigram forms a temple in which people are safe from the pit [the lower trigram]; its middle line [five] signifies the King. The implication is that we should employ spiritual or moral means to preserve ourselves from the danger threatened by the lower trigram. (7) The implication is similar to that explained in note six. (8) Namely a group of people who have proved themselves inimicable to the public good. (9) This is an auspicious time to 'cast our bread upon the waters'. Acts of great generosity are now essential to our success. (10) One additional commentary suggests that perspiration comes from illness and anxiety and that the meaning is: 'The King rids himself of cause for anxiety by ordering that his goods be dispersed among the needy.' Again, large generosity is required for our success. (11) The text of the original is so unclear that the additional commentaries all disagree as to the meaning of dispersing blood, but the general idea is perfectly clear from the commentary on the line.

HEXAGRAM 60
CHIEH   RESTRAINT[1]

Component trigrams:
Below: TUI, *a body of water, pool, marsh, joy.*
Above: K'AN, *water, a pit.*

TEXT   Restraint—success! It is wrong to persist in harsh restraint.

COMMENTARY ON THE TEXT   This hexagram signifies success because the firm and yielding lines are equal in number and the firm (fifth line) is central (to the upper trigram). Harsh restraint must not be persistently applied because it leads to exhaustion. Joy is experienced in undertaking what is dangerous.[2] The central line (of the upper trigram) is correctly placed and (signifies) reaching (our) goal. It is through the restraint of the celestial and terrestrial forces that the four seasons arrive each at its proper time. When restraint is exercised in the work of governing, property suffers no damage and the people are not harmed.

SYMBOL   This hexagram symbolizes water (held by a dyke) above a marshy lake.[2] The Superior Man employs a system of regulations in his plans for the (widespread) practice of virtue.

CHIEH RESTRAINT

The Lines

9 FOR THE BOTTOM PLACE   He goes not forth from the outer gates and courtyards (of his home)—no error!   COMMENTARY   He acts thus from his knowledge of when things can be carried through (to their end) and when they will be blocked.³

9 FOR THE SECOND PLACE   He goes not forth from the inner gates and courtyards (of his home)—misfortune!   COMMENTARY   Misfortune because he neglects to take advantage of an opportunity now presenting itself.⁴

6 FOR THE THIRD PLACE   Sighing over an apparent lack of restraint—no error!   COMMENTARY   Who would find fault with that?⁵

6 FOR THE FOURTH PLACE   Peaceful restraint—success!   COMMENTARY   Success is indicated by the firm line immediately above this one.

9 FOR THE FIFTH PLACE   Voluntary restraint—good fortune! Advancing now wins praise.⁶   COMMENTARY   This is indicated by the central position of this ruling line.

6 FOR THE TOP PLACE   Painful restraint—persistence brings misfortune! However, regret will cease later.   COMMENTARY   Misfortune in the sense that the road we are following peters out.⁷

NOTES   (1) Like several other hexagrams, this one reminds us that there are times when non-action is the best action we can take.   (2) A reference to the component trigrams. The insertion about the dyke is pure guesswork on my part.   (3) The implication is that we should now hold back.   (4) The implication is that it would be wrong to hold back now.   (5) It is salutary to regret lack of restraint in ourselves or others.   (6) Presumably this means that we have rightly exercised restraint and that the time has now come for us to continue our advance.   (7) This implies that we should stop following our present course and that, by doing so, we shall eliminate the cause of our present worry or regret.

HEXAGRAM 61

CHUNG FU   INWARD CONFIDENCE AND SINCERITY

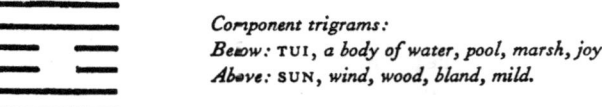

Component trigrams:
Below: TUI, *a body of water, pool, marsh, joy.*
Above: SUN, *wind, wood, bland, mild.*

TEXT   Inward Confidence and Sincerity. Dolphins—good fortune! It is advantageous to cross the great river (or sea). Persistence in a right course brings reward.

COMMENTARY ON THE TEXT   The yielding lines are inside the hexagram and there are firm lines central (to each of the component trigrams). Joyfulness and gentleness are conjoined and there is sufficient confidence to ensure the smooth development of the realm. The good fortune symbolized by dolphins is that of winning the confidence of every creature. That it is advantageous to cross the great river (or sea) implies making use of an unloaded boat (or ship). Persistence is always advantageous when it is accompanied by confidence, for then it accords with heaven ('s decrees).

SYMBOL   This hexagram symbolizes wind blowing over a marshy lake.[1] The Superior Man devotes careful thought to his judgements and is tardy in sentencing people to death.

The Lines

9 FOR THE BOTTOM PLACE   The officer in charge of hunting and fishing[2]—good fortune! The presence of others would give rise to anxiety.[3]   COMMENTARY   The good fortune presaged by this line implies that our purpose remains unaltered.

9 FOR THE SECOND PLACE   A crane sings in the shade; its young

CHUNG FU INWARD CONFIDENCE

ones follow suit.⁴ I have a fine goblet and will share it with you.⁵
COMMENTARY 'Its young ones follow suit' indicates heartfelt desire.

6 FOR THE THIRD PLACE He makes an enemy. Beating a drum by fits and starts, he weeps and sings in turn.⁶ COMMENTARY His beating the drum by fits and starts is indicated by the unsuitable position of this line.

6 FOR THE FOURTH PLACE A team of horses strays just before the full moon—no error! COMMENTARY The straying of the horses signifies rising above those of our own kind.

9 FOR THE FIFTH PLACE He seems to be pulled forward by his confidence (in what he is doing)—no error! COMMENTARY This is indicated by the correct position of this ruling line.

9 FOR THE TOP PLACE The noise of cocks crowing rises to the sky—to persist now would bring misfortune.⁷ COMMENTARY For how could this continue for long?

NOTES (1) A reference to the component trigrams. (2) The whole of this phrase translates a single Chinese word. The additional commentaries in my possession differ widely in their interpretation of this character (which has several other meanings) and of the passage as a whole. None of them gives what seems to me a satisfactory explanation and I must confess myself unable to interpret the meaning. (3) In the light of the commentary on the line which follows, this could also be taken to mean: 'Any other way (than the way we are following) would make us lose our peace of mind.' (4) This symbolizes a longing in which others share. (5) We should allow others to benefit from something or some circumstance which is valuable to us. (6) We are conscious of having made an enemy, but we cannot make up our minds what to do about it. The implication is that we should have more courage. (7) This suggests that we are overconfident and inclined to crow about our good fortune; but we should remember that triumph seldom lasts long and avoid seeking even greater triumphs at this time.

HEXAGRAM 62
HSIAO KUO   THE SMALL GET BY

Component trigrams:
Below: KÊN, *a mountain, hard, obstinate, perverse.*
Above: CHÊN, *thunder, movement, to sprout or quicken.*

TEXT   The Small Get By—success! Persistence in a righteous course brings reward. Small things can be accomplished now, but not great ones. When birds fly high, their singing is out of tune.[1] The humble, but not the mighty, are favoured now with great good fortune.

COMMENTARY ON THE TEXT   This hexagram augurs success for the small; their persistence is rewarded and their actions accord with the times. The yielding (fifth line) obtains the central place (in the upper trigram); it is this which indicates good fortune in small matters. The firm (fourth line) fails to get a commanding position and is not central; hence, important matters should not be undertaken now. The image of a bird has been chosen; for, when birds fly high, they cannot sing harmoniously. That the humble, but not the mighty, are greatly favoured by fortune indicates that those ascending now will meet with difficulty, whereas those descending will find their way smooth.[2]

SYMBOL   This hexagram symbolizes thunder over the mountains.[3] The Superior Man now acts with too much reverence, experiences too much sorrow from bereavement and is over thrifty in satisfying his needs.[4]

The Lines

6 FOR THE BOTTOM PLACE   A bird in flight brings misfortune.
COMMENTARY   There is nothing we can do about it.[5]

6 FOR THE SECOND PLACE   Passing by (the spirit tablets of) his ancestors, he encountered (the ghost of or else the tablet of) his late

HSIAO KUO THE SMALL GET BY

mother.⁶ He did not get as far as the Prince but encountered one of the ministers—no error! COMMENTARY He did not reach the Prince because he was unable to get by the minister.⁷

9 FOR THE THIRD PLACE Unless he takes appropriate precautions, one of his subordinates may slay him⁸—misfortune! COMMENTARY Were that to happen, it would indeed be misfortune!

9 FOR THE FOURTH PLACE No error! Instead of passing him by, he accosts him. Advancing now entails dangers which have to be guarded against. This is not a time for action, but for unwavering determination. COMMENTARY Accosting someone instead of passing him by is now inappropriate (or, is indicated by the unsuitable position of this line). The danger of going forward and the need for precaution imply that we should not continue long in our present course.

6 FOR THE FIFTH PLACE Dense clouds come from the western outskirts,⁹ but no rain falls. The prince shoots an arrow and hits someone in a cave.¹⁰ COMMENTARY Dense clouds and no rain points to their having risen too high.¹¹

6 FOR THE TOP PLACE Instead of accosting him, he passed him by, The bird flew away from him—misfortune in the form of natural calamity and deliberate injury. COMMENTARY The first sentence suggests that we behave too arrogantly.

NOTES (1) A picturesque way of saying that to aim high now would be to put ourselves out of accord with the times. (2) Far from aiming higher, we should deliberately draw in our horns for the time being. (3) A reference to the component trigrams. (4) This is almost the only place in the book where fault is found with the Superior Man. Even he is human enough to go too far at times. (5) The bird is merely a symbol; we are due to encounter misfortune which we are powerless to avert. (6) The additional commentaries do not make the meaning clear. Presumably, we can take it to mean very much the same as the sentence which follows. (7) We fail, but through no fault of ours, to reach as high as we had hoped. This is a time to be content with modest success. (8) We are liable to be injured by a subordinate. (9) See note three to Hexagram 9. (10) The prince symbolizes the fifth line; the two yielding lines at the top suggest a cave. The meaning is that something is gained, but nothing of much importance. (11) Something which could have been of great help to us passes us by.

HEXAGRAM 63
CHI CHI AFTER COMPLETION

The component trigrams:
Below: LI, *fire, brilliance, beauty.*
Above: K'AN, *water, a pit.*

TEXT   After Completion—success in small matters! Persistence in a righteous course brings reward. Good fortune at the start; disorder in the end![1]

COMMENTARY ON THE TEXT   This hexagram presages success in small matters. That right persistence will be rewarded is indicated by the correctness and suitable arrangement of the firm and yielding lines. Since the yielding (line 2) is central (to the lower trigram), it is clear that good fortune will accompany the start; but, ultimately, affairs will be halted amid disorder because the way peters out.[2]

SYMBOL   This hexagram symbolizes water above fire.[3] The Superior Man deals with trouble by careful thought and by taking advance precautions.

The Lines

9 FOR THE BOTTOM PLACE   He brakes the wheel of his chariot and gets the rear part wet—no error!   COMMENTARY   This passage means that (since we manage to stop at the right moment) we are not to blame (for what happens).

6 FOR THE SECOND PLACE   The lady loses the blind from her chariot window. She should not go in search of it, for she will recover it in seven days.   COMMENTARY   Her getting it back after seven days suggests that restraint or (moderation) will be rewarded.

9 FOR THE THIRD PLACE   The Illustrious Ancestor (namely, the

CHI CHI AFTER COMPLETION

Emperor Wu Ting, 1324 BC) carried out a punitive expedition in Kuei Fang (literally, the Land of Devils) and conquered it after three years—men of mean attainments would have been useless![4] COMMENTARY His taking three years to conquer it indicates great fatigue.[5]

6 FOR THE FOURTH PLACE Amidst the fine silk are ragged garments[6]—be cautious throughout the livelong day! COMMENTARY This indicates that doubt and suspicion are now prevalent.

9 FOR THE FIFTH PLACE In terms of benefits, the neighbour to the east gained less from sacrificing an ox than the neighbour to the west obtained from carrying out the spring sacrifice. COMMENTARY Because the former's sacrifice (though bigger) was less timely.[7] The benefits obtained by the neighbour to the west betoken that good fortune is on its way to us.

6 FOR THE TOP PLACE His head gets wet—trouble! COMMENTARY But this sort of trouble can scarcely last long.[8]

NOTES (1) Perhaps persistence may help to lessen the disorder that threatens to come upon us after some initial success. (2) Hence, we should not try to advance very far. 'The way peters out' can also be taken to mean that our stock of merit becomes exhausted. (3) A reference to the component trigrams. (4) The Land of Devils was probably a territory inhabited by non-Chinese tribes. The implication is that only a man of outstanding capability should attempt any difficult task now. (5) Even if we do feel capable of undertaking an extremely difficult task, we must expect it to occupy us for so long as to make us feel exhausted. (6) This corrupt passage is variously interpreted in the additional commentaries. In any case it signifies a need for caution. (7) This is one of the favourite themes of the *Book of Change*, namely the importance of timeliness. A small effort at the right time will win for us more benefit than a gigantic effort at the wrong time. (8) We must expect some trouble, but perhaps not very serious and not likely to endure.

o

HEXAGRAM 64
WEI CHI   BEFORE COMPLETION[1]

Component trigrams:
Below: K'AN, *water, a pit.*
Above: LI, *fire, brilliance, beauty.*

TEXT   Before Completion—success! Before the little fox has quite completed its crossing (of the ice), its tail gets wet.[2] No goal (or destination) is favourable now.

COMMENTARY ON THE TEXT   This hexagram presages success because the yielding line (line five) occupies a central position (in the upper trigram). That the little fox does not quite complete its crossing (before getting its tail wet) indicates that we have not yet succeeded in getting beyond the middle (of the matter forming the subject of our enquiry). The wetting of its tail and the absence of any favourable goal (or destination) imply that our affairs cannot be pushed through to completion.[3] The firm and the yielding lines, although not appropriately placed, accord with one another.

SYMBOL   This hexagram symbolizes fire above water.[4] The Superior Man takes care to distinguish between things before arranging them in order.

The Lines

6 FOR THE BOTTOM PLACE   Its tail gets wet—disgrace![5]   COMMENTARY   This also implies that we do not know how to take advantage of opportunities.

9 FOR THE SECOND PLACE   He brakes the wheel of the chariot—righteous persistence brings good fortune![6]   COMMENTARY   Namely, the good fortune of being able to steer a middle course and go straight forward.[7]

WEI CHI BEFORE COMPLETION

6 FOR THE THIRD PLACE   The crossing is incomplete, so to advance now would bring misfortune; (yet) it will be advantageous to cross the great river (or sea).⁸   COMMENTARY   The first part of this passage is suggested by the line's unsuitable position.

9 FOR THE FOURTH PLACE   Persistence in a righteous course brings reward and regret vanishes. The subjugation of the land of Kuei involved tremendous activity; but, at the end of three years, great territories were bestowed (upon the successful generals).⁹   COMMENTARY   The reward to be gained by persistence and the disappearance of regret both imply that what we will will come about.

6 FOR THE FIFTH PLACE   Persistence in a righteous course brings good fortune and absence of regret. The lustre of the Superior Man wins people's confidence—hence the good fortune!   COMMENTARY   The Superior Man has the glorious custom of distributing his good fortune (among the needy).¹⁰

9 FOR THE TOP PLACE   Those in whom the people repose their trust may feast themselves without doing wrong; but if they allow their heads to get wet they will forfeit that trust.¹¹   COMMENTARY   Because that would indicate lack of restraint.

NOTES   (1) That the LAST of the sixty-four hexagrams should be Before Completion rather than After Completion (H.63) may seem surprising until it is recalled that there is nothing final about it; the cycle of change continues, passing from H.64 onto the first hexagram, and so on eternally.   (2) This implies that we are to expect a setback in our plans.   (3) Hence this is a time for waiting and for drawing in our horns.   (4) A reference to the component trigrams.   (5) If we receive this moving line, the setback is likely to be discreditable to us.   (6) But note that he uses his brake; i.e. our persistence must be in the form of determination to halt now and proceed later.   (7) See note six, just above this one. If events permit us to interpret the braking of the wheel as a recent success in preventing ourselves being dragged into a wrong course, then all is well and there is no need to halt now.   (8) The second and third clauses of this passage appear contradictory; but not if we interpret them to mean that, though we must halt for a while, we should preserve our determination to go forward to the end when conditions warrant an advance.   (9) This implies that we must work and, perhaps, suffer much in order to gain the fulfilment of our will promised in the commentary on this line.   (10) From the point of view of divination, this implies that we should be very generous in sharing the promised good fortune.   (11) This is a warning against excess. We have every right to enjoy our good fortune within reasonable bounds; but, if we are guilty of an excess comparable to that of drunken men who pour wine over one another's heads, we shall forfeit the high esteem in which we are (or soon will be) held.

O*

POSTSCRIPT

The Chinese original of the *Book of Change* contains a further section which is omitted here. This consists of various commentaries and essays of great significance with regard to the deeper aspects of the book, but not helpful to those whose concern with it is centred on divination. It has been omitted partly for this reason and partly because I doubt my ability to do it justice. Those whose interest in the *Book of Change* goes beyond divination to its religious, philosophical and metaphysical implications will find a complete translation in Wilhelm's version. As indicated previously, I have not found his rendering reliable and my doubts about it are shared by those Chinese scholars with whom I have discussed the matter; but it will surely give a good idea of the general scope of the final section.

I never enjoy casting aspersions on the work of someone else, and in this case I can truthfully add that I am far from satisfied with my own rendering. The fact is that a complete and really accurate translation of the *Book of Change* would almost certainly have to be the work of a group of people. Ideally, it should comprise one or more Chinese well versed in the traditional approach to the *I Ching*, at least one Chinese with a reasonable knowledge of this approach and a fine command of English, and at least one native English speaker competent in Classical Chinese who has specially prepared himself for the task. There was a time when this method of translating valuable works was quite usual. The admirable Chinese and Tibetan translations of Sanscrit Buddhist sutras were, in many cases, accomplished by groups of no less than twelve or fifteen people; they included Indian Sanscritists who knew no Chinese or Tibetan at one end and skilled native writers of Chinese or Tibetan ignorant of Sanscrit at the other; in the middle were people with a fair knowledge of Sanscrit and of the language into which they were rendering the texts. In these days, alas, few books are published unless there is a reasonable hope that they will be easy to sell, so we may have to wait a long time before the perfect English translation of the *Book of Change* comes into being!

APPENDIX
TABLES AND DIAGRAMS FOR ASSISTING INTERPRETATION

These tables and diagrams are not required for divination by the ordinary method described in this book. They would be useful for working out meanings directly from the hexagrams themselves without paying attention to the Texts and Commentaries, were this difficult task within the range of our abilities, which can seldom be the case. By studying them, however, we can learn a little of the means by which the authors of the *Book of Change* deduced the Texts and Commentaries from each hexagram and each component line. Diagram Eleven is of special interest; by reading the columns both horizontally and vertically, we can discover various relationships subsisting between hexagrams. It was these relationships which helped to determine the sequence in which the hexagrams occur in the *Book of Change* and assisted in clarifying their meanings. I have not seen any one Chinese edition which contains all the tables and diagrams given here, but those attributed to King Wên and to the Emperor Fu Hsi are to be found in almost every edition, even the smallest and least carefully annotated.

By studying these diagrams, the reader will see for himself how the arrangements of component lines cause some KUA (trigrams and hexagrams) to be in harmony with or antagonistic to certain others, in degrees ranging from the utmost compatibility to profound antagonism, just as in nature we find different forces working with or against one another in varying degrees. It will also be seen that the relationship between one hexagram and its neighbours helps to determine its meaning, according to whether one seems to merge into another or develop away from it. The number of possible relationships between the hexagrams must be enormous; some Chinese editions deal exhaustively with them; others discuss only the most obvious, since these are also the most important.

Even without much background knowledge, we can spend many happy hours comparing the KUA, tracing out some of their relationships and speculating as to what these portend. A much more fascinating exercise is to try to determine what analogies exist between the interplay of natural forces and the relationships between compatible and incompatible KUA; this study may even lead some of us to have as deep an insight into the symbolism of the KUA as if we had digested several ponderous tomes on the subject.

To understand much about the hexagrams, we must first have some knowledge of the significance of each of the eight trigrams; hence, in the following pages, the trigrams are dealt with first.

1. The Trigrams Listed in Their Most Usual Order With Their Principal Attributes

1 Ch'ien — Heaven	sky	cold		creative active strong firm light	father
2 Tui — lake	marsh	rain	autumn	joyful pleasurable	Youngest daughter
3 Li — fire	lightning	sun	summer	beautiful depending clinging	Middle daughter
4 Chên — thunder	thunder		spring	active moving arousing	Eldest Son
5 Sun — wind	wood			gentle penetrating	Eldest daughter
6 K'an — water	cloud a pit	moon	winter	enveloping dangerous	Middle Son
7 Kên — mountain	thunder			stubborn immovable perverse	Youngest Son
8 K'un — earth		heat		receptive responsive yielding passive weak dark	Mother

Some additional meanings which will help to explain how the texts of certain individual lines were arrived at are:—

1. head, horse. 2. mouth, sheep (goat). 3. eye, pheasant. 4. foot, dragon. 5. thigh, cock. 6. ear, boar (pig). 7. hand, dog. 8. belly, cow.

APPENDIX 217

It should be noted that, in certain less usual arrangements, some of the attributes and several of the family relationships change. Fortunately, the *I Ching's* interpretations of the hexagrams are all (or very nearly all) based on the above system, so there is not much room for confusion.

2. Fu Hsi's Arrangement of the Trigrams

8	7	6	5	4	3	2	1
K'un earth	Kên mountain	K'an water	Sun wind	Chên thunder	Li fire	Tui lake	Ch'ien Heaven

Great Yin	Lesser Yang	Lesser Yin	Great Yang

YIN NEGATIVE PRINCIPLE	YANG POSITIVE PRINCIPLE

T'AI CHI THE ABSOLUTE IN UNDIFFERENTIATED FORM

3. Fu Hsi's Circular Arrangement of the Trigrams in Pairs of Opposites

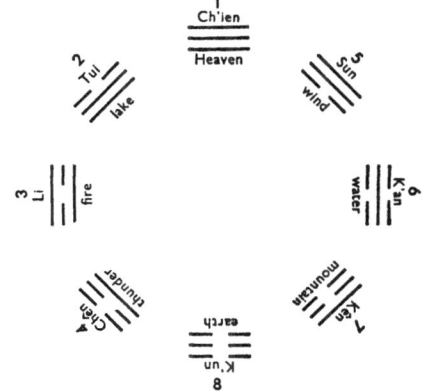

4. King Wên's Arrangement of the Trigrams in Family Relationships

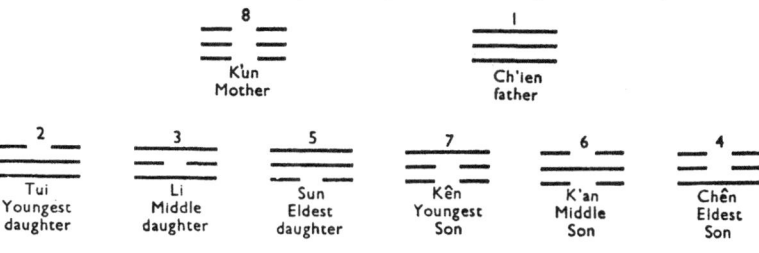

THE BOOK OF CHANGE

These relationships are easy to memorize so that they can be recalled when studying the hexagrams containing various pairs of family members. The symbols for the father and the mother are the same as those for Yang and Yin. With the children, it is the odd line which determines their sex; thus all the sons have one Yang line and all the daughters one Yin line. As KUA are always read from the bottom up, it stands to reason that the sex line at the bottom indicates the eldest son or daughter and the sex line at the top the youngest. The fact that the sons have more Yin lines than Yang and the daughters more Yang lines than Yin illustrates one of the *I Ching's* principal concepts, namely the close interrelationship of everything with its own opposite.

5. King Wên's Circular Arrangement of the Trigrams

It is difficult to see the logic of this arrangement; but, since it is found in all Chinese editions of the *I Ching*, I have included it here. It is said in China that beings above the level of humans are able to discover the meaning of this order, whereas humans are no longer able to do so.

6. The Trigrams in the Arrangement Used in Charms for Warding off Evil

It is possible that this arrangement resulted from the ignorance of some fortune-teller at the popular level; there may well be a better reason for it, but it is not immediately apparent.

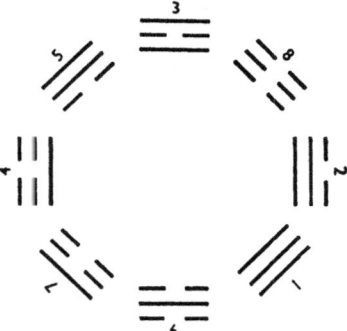

7. Parallel Diagrams Revealing the Interaction of Yin and Yang

These diagrams are often drawn side by side. The first indicates the normal process of action and interaction; the second shows one type of change which may be expected under certain conditions and accounts for an alternative sequence of trigrams sometimes used for divination.

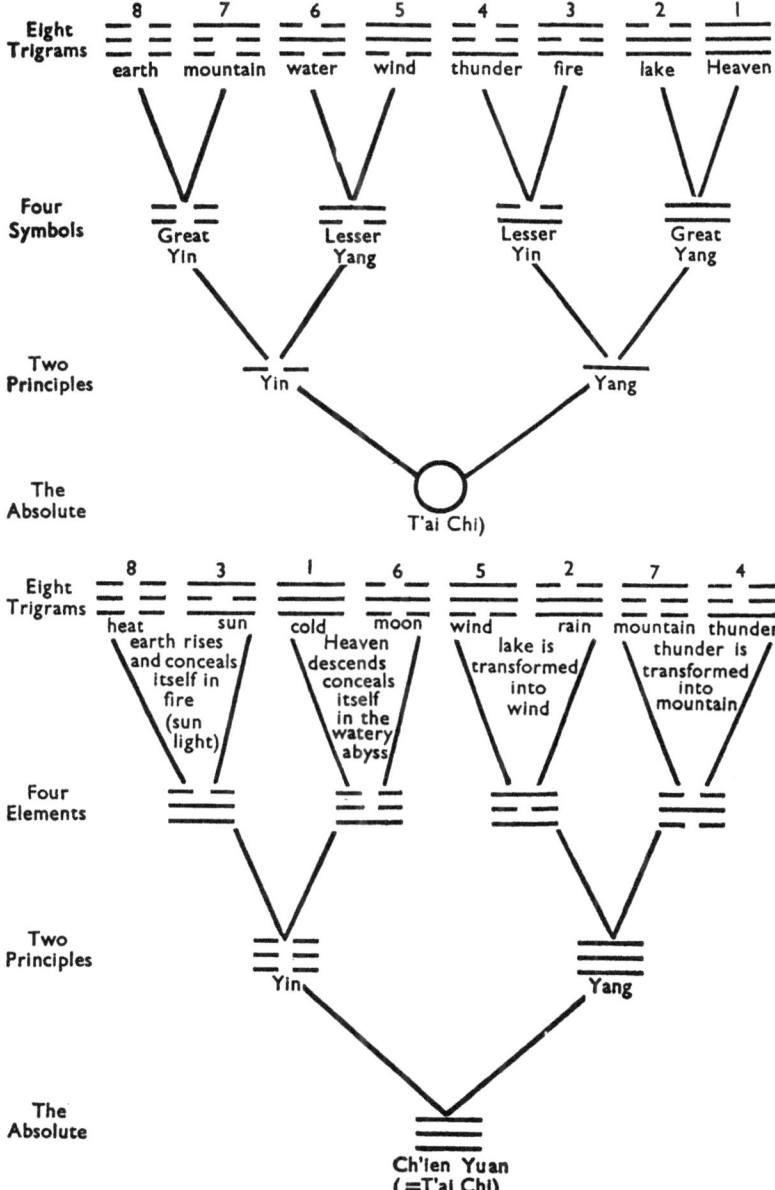

8. The Hexagrams in the Sequence in which They Occur in the Book of Change

1 Ch'ien — The Creative Principle	15 Ch'ien — Modesty	29 K'an — The Abyss
2 K'un — The Passive Principle	16 Yü — Repose	30 Li — Flaming Beauty
3 Chun — Difficulty	17 Sui — Following	31 Hsien — Attraction
4 Mêng — Immaturity	18 Ku — Decay	32 Hêng — The Long Enduring
5 Hsü — Calculated Inaction	19 Lin — Approach	33 Tun — Yielding
6 Sung — Conflict	20 Kuan — Looking Down	34 Ta Chuang — The Power of the Great
7 Shih — The Army	21 Shih Ho — Gnawing	35 Chin — Progress
8 Pi — Unity	22 P'i — Elegance	36 Ming I — Darkening of the Light
9 Hsiao Ch'u — The Lesser Nourisher	23 Po — Peeling off	37 Chia Jên — The Family
10 Lu — Treading, Conduct	24 Fu — Return	38 K'uei — The Estranged
11 T'ai — Peace	25 Wu Wang — Integrity	39 Chien — Trouble
12 P'i — Stagnation	26 Ta Ch'u — The Great Nourisher	40 Hsieh — Release
13 T'ung Jên — Lovers, etc.	27 I — Nourishment	41 Sun — Loss
14 Ta Yü — Great Possessions	28 Ta Kuo — Excess	42 I — Gain

APPENDIX

43 Kuai — Resolution	51 Chên — Thunder	59 Huan — Scattering
44 Kou — Contact	52 Kên — Desisting	60 Chieh — Restraint
45 Ts'ui — Gathering together	53 Chien — Gradual Progress	61 Chung Fu — Inward Confidence and Sincerity
46 Shêng — Ascending	54 Kuei Mei — The Marriageable Maiden	62 Hsiao Kuo — The Small Get By
47 K'un — Adversity	55 Fêng — Abundance	63 Chi Chi — After Completion
48 Ching — A Well	56 Lü — The Traveller	64 Wei Chi — Before Completion
49 Kê — Revolution	57 Sun — Willing Submission	
50 Ting — Sacrificial Vessel	58 Tui — Joy	

9. The Hexagrams Arranged According to the Base Structure

Each trigram forms the base of eight hexagrams. The following arrangement helps to illustrate one of the main factors by which the significance of each hexagram is determined. The horizontal sequence is arranged so that each base trigram is first surmounted by its own double and then by seven others in the order shown in the left hand column, but always starting from the one just below it in that column.

Chinese versions of the *I Ching* often contain a metrical arrangement of words based on this sequence and consisting of sixty-four lines of three syllables each. Once it has been memorized, it is possible to name every hexagram at sight or, alternatively, to draw each hexagram correctly just from hearing or reading its name. Most unfortunately, the polysyllabic English language does not lend itself to this excellent method of memorizing.

	1	11	34	26	14	5	43	9
1 Heaven								
8 earth	2	16	23	35	8	45	20	12
4 thunder	51	27	21	3	17	42	25	24
7 mountain	52	56	39	31	53	33	15	62
3 fire	30	63	49	37	13	36	55	22
6 water	29	47	59	6	7	40	4	64
2 lake	58	61	10	19	54	41	38	60
5 wind	57	44	46	32	18	50	48	28

If this arrangement is read line by line horizontally, it will be found that the Yin and Yang lines form a number of symmetrical patterns. Chinese scholars seek for many kinds of symmetry in these hexagrams, reading them now one way and now another. Each type of symmetrical connection between groups of hexagrams has its peculiar significance.

APPENDIX

10. *Fu Hsi's Diagram of the Derivation of the Sixty-Four Hexagrams*

11. The Hexagrams Arranged According to the Number of Yang Lines In Each

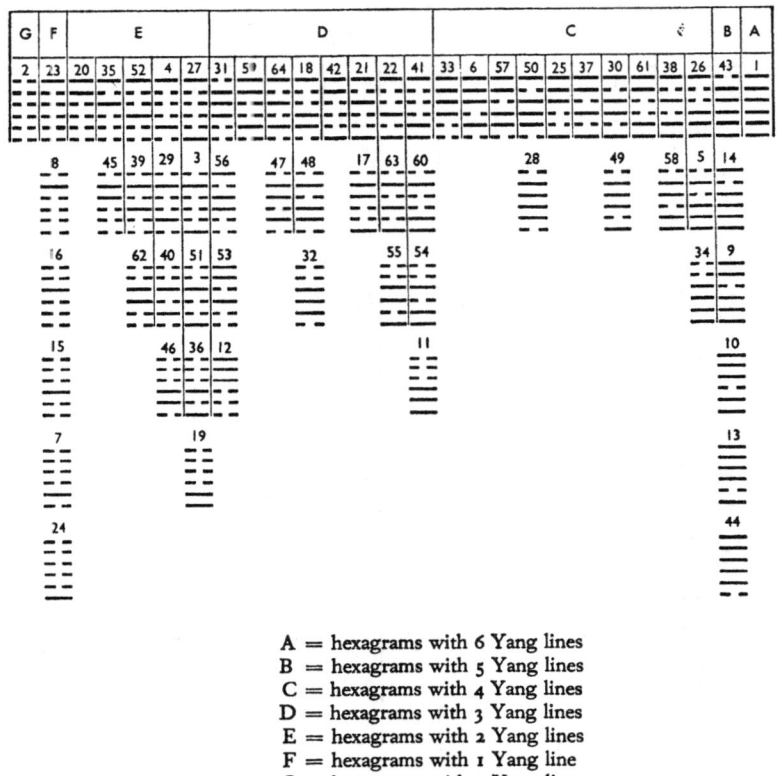

A = hexagrams with 6 Yang lines
B = hexagrams with 5 Yang lines
C = hexagrams with 4 Yang lines
D = hexagrams with 3 Yang lines
E = hexagrams with 2 Yang lines
F = hexagrams with 1 Yang line
G = hexagrams with 0 Yang lines

The Chinese version of this arrangement is longer, as those hexagrams with four, three or two Yang lines are repeated in categories labelled two, three and four Yin lines respectively. This is done to enable the student to trace relationships between neighbouring hexagrams. In the complete version, various lines are seen to proceed downwards as we look at one hexagram after another and then upwards again in the reverse order. However, this abbreviated arrangement (which, nevertheless, contains all sixty-four hexagrams) should be sufficient for most purposes. For the Chinese, this table has an additional purpose. In most Chinese editions of the *Book of Change*, the hexagrams are not numbered, so it is by looking at the Chinese characters which replace the numbers used here that the reader discovers the name of a given hexagram.

APPENDIX

12. The Seasonal Correspondences

The traditional Chinese calendar, which remained in use until not many decades ago and which is still preferred by Chinese farmers because of its accuracy in forecasting each minor seasonal change, is a lunar calendar. Each month begins on the first day of a new cycle of the phases of the moon. The fifteenth of the month always corresponds with full moon and there are thirty days to each month. In order to keep the calendar closely in accord with the seasons of the year (i.e. with the solar progression) an extra month is inserted every four years. The pages of most versions of this calendar are marked with weather forecasts, such as lesser heat, great heat, first snow and so on, which in North China are so astonishingly accurate as to make it appear that the deity or deities responsible for such changes have the utmost respect for this man-made, but perhaps divinely inspired, calendar.

As with the Easter festival in the West, there is no exact correspondence between Chinese lunar months and the solar months to which we are accustomed. For interpreting this table and any references to months or seasons in the text of the *Book of Change,* those who are unable to obtain a Chinese calendar for the current year are compelled to use the rough and ready method of regarding each Chinese month as being approximately one month later than the corresponding solar month. According to this system, the First Month corresponds to February, the Eighth Month to September, the Twelfth Month to January, etc. The following table gives a list of the lunar months with which each of the hexagrams has a special correspondence. However, it should not be understood that anything forecast by a particular hexagram will certainly occur in that part of the year to which it is related, unless the text expressly indicates this. On the other hand, if we put to the *I Ching* the question 'In which month will so and so happen?' the answer will be found in this table.

First Month (approximately February) — hexagrams	11	5	17	35	40	52
Second Month (approximately March) — hexagrams	34	16	6	18	45	
Third Month — hexagrams	43	56	7	8	9	↓
Fourth Month — hexagrams	1	14	37	48	31	30
Fifth Month — hexagrams	44	50	55	59	10	
Sixth Month — hexagrams	33	32	60	13	41	↓
Seventh Month — hexagrams	12	57	49	26	22	58
Eighth Month — hexagrams	20	54	25	36	47	
Ninth Month — hexagrams	23	51	63	21	28	↓
Tenth Month — hexagrams	2	64	39	27	61	29
Elventh Month — hexagrams	24	3	15	38	46	
Twelfth Month — hexagrams	19	62	4	42	53	↓

For those who are able to obtain a Chinese calendar for the current year (which will certainly have the corresponding Western calendar dates marked on each page), the use of this table is much greater. As each lunar month has exactly thirty days and as there are five hexagrams to each month, it will be seen that each hexagram governs six particular days. Furthermore, each line of that hexagram will be found to govern one of those six days. Thus a moving line four in Hexagram 5 would indicate the tenth day of the First Month; a moving line six in Hexagram 53 would indicate the last day of the Twelfth Month and so on. It will be noticed that four of the hexagrams govern a whole three month period each. This table and means of reckoning is based upon an elaborate circular diagram attributed to the legendary Emperor Fu Hsi. A remarkable fact is that the Chinese calendar, which, as explained above, is very accurate in forecasting changes of weather in North China, is drawn up in strict accordance with this many thousand year old diagram.

13. Table of Ruling Lines

Each hexagram has one and sometimes two so-called 'ruling lines' whose nature and position played a part in the interpretations of its meaning found in the traditional texts and commentaries. The places occupied by the ruling lines were determined by complicated considerations which lie outside the scope of this book. However, as there are several references to them in the Confucian commentaries, the following table for identifying them has been prepared. The numbers from 1 to 64 are those of the hexagrams; those in brackets indicate the position of the ruling line or lines in each of them.

1(5); 2(2); 3(1 and 5); 4(2 and 5); 5(5); 6(5); 7(2 and 5); 8(5); 9(5); 10(5); 11(2 and 5); 12(2 and 5); 13(2 and 5); 14(5); 15(3); 16(4); 17(1 and 5); 18(5); 19(1 and 2); 20(5 and 6); 21(5); 22(2 and 6); 23(6); 24(1); 25(1 and 5); 26(5 and 6); 27(5 and 6); 28(2 and 4); 29(2 and 5); 30(2 and 5); 31(4); 32(2); 33(5); 34(4); 35(5); 36(2 and 5); 37(2 and 5); 38(2 and 5); 39(5); 40(2 and 5); 41(5); 42(2 and 5); 43(5); 44(2 and 5); 45(4 and 5); 46(5); 47(2 and 5); 48(5); 49(5); 50(5 and 6); 51(1); 52(6); 53(2 and 5); 54(5); 55(5); 56(5); 57(5); 58(2 and 5); 59(5); 60(5); 61(5); 62(2 and 5); 63(2); 64(5).

14. Table of Approximate English Phonetic Equivalents of the Names of the Hexagrams

Throughout this book, the Wade System of transliterating Chinese sounds has been used in in preference to any other systems, because its use is widespread in English-speaking countries and because it is employed by most of the Chinese-English dictionaries which readers acquainted with Chinese may wish to consult. The following is a list of the hexagrams in their usual order with the names transcribed both according to the Wade System and according to a rough and ready system of my own which may prove helpful to those higherto unacquainted with these names. Each of the names underlined belongs also to one of the eight trigrams.

APPENDIX

1. Ch'ien   (Chee'en)
2. K'un (Kwên; vowel so short as to be almost non-existent)
3. Chun   (Jwên; vowel as in 2 above)
4. Mêng   (Mêng; vowel as in 2 above)
5. Hsü   (Shü; vowel as in the French 'Tu')
6. Sung   (Soong)
7. Shih   (Shrrr)
8. Pi   (Bee)
9. Hsiao Ch'u   (She-au Choo; the second vowel as in 'House')
10. Lü   (Lü; vowel as in the French 'Tu')
11. T'ai   (Tie, as in 'Necktie')
12. P'i   (Pee)
13. T'ung Jên   (Toong Rên; vowel as in 2 above)
14. Ta Yu   (Dah You)
15. Ch'ien   (Chee-en)
16. Yü   (Yü; vowel as in the French 'Tu')
17. Sui   (Sway)
18. Ku   (Goo)
19. Lin   (Lin)
20. Kuan   (Gwun; rhymes with 'Fun', 'Done', etc.)
21. Shih Hô   (Shrrr Her; but with the 'r' of 'Her' not pronounced)
22. P'i   (Bee)
23. Po   (Por; but with the final 'r' not pronounced)
24. Fu   (Foo)
25. Wu Wang   (Woo Wung; rhymes with 'Flung')
26. Ta Ch'u   (Dah Choo)
27. I   (Yee)
28. Ta Kuo   (Dah Gwor; but with the final 'r' not pronounced)
29. K'an   (Cun, as in 'Cunning')
30. Li   (Lee)
31. Hsien   (Shee-en)
32. Hêng   (Hêng; vowel as in 2 above)
33. Tun   (Doon: but with a short vowel as in 'Book')
34. Ta Chuang   (Dah Jwung; with the vowel as in 'Hung')
35. Chin   (Jin)
36. Ming I   (Ming Yee)
37. Chia Jên   (Jee-ah Rên; last vowel as in 2 above)
38. K'uei   (Kway)
39. Chien   (Jee-en)
40. Hsieh   (Shee-ay; the second vowel rhymes with 'Hay')
41. Sun   (Soon; but with a short vowel as in 'Book')
42. I   (Yee)
43. Kuai   (Gwy; rhymes with 'Buy')

44. Kou   (Go)
45. Ts'ui   (Tswey)
46. Shêng   (Shêng; vowel as in 2 above)
47. K'un   (Kwên; vowel as in 2 above)
48. Ching   (Jing)
49. Kô   (Ger; but with the final 'r' not pronounced)
50. Ting   (Ding)
51. Chên   (Jên; vowel as in 2 above)
52. Kên   (Gên; vowel as in 2 above)
53. Chien   (Jee-en)
54. Kuei Mei   (Gway May)
55. Fêng   (Fêng; vowel as in 2 above)
56. Lü   (Lü; vowel as in the French 'Tu')
57. Sun   (Soon; but with the vowel short as in 'Book')
58. Tui   (Dway)
59. Huan   (Hwun; the vowel rhymes with 'Fun', 'Done', etc.)
60. Chieh   (Jee-eh)
61. Chung Fu   (Joong Foo)
62. Hsiao Kwo (Shee-au Gwor; but with the final 'r' not pronounced)
63. Chi Chi   (Jee Jee)
64. Wei Chi   (Way Jee)

For Product Safety Concerns and Information please contact our EU representative GPSR@taylorandfrancis.com
Taylor & Francis Verlag GmbH, Kaufingerstraße 24, 80331 München, Germany

www.ingramcontent.com/pod-product-compliance
Lightning Source LLC
Chambersburg PA
CBHW070604300426
44113CB00010B/1395